Morning Glory 2

366 Devotionals like no other!

Dr. Sheila Hayford

Book Title: Morning Glory 2

366 Devotionals like no other!

Copyright © 2016, 2017, 2018, 2019, 2020 by Dr. Sheila Hayford

2020 Edition

Published By: Dr. Sheila Hayford, What A Word Publishing and Media Group

http://www.whatawordpublishing.com

Email: info@whatawordpublishing.com

ISBN: 978-1-7328240-3-4

All rights reserved. No part of this book may be reproduced or transmitted in any form or by any means without written permission from the author, Dr. Sheila Hayford. Permission Requests should be addressed to: info@whatawordpublishing.com

You may also contact the author via the Publisher's website by visiting http://www.whatawordpublishing.com

*** Excerpt from 2017 Edition of Morning Glory -365 Devotionals like no other! By Dr. Sheila Hayford. Used with permission.

Scripture verses are from the King James Version Translation of the Bible unless otherwise indicated.

New International Version (NIV)

Holy Bible, New International Version®, NIV® Copyright ©1973, 1978, 1984, 2011 by Biblica, Inc.® Used by permission. All rights reserved worldwide.

"Scripture quotations taken from the Amplified® Bible (AMPC), Copyright © 1954, 1958, 1962, 1964, 1965, 1987 by The Lockman Foundation

Used by permission. www.Lockman.org"

This book is intended to be used as a spiritual guide from a Christian perspective. For your specific needs, seek expert professional advice.

Printed in the United States of America.

This book is dedicated to:

Mum and Dad

With heartfelt thanks to my Mum and Dad for introducing me to and nurturing my love of reading and writing. Mum is an educator and growing up as a child, I would receive volumes of Shakespeare and Readers Digest books in addition to the dolls as gifts on special occasions. I so enjoyed the books I would bring them to the dinner table to continue reading. Then, I would be reminded to eat my food! Dad was well learned, very eloquent, hardworking and had high expectations of excellence. My dad taught his kids poems he enjoyed as well as how to recite them with accompanying actions. When Dad's friends came to visit, Dad would have us recite the poems with their accompanying gestures and we loved it. I can still recite his favorite one! Afterwards we would smile, take a bow and curtsy and then take our leave of the grown-ups. I still love and enjoy plays and theatrical performances, reading and writing and am so grateful to both of you.

Sheila.

Index of Featured Businesses

1. Barksdale & Affiliates Realty ....page 50
Home Buying and Selling. Free Home Market Analysis.

2. Wealth Wisdom Group ....page 51
Tax and Income Planning.

3. Dance Delaware Studios ....page 62
Dance. Tap. Ballet. Jazz. Hip-Hop. Acrobatics.

4. U. S. Tax Pros ....page 66
Tax, Accounting and Business Support.

5. Laurece West ....page 80
Voice Coach. Singer. Speaker.

6. Mr. Income Tax ....page 86
Personal and Business Taxes, Small Business Accounting.

7. Simpsons Hobbies and Gifts ....page 188
Toys. Collectibles. Antiques. Gifts. Repairs.

8. Tina's Timeless Threads ....page 221
Clothing. Accessories and Novelty Gifts.

9. Power Up 4 Success ....page 269
Monthly Training Meetings.

January 1
A Lesson In Contrasts – David Versus Joseph

Deuteronomy Chapter 5, verse 33:
Walk in obedience to all that the LORD your God has commanded you, so that you may live and prosper and prolong your days in the land that you will possess. (NIV)

John Chapter 10, verses 9, 10:
I am the gate; whoever enters through me will be saved. They will come in and go out, and find pasture. The thief comes only to steal and kill and destroy; I have come that they may have life, and have it to the full. (NIV)

Prayer: Dear God, you have blessed us with the gift of A New Year and the opportunity to advance in our God given destiny in Christ. In your mercy, you give us the solid foundations we need to live life fully. Enable us to always walk humbly and in obedience to you. In Jesus' Name we pray, Amen.

David and Joseph in the Bible both started out in life with similar situations. God called Joseph and David in their teenage years for greatness in order to manifest the plans, purposes and glory of God. They were both young and disliked by their siblings. David's siblings despised David and showed their disdain for him when he showed up in the battle against Goliath and David's father, Jesse, did not even consider David as kingly potential when the prophet Samuel came to Jesse's house to anoint the future king. Joseph's siblings hated Joseph so much they tried to kill him but decided to sell Joseph into slavery instead. Joseph and David both had extraordinary experiences with God in their young tender years. For David, that included rescuing a lamb out of the mouth of a lion and a bear and killing the lion and the bear with his bare hands. For Joseph it was having those amazing dreams that earned him the nickname "dreamer" by his siblings. No doubt Joseph and David both realized that not everyone had the talents, gifts and abilities they had and with that came the temptation to become prideful and arrogant. When David stood before Goliath, not a single person in the entire army of Israel was willing to take on Goliath. David probably thought, "What is wrong with "these" people, allowing Goliath to talk badly and berate them and their God like that?" And with that came the temptation to look down and demean his fellow man. As they grew up, both David and Joseph were treated unfairly by others. With their God given abilities and gifts it was easy for people to become envious and jealous of them and they were wronged in numerous ways. King Saul was jealous of David and tried to kill David such that David had to flee for his life. Joseph was lied on by someone in a position of power and thrown into prison for a crime he did not commit. Nevertheless, the God who had invested in the lives of David and Joseph preserved both of them because of the great purpose he had called them to and for the benefit of many.

With God's intervention through extraordinary sets of events, David became King of Judah and then King of Israel and Joseph was promoted to second in command to King Pharaoh at the time, or what you might call in today's language, the Prime Minister in Egypt. That was when this lesson in contrasts between David and Joseph became evident. King David had not fully dealt with or mastered the temptations of pride and arrogance, nor the temptation to look down on those who were not as motivated, talented or as driven as he was. And when he became king, King David became complacent instead of stepping up to his responsibilities. At the time when kings were supposed to be in battle, King David stayed home. And while he was home, he saw Bathsheba and wanted her as his wife. Now Bathsheba was someone else's wife and the Ten Commandments speak against coveting someone else's wife but King David felt he was king and entitled to whatever he wanted when he wanted it, even if that meant committing adultery and murder to get what he wanted. This is a man who has known and walked with God from his youth but King David failed to take his character flaws seriously. King David committed adultery with Bathsheba, got her pregnant, orchestrated the murder of Bathsheba's husband, Urriah, who was killed and then took Bathsheba to be his wife. Sadly, at this point, King David thought nothing about this action until God sent the prophet Nathan to confront him. God was so displeased with what King David did that God said the sword would never depart from King David's house. Absalom who was King David's son ended up killing his sibling, started an insurrection to take the kingdom out of the reign of King David and then died in battle at the hands of his father King David's army. King David wanted to build a house for God but God said, No! King David's son, Solomon, would build it instead. However, Solomon, the child of King David and his mother Bathsheba, was so sexually addicted that he had seven hundred wives as well as three hundred concubines. And in King David's old age, instead of being surrounded by loving wonderful family and friends, Adonijah tried to usurp Solomon from becoming King and a young maiden was chosen to keep King David warm. The pleasures of sin are never worth the consequences of sin and King David experienced so much pain and turmoil as the result of his careless decisions involving Bathsheba that you have to have great compassion for him.

Contrast all King David's issues with Joseph. By the time Joseph was promoted by King Pharaoh, Joseph had faced and dealt with the temptation to become proud and arrogant. When Potiphar's wife tempted Joseph, Joseph did not feel he deserved to be in the place of her husband and shunned her, fleeing from her presence. Potiphar's wife then falsely accused Joseph of a crime he did not commit and it cost Joseph his reputation and time in prison. In prison, Joseph continued to serve and to share his gifts with his fellow men. He developed his God given gifts and began interpreting the dreams of those in prison. When those who promised to help Joseph after they left prison initially forgot about him and it seemed Joseph's destiny was being curtailed Joseph forgave them and kept on living for God. Joseph was developing and mastering the character of humility. So when Joseph left prison and was immediately promoted, he went to work diligently and with great humility. Joseph was an immigrant in a great position of authority, yet when he wanted his family to come to Egypt he did not demand that of Pharaoh. Joseph's excellent attitude, work and humility caused Pharaoh to show him great favor so Pharaoh had Joseph bring his whole family to Egypt where they would be given good land and plenty of provision. The entire world at the time was saved from starvation during the famine because of Joseph.

God's investment in the lives of David and Joseph was poured into individual soup containers that housed their spirit, soul, body, seasonings from tests and trials, experiences, relationships and character combined and made into a unique soup that was to provide nourishment by the time they reached their leadership roles. King David cracked his container with his character flaws over Bathsheba and out poured the soup, leaving King David with his core self as a spiritual child of God. Joseph's soup container remained intact and the known world at that time was able to draw soup from that container for food and other benefits for the remainder of his life here on earth and no doubt for eternity. This Lesson in Contrasts is summarized in four words:

C - Complacency; H - Humility; A – Arrogance; P - Pride

The CAP of Complacency, Arrogance and Pride will pull you down but Humility towards God and meekness towards your fellow human will lift you up.

Hold on! God was not done with King David! God said to King David; I'll tell you what, King David, even though you will not build my earthly temple made with human hands, I will use you to build my eternal temple not made with human hands. Out of your descendants will come the King of Kings and the Lord of Lords, my Son Jesus Christ who will save you and all who receive him from sin and you will live and reign with him forever! Hallelujah! So when we sin, we confess our sins to God, receive forgiveness through our Lord Jesus Christ and grow in grace and maturity in our faith and relationship with God. Let us determine and resolve that we will live this year and every year being who God has called us to be, speaking what God tells us to say and doing all God is calling us to do. We must not shortchange ourselves in any area so our soup pot containing the life-giving nourishing soup in us remains intact; for the glory of God and the saving and benefit of humankind.

© By Dr. Sheila Hayford.

January 2
Faith Finds

Matthew Chapter 17, verse 20:

He replied, "Because you have so little faith. Truly I tell you, if you have faith as small as a mustard seed, you can say to this mountain, 'Move from here to there,' and it will move. Nothing will be impossible for you." (NIV)

Prayer: Dear Lord Jesus, thank you for these words of encouragement. You say that even with little faith, great things can be accomplished. Whatever the challenges we face, may we boldly advance and experience the joys of seemingly impossible achievements. Amen.

It was going to be a busy day. I decided to take the Inter-county bus and set out to the station. The Holy Spirit asked me to move my keys from my handbag to my pocketbook earlier and I made a mental note to do so but I had not done so. I caught the bus and the ride was smooth. A mile or so from the Transit hub, a passenger on the bus appeared unsure of where he wanted to go and kept distracting the driver. The driver was on a time schedule but was patient with him. After the passenger alighted, the driver struck up a conversation. He had been working for the company for thirty-five years. That was impressive! Soon we were at the Transit hub. I walked nearby to a connecting bus and got on that bus. As the bus started to move, I noticed I was missing my handbag! I signaled to the bus driver to stop, explained why, got off and walked to the Inter-county bus scheduled to leave in ten minutes. The driver and I went back into the bus. There were two people seated since the time I got off and we asked if anyone had seen my handbag. Both said "No!" I walked to the areas where I was seated and looked but did not see my handbag. Remember, my keys were in it! Did my bag fall on my way to the connecting bus? I retraced my steps quickly but didn't see it. I decided to go back to the Inter-county bus; but this time I commanded my handbag to return to me in the Name of Jesus. I told the driver I would look again. This time the driver was on his knees looking under the seats. He walked to one of the passengers and boldly asked him if he could look around. The guy said "Yes!" The driver moved the passenger's book bag out of the way and pulled up my blue polka dot handbag. It was now about three minutes before the bus would leave. I was elated and thanked the driver profusely! I saw my keys and nothing had been taken from my handbag. Thank God for favor with God and man and for the Word of God. What is that impossible dream or goal you desire? We honor God when we bring to God our seemingly impossible goals and dreams. Believe God. Believe God's Word. Agree with God in your words. Faith finds!

© By Dr. Sheila Hayford.

January 3
Patience - She Pays!

James Chapter 1, verse 4:
But let patience have her perfect work, that ye may be perfect and entire, wanting nothing.

Prayer: Dear God: Thank you for the gift of the Holy Spirit in us, enabling us to be patient with you and with our fellow man. We choose whether we will reap the benefits of our patience or experience the frustrations of impatience so help us to choose wisely. In Jesus' Name, Amen.

The elderly woman was in front of me at the cashier in the department store. She had a few items, each of which was being rung up wrong and she wanted to make sure she got the discounted prices they had advertised in store. For one of the items, the cashier had to walk to the area where the woman bought it to verify the sale price. The woman looked at me and apologized for taking so much of my time. "No problem!" I said, as I smiled. The cashier came back, corrected the price and proceeded to ring the last item. It turned out it was an item I came to buy that was marked down to $2.49, over 90% discount. That caught my attention! The woman told the cashier the store sale was so good she couldn't walk past it and just had to purchase it. "Excuse me," I asked, "where did you buy that? I have a similar item on hold. Could you show me?" She graciously agreed to. After her item was rang up and paid for, she showed me rows of the items heavily discounted. I realized this was a God ordained sale. I was able to purchase the item I wanted and more with some of the savings.

Sometimes when one is going through a challenge, it can seem like a wasted experience. But that is not what God says. God can and will work all things out for the good of his born again children. All God asks us from us is our faith, trust, obedience and yes, our patience. Can we do all of this in our own strength? No! That is why God the Holy Spirit, our enabler, lives within us. As we yield to the Holy Spirit, the fruit of the Holy Spirit, which includes the "patience" fruit, grows and matures. So do not despair, whatever your circumstances. In God's time, on this earth or on the other side of eternity, we will be thankful that God indeed worked all things out for our good.

© By Dr. Sheila Hayford.

January 4
Make It Plain

Habakkuk Chapter 2, verse 2:
And the Lord answered me, and said, Write the vision, and make it plain upon tables, that he may run that readeth it.
1 John Chapter 5, verses 11, 12:

And this is the record, that God hath given to us eternal life, and this life is in his Son. He that hath the Son hath life; and he that hath not the Son of God hath not life.

Prayer: Dear God: Thank you for the simplicity of your Word. In Jesus' Name. Amen.

The little boy was in the Art Gallery with his older brother looking at various paintings. He had a frustrated look as he stared at one particular picture. Finally, he said to his older brother: "I am confused, I don't get it! What is that picture supposed to mean?" The older brother, who seemed to be in his preteens, mumbled something about the painting signifying the ocean waves. "Oh!" the little boy said, not very convinced. Sometimes we make our relationship with God and the reading of the Bible complicated when it should be easily understood. A child may not understand everything his parents ask him to do, but he understands love and the child is full of trust. God has revealed his love and desires for humankind through His Son, the Lord Jesus Christ. All God asks of us is to love, trust and obey God. If we love God, we will love our fellow man and study the Holy Bible to find out what God says. We will take the time to have conversation with God in prayer. Trust is an extension of faith. If we have faith in God and trust God with our wellbeing, we will desire to obey God. In Christ, we are given the gift of the Holy Spirit to help us live for God. Let's keep God's message simple!

© By Dr. Sheila Hayford.

January 5
Purposeful

Genesis Chapter 1, verses 26 - 31:
And God said, Let us make man in our image, after our likeness: and let them have dominion over the fish of the sea, and over the fowl of the air, and over the cattle, and over all the earth, and over every creeping thing that creepeth upon the earth. So God created man in his own image,

in the image of God created he him; male and female created he them. And God blessed them, and God said unto them, Be fruitful, and multiply, and replenish the earth, and subdue it: and have dominion over the fish of the sea, and over the fowl of the air, and over every living thing that moveth upon the earth. And God said, Behold, I have given you every herb bearing seed, which is upon the face of all the earth, and every tree, in the which is the fruit of a tree yielding seed; to you it shall be for meat. And to every beast of the earth, and to every fowl of the air, and to every thing that creepeth upon the earth, wherein there is life, I have given every green herb for meat: and it was so. And God saw every thing that he had made, and, behold, it was very good. And the evening and the morning were the sixth day.

Matthew Chapter 20, verses 6, 7:

And about the eleventh hour he went out, and found others standing idle, and saith unto them, Why stand ye here all the day idle? They say unto him, Because no man hath hired us. He saith unto them, Go ye also into the vineyard; and whatsoever is right, that shall ye receive.

Prayer: Dear God, you will not ask us to do anything we are not capable of doing, no matter how daunting or difficult the task may appear. Help us to trust you and move forward in your plans and purpose for our lives. In Jesus' Name, Amen.

Have you noticed that everything God does is **purposeful**? No actions stemming from distractions, no idle words, no wasted time. The creation of humankind was God's idea. That idea progressed to God's intent. However, it was intent with purpose. And what was that intent? **It is what I call the three A's God established for humankind; Authority, Assignment and Accountability**.

God has a vast universe and he assigned authority to humankind on this earth over an assigned territory. Then God gave humankind an assignment with the do's and do not's of that assignment. Finally, God gave humanity accountability; accountability first to God and then to humanity. God's humankind project was not without risk. In fact, God had risk built into the project; create humankind in robot like fashion to only do God's bidding, or create humankind with free will. God chose the latter. Obedience to God would come with blessings and benefits and disobedience to God would come with judgement and punishment. That was a risk with the potential to mess up God's original plan. But God had a plan B for the risks should humankind disobey God; in the person of his Son, the Lord Jesus Christ. So with a plan that took into account the risks, God shared his plan with the Lord Jesus and the Holy Spirit; essential in bringing about the implementation of the plan. After humankind was created, God inspected his plan to make sure it was what he intended. And God continually assessed his plan, making a change to Plan B. Now and for eternity God's Plan B will continue.

God, in his mercy, chose to allow us to enter into this New Year. **What are your New Year Resolutions that you want to implement with God's help?**

- Write them down for every area of your life; health and wellness, family, finances, work, spiritually, community, etc.
- Write down who you are going to share them with in order to bring about the implementation. Those you share them with should be qualified and capable of helping you bring your plans into reality.
- Then take action and make an appointment to meet with them, whether it be a Nutritionist, Physician, Fitness trainer, Financial planner, Realtor, Pastor or an organization.
- Be sure to do what is needed to bring that plan into reality.
- Monitor and work your plan.
- Set up times during the year to assess and take stock of your plan.

Remember, since your first accountability is to God, be sure to consult with God before, during and after the plan becomes a reality. For you are a part of God's ultimate plans and purpose.

© By Dr. Sheila Hayford.

January 6
God's Creative Genius

Psalm 89, verse 11:
The heavens are yours, and yours also the earth; you founded the world and all that is in it. (NIV)

Mark Chapter 4, verse 39:
And he arose, and rebuked the wind, and said unto the sea, Peace, be still. And the wind ceased, and there was a great calm.

Prayer: Dear heavenly Father: I am so amazed as I behold your wondrous works; the skies, the seas and this beautiful earth. Help me not to take such beauty for granted and to do my part as a good steward of all you have entrusted to me. In Jesus' Name, Amen.

I love to travel and behold God's amazing creative genius so when I had the opportunity to attend a three day conference in Bermuda, I was all for it. On the last day of the conference, I would have time to explore this beautiful island and I was looking forward to that. Well, on the second day of the conference as I was walking back to the hotel, a car drove right through a puddle of water on the street and splashed the road water all over my clothes. I was upset and began to complain about the driver (I didn't curse the driver!) when one of the persons nearby said that puddle of water was nothing and that a hurricane was supposed to hit the island the next day. What? That was my day for exploring the island! I was thankful for the announcement because now I knew how to pray. When I got back to the hotel there were several signs posted stating that the airlines were offering flights out of the island that evening for those who wished to depart earlier because of the forecasted hurricane. What should I do? I decided I would do what the Lord Jesus did. I would command the wind to calm down and pray for nice weather so I went to bed. When I woke up the next morning and went outside, the wind was so strong it picked me up and I had to hold onto a nearby pole. Then I spoke to the wind to calm down in the Name of Jesus and prayed for nice weather. Do you know? The wind calmed down and the sun came out. I was able to crisscross one end of the island to the other in the gorgeous sunshine weather, visiting tourist and local sites. I met the locals and they were joking about the nice weather and no hurricane. Of course, I was excited and shared my story with anyone who would listen. Some smiling said, "Oh! So we have you to thank for the nice weather!" Back in the United States as I was sharing my wonderful experience, an acquaintance said that God had sent me to Bermuda to protect the people of that island. That was a profound revelation to me. While I was admiring and enjoying God's creative genius, God had a larger purpose for my visit and it was for the saving of life and property. Each one of us is a visitor on this earth and we will all be here for a finite period of time. God has a purpose and plans for our lives and it always include service. Yes, God provides the fun and God provides the funds but most importantly, God provides the plans and purpose. Travel with God today!

© By Dr. Sheila Hayford.

January 7
Persuadable or Unpersuadable

John Chapter 3, verse 16:

For God so loved the world, that he gave his only begotten Son, that whosoever believeth in him should not perish, but have everlasting life.

Romans Chapter 5, verse 8:

But God commendeth his love toward us, in that, while we were yet sinners, Christ died for us.

Romans Chapter 8, verses 38, 39:

For I am persuaded, that neither death, nor life, nor angels, nor principalities, nor powers, nor things present, nor things to come, Nor height, nor depth, nor any other creature, shall be able to separate us from the love of God, which is in Christ Jesus our Lord.

Romans Chapter 6, verse 23:

For the wages of sin is death; but the gift of God is eternal life through Jesus Christ our Lord.

2 Chronicles Chapter 30, verse 8:

Now be ye not stiffnecked, as your fathers were, but yield yourselves unto the Lord, and enter into his sanctuary, which he hath sanctified for ever: and serve the Lord your God, that the fierceness of his wrath may turn away from you.

Psalm 33, verse 4:

For the word of the Lord is right; and all his works are done in truth.

Prayer: Dear God: You are the true and faithful God and you watch your words come to pass. Help us to always humble ourselves before you and take seriously what you have to say to us. In Jesus' Name. Amen.

God is fully love and fully just. Thus, God has to judge and punish sin. When Adam and Eve sinned against God, they brought God's wrath and punishment for sin on themselves and all humankind. God's judgement for sin included death and separation from God. God, in his love for humankind, sent his Son, the Lord Jesus Christ to earth to take the punishment for our sins by dying on the cross. Anyone who is sorry and repentant for their sins and believes in the Lord Jesus can invite the Lord Jesus into their life as Lord and Savior. This is a freewill choice. All who accept the Lord Jesus' work in taking on the punishment for their sin have a new relationship with God and all the benefits therein. Those who reject the Lord Jesus Christ choose to live with the consequences of their action, for God's love for them compels God to respect their freewill. Are you persuadable or unpersuadable when it comes to God and the Word of God? Let us all heed Psalm 33, verse 4 which reads, "For the word of the Lord is right; and all his works are done in truth."

© By Dr. Sheila Hayford.

January 8
The Three Dresses

1 Chronicles Chapter 17, verse 26:
You, Lord, are God! You have promised these good things to your servant. (NIV)

Prayer: Dear God: I am grateful for all that you have done and continue to do for me. Words are never enough to express my heartfelt thanks but I still say, Thank You! In Jesus' Name, Amen.

I had just finished an appointment with my client and had planned to head home. The Holy Spirit asked me to go to a nearby store. My first thought was, "You mean, you want me to spend some money!" It was a nice store and they always had beautiful clothes but that was not where I wanted to go at that time. However, I chose to obey God and headed to the store. When I got there I was pleasantly surprised. That store was going out of business and the prices were slashed. I noticed a famous designer's clothes on sale at unbelievably ridiculously low prices. And they were stylish, as in the same style and color I had seen on royalty! I saw one I would buy and the Holy Spirit said to buy three items. So I chose a few clothes to try on at the fitting area. Well, next to me was another lady who was applying to places to do her postgraduate medical residency training course and she was trying on clothes she could wear for interviews. Her friend was with her. Since we were about the same size, we would come out after trying on the clothes and her friend would give her review. Soon her friend started talking about spiritual things and I mentioned my Morning Glory book to which this book is the sequel. Her friend wanted to buy the book after browsing through my copy and we made an appointment to meet later. I bought three beautiful clothes for less than $20.00 and left the store satisfied. Her friend and I met later and it was a blessing. Do not put God in a box. Allow God to surprise you and experience the wonderful things God has in store for you!

© By Dr. Sheila Hayford.

January 9
Pure Love, Sheer Joy!

Luke Chapter 10, verse 27:
And he answering said, Thou shalt love the Lord thy God with all thy heart, and with all thy soul, and with all thy strength, and with all thy mind; and thy neighbour as thyself.

Prayer: Dear Lord Jesus: You are coming back again and that is great news! Help us share this good news with many and live holy. We love you! Amen.

It was a busy summer weekend and many families were travelling. The chatter of excited children filled the bus, many of them looking forward to spending time with their cousins, extended family and friends. As the bus pulled into the "Park and Ride" bus stop I noticed a casually dressed gentleman by his car with the driver's side door open. I thought he was expecting one of the excited families. Shortly before the bus came to a stop, he opened the back door on his side and out jumped this beautifully dressed African-American little girl. She quickly made her way to the front of the car and began jumping excitedly up and down. She was overjoyed! When the bus stopped, the little girl began waving both hands and pointing in her direction as she continued to jump up and down. She was oblivious to the spectators; her focus was on the children on the bus she was expecting. Or so I thought! Suddenly an older woman came off the bus. She looked frail and walked slowly with her walking cane in the direction of the little girl. The little girl couldn't help but express her sheer joy. She began running towards the woman. She hugged the woman with her little arms and after a few shared words, they walked back slowly together towards the car, hand in hand. It was a beautiful scene! Our Lord Jesus is coming back again. Are we dressed in proper attire and ready to meet him? Are we excited? Are we full of sheer joy in anticipation of his coming? The Holy Spirit has opened the driver's door of our lives in anticipation of Christ's return. God's assigned holy angels will accompany our Lord Jesus when he comes back to earth. Soon the heavenly cloud doors will open for us and our precious Lord and Savior Jesus Christ will appear. This time we will not be bringing him to our earthly home; the Lord Jesus will take us to be with Him forever. Pure love! Sheer joy! Are you ready?

© By Dr. Sheila Hayford.

January 10
Sure, There Are!

Philippians Chapter 4, verse 8:
Finally, brethren, whatever things are true, whatever things are honest, whatever things are just, whatever things are pure, whatever things are lovely, whatever things are of good report, if there is any virtue and if there is any praise, exercise yourselves in these things.

Psalm 34, verses 12-13:
Whoever of you loves life and desires to see many good days, keep your tongue from evil and your lips from telling lies. (NIV)

Prayer: Dear heavenly Father, we expect good from you and receive more good than we thought was possible. Help us to extend your grace to our fellow man. In the Name of Jesus, we pray. Amen.

The room was filled to capacity and hardly a seat could be found. I had some work to follow up on and so I stood. Suddenly, I saw a tall gentleman walking from one end of the room in my direction. He was carrying a chair. He placed the chair right in front of me. I asked smiling, "Is this for me?" "Yes!" he said, "there are still some (good men) left." "Sure, there are!" was my reply as I gratefully accepted the chair. These verses in the book of Philippians are a wonderful reminder of what we should focus our thoughts on. When you expect good, you will look for good and find good. When you focus on misery, you will live misery and project misery. I have learned to live expecting the best in a person unless or until they give me cause to believe otherwise and I find that very liberating. I do not determine a person's character based on hearsay or gossip and being a very direct person, I have zero tolerance for gossip and backbiting. I find that most people live up to the good you expect of them. When we look at where God wants us to be in our relationship with him and in our service to God and humanity, can we afford to spend our thoughts and our time focusing on the flaws of other people? We would all do better by allowing the Holy Spirit to perfect God's work in us.

© By Dr. Sheila Hayford.

January 11
Hypocrisy – Mired In Contradictions

2 Chronicles Chapter 7, verse 14:
If my people, which are called by my name, shall humble themselves, and pray, and seek my face, and turn from their wicked ways; then will I hear from heaven, and will forgive their sin, and will heal their land.

John Chapter 17, verse 17:
Sanctify them by the truth; your word is truth. (NIV)

Prayer: Dear God, your word is absolute truth and the perfect standard for life and living. Help us to look in the mirror of the Holy Bible and make the necessary changes we need to apply by an act of our will and in the Holy Spirit's power. In Jesus Name, I pray. Amen.

One of the things the President Trump presidency has brought out is the hatred and hypocrisy of many. Some who for years were adamant that the accused had a right to face their accuser failed to apply that same standard when it came to their political opponent. Others, who knew better because they were raised in humble beginnings, began to stereotype the poor as lazy and always seeking handouts. Tolerance and civility in political conversations which many had intellectually espoused as vitally necessary in a civilized society suddenly was applied by some only if it was in relation to those who shared their political ideology. Even some who had previously paraded their joy in living in a democratic country suddenly proclaimed duly elected President Trump was "not my president." How could some Christian leaders fail to live up to what they preached? In other words, did they put their political party allegiance before their allegiance to God and the Word of God? After preaching that the Bible says we should pray for those in authority and it does, they began to criticize those who went to the White House to pray for and with President Trump. How can a person expect to effect change without engagement? I firmly believe and say that the state of any nation reflects the collective state of the Christian believers in that nation. So, we all need to look in the mirror. The Scripture verses above clearly say that if Christians will humble ourselves, pray, seek God and turn from evil, God will heal the land. If someone does not know better you might understand where that person is coming from, but if we say we speak for God, then God help us put into practice what we preach. It is time to heal the land!

© By Dr. Sheila Hayford.

January 12
Heed God's Promptings

Romans Chapter 8, verse 14:
For those who are led by the Spirit of God are the children of God. (NIV)
Prayer: Dear God; your way is always the best way to get to our destination. Help us to heed the Holy Spirit's promptings. In Jesus' Name. Amen.

I had like to shop on sale so I planned to go to three different places to buy what I needed; one for household items, another for groceries and I needed to go to a third store for business services. The Holy Spirit said to go to the grocery store and then take care of the business services but nothing about going to the store for my household items. I decided to heed the Holy Spirit's promptings and headed to the grocery store first. In addition to the grocery items I came to buy I was very surprised to find out that the **exact** household item brand I was going to buy at the household items store was heavily discounted at the grocery store for $0.99 to $1.49 if you bought 5 items and you could mix and match the items. I bought 5 for a little over the price of 1! The lemonade was buy 1 get 1 free, my favorite barbeque sauce was buy 1 get 1 free, all items on my list. There was no need to go to the household items store! I took care of the business services and headed home, thankful I had obeyed God. Heed God's promptings! The way God said to do it is the way to do it!

© By Dr. Sheila Hayford.

January 13
*** Corporate Prayer, Forgiveness And Communion Day

Mark Chapter 15, verses 25, 26:
And when ye stand praying, forgive, if ye have ought against any: that your Father also which is in heaven may forgive you your trespasses. But if ye do not forgive, neither will your Father which is in heaven forgive your trespasses.

Prayer: Dear Lord God, forgive us for the many times we have asked your forgiveness while harboring unforgiveness in our hearts towards our fellow man. Help us to repent and take the command of forgiveness by the Lord Jesus Christ seriously. Enable us to walk in love and refuse to allow any bitterness in our lives. We pray in Jesus' Name, Amen.

It is amazing how fellow born again believers can attend church services and events and not be on talking terms with a believer in the same or other congregation for years. And then take communion while harboring unforgiveness. It might be the reason the Apostle Paul says in the book of 1 Corinthians Chapter 11, verse 30 that some are sick, weak or have died. If the Lord Jesus Christ forgives us in spite of what we did to him on the cross of Calvary, do we have any right to hold unforgiveness against another person? I suggest that we each set aside a day a month for Corporate Prayer, Forgiveness and Communion where we take time to make it right with those we have offended or who have offended us. Will everyone willingly grant your request for forgiveness? Maybe not, but you will have done your part and exercised your clear conscience towards God in that respect.

If you would like to take the pledge for Corporate Prayer, Forgiveness and Communion for you, your family, your church and your organization here it is:

Corporate Prayer, Forgiveness and Communion Day Pledge:
I pledge by the power of God the Holy Spirit to walk in forgiveness even as my Lord Jesus Christ has forgiven me. I know it is not easy and that it may go against my natural instinct to seek immediate or long-term revenge or redress of an issue. However, I believe the Word of God that tells me I can do all things through Christ who strengthens me. I make the conscious decision to forgive ALL who have wronged me and I seek forgiveness from those I have wronged. So help me, dear Holy Spirit. In the Name of Jesus, Amen.

If you would like to let us know you took the pledge and would like to share the Corporate Prayer, Forgiveness and Communion Day Pledge with others visit forgivenesspledge.org. God thanks you!

© By Dr. Sheila Hayford.

*** Excerpt from 2017 Edition of Morning Glory -365 Devotionals like no other! By Dr. Sheila Hayford. Used with permission.

January 14
Disobedience to God - Lessons from Lot's Wife

Genesis Chapter 19, verses 12-22, 26:

The two men said to Lot, "Do you have anyone else here - sons-in-law, sons or daughters, or anyone else in the city who belongs to you? Get them out of here, because we are going to destroy this place. The outcry to the Lord against its people is so great that he has sent us to destroy it." So Lot went out and spoke to his sons-in-law, who were pledged to marry his daughters. He said, "Hurry and get out of this place, because the Lord is about to destroy the city!" But his sons-in-law thought he was joking. With the coming of dawn, the angels urged Lot, saying, "Hurry! Take your wife and your two daughters who are here, or you will be swept away when the city is punished." When he hesitated, the men grasped his hand and the hands of his wife and of his two daughters and led them safely out of the city, for the Lord was merciful to them. As soon as they had brought them out, one of them said, "Flee for your lives! Don't look back, and don't stop anywhere in the plain! Flee to the mountains or you will be swept away!" But Lot said to them, "No, my lords, please! Your servant has found favor in your eyes, and you have shown great kindness to me in sparing my life. But I can't flee to the mountains; this disaster will overtake me, and I'll die. Look, here is a town near enough to run to, and it is small. Let me flee to it - it is very small, isn't it? Then my life will be spared." He said to him, "Very well, I will grant this request too; I will not overthrow the town you speak of. But flee there quickly, because I cannot do anything until you reach it." (That is why the town was called Zoar. But Lot's wife looked back, and she became a pillar of salt.

Luke Chapter 17, verse 32:

Remember Lot's wife.

Prayer: Dear Lord Jesus; your desire for us is to avoid the tragic consequences of disobedience to God's words. You have given us the gift of God the Holy Spirit to help us live for God and you forgive us when we repent of and confess our sins. Let us not walk in fear, but in faith and obedience to God. Amen.

When we read about the tragic end of Lot's wife it is very sobering. Here is a woman who with her husband and daughters were favored by

God to escape the punishment that God was about to send on Sodom and Gomorrah. The angels of God literally walked them safely out of the city and they had only two instructions from God at that time. Run or flee for your lives and do not look back. What did Lot's wife do? She partially obeyed God which is the equivalent of disobedience to God. Lot's wife run but she looked back and turned into a pillar of salt, a memorial to her act of disobedience to the Word of God. Sometimes when temptation and tests show up, satan wants us to think that God's commandments can be toyed or played with. Lot's sons-in law thought God's commandments were a joke until they were destroyed when God destroyed Sodom and Gomorrah. When God commands us to forgive, it is for our own good. God knows how to punish the adversary or the enemy. We have to do our part to obey God and follow God's instructions as to what we should do in any temptation or challenge. The lesson from Lot's wife is this: Disobedience to God may cost you your life. The Lord Jesus reinforces this lesson with the reminder, "Remember Lot's wife."

© By Dr. Sheila Hayford.

January 15
Even The devils Believe

James Chapter 2, verses 19-20:

Thou believest that there is one God; thou doest well: the devils also believe, and tremble. But wilt thou know, O vain man, that faith without works is dead?

Prayer: Dear Lord Jesus, you have done so very much for humankind. May we apply the corresponding works to our professions of faith in you and thus receive salvation, deliverance and victory in every area of our lives. Amen.

A person may believe that the chair they see may be able to bear their weight when they sit on it. However, if they remain standing when they should be sitting on that chair their belief in the chair is practically useless to them. The chair has a useful function and would benefit them if they used it, but their lack of action or works to accompany their belief make their faith or belief useless. It is the same way when it comes with spiritual things. Some will be quick to tell you they believe the Lord Jesus is the Son of God. When you ask them if they have accepted the Lord Jesus personally as their Lord and Savior, their answer is "No!" And their living or their works prove that they have made salvation through the Lord Jesus of null effect in their lives. The devils recognized the Lord Jesus as God but their works have condemned them to an eternal hell. Never let that be said of you. If you have not yet applied action to your belief and invited the Lord Jesus Christ as your Lord and Savior, now is the time to receive Christ's offer of your salvation and be welcomed into the family of God.

© By Dr. Sheila Hayford.

January 16
Don't Blow it - It's Yours To Win!

1 Corinthians Chapter 15, verse 57:
But thanks be to God, which giveth us the victory through our Lord Jesus Christ.

Prayer: Dear God; in Your Son, Jesus Christ, we have everything we need to be victorious in life. When we sin or fumble, we can repent and confess our sins, receive your forgiveness and advance. Help us not take this victory lightly. Enable us to be diligent in enforcing what is already ours through our Lord Jesus Christ in the power of the Holy Spirit. In Jesus' Name we pray. Amen.

It was the football game between the Philadelphia Eagles and the Washington Redskins and the Redskins were up by 20 points. True, teams have come back from behind to win the game, but with the advantage of such a wide score, the game was in place for the Redskins to win. However, the Redskins failed to maximize their half-time advantage and ended up losing the game to the Eagles with a final score of 29-27. Finally, after zero wins and five losses for the season, Daniel Snyder, the Washington Redskin's owner fired the Redskin's coach, Jay Gruder. What is the point here? The Lord Jesus came to this earth and conquered sin, sickness, disease, every form of oppression and death on behalf of humankind. And he gives everyone who receives the Lord Jesus as Lord and Savior the opportunity to experience Christ's victory in every area of life. What do you do in the game of your life when tests, temptations, challenges, opposition seem to knock you down? Do you quit living mentally and spiritually, roll over and play dead instead of asking God the Holy Spirit to strengthen you, renew and refresh you and help you experience your victory through Christ? You are already positioned to win in life because of the finished work of the Lord Jesus Christ. Yours is to enforce that victory. So speak life, speak victory, live in hopeful expectation of the manifestation of God's goodness and victory in your life. If you fall short, confess your sins to God, ask for and experience God's forgiveness, then move forward with God. Remember, victory through Christ is yours to win!

© By Dr. Sheila Hayford.

January 17
Miriam: How Dare You?

Numbers Chapter 12, verses 1-2, 5-14:

And Miriam and Aaron spake against Moses because of the Ethiopian woman whom he had married: for he had married an Ethiopian woman. And they said, Hath the Lord indeed spoken only by Moses? hath he not spoken also by us? And the Lord heard it. And the Lord came down in the pillar of the cloud, and stood in the door of the tabernacle, and called Aaron and Miriam: and they both came forth. And he said, Hear now my words: If there be a prophet among you, I the Lord will make myself known unto him in a vision, and will speak unto him in a dream. My servant Moses is not so, who is faithful in all mine house. With him will I speak mouth to mouth, even apparently, and not in dark speeches; and the similitude of the Lord shall he behold: wherefore then were ye not afraid to speak against my servant Moses? And the anger of the Lord was kindled against them; and he departed. And the cloud departed from off the tabernacle; and, behold, Miriam became leprous, white as snow: and Aaron looked upon Miriam, and, behold, she was leprous. And Aaron said unto Moses, Alas, my lord, I beseech thee, lay not the sin upon us, wherein we have done foolishly, and wherein we have sinned. Let her not be as one dead, of whom the flesh is half consumed when he cometh out of his mother's womb. And Moses cried unto the Lord, saying, Heal her now, O God, I beseech thee. And the Lord said unto Moses, If her father had but spit in her face, should she not be ashamed seven days? let her be shut out from the camp seven days, and after that let her be received in again.

Prayer: Dear God, the lesson here from Miriam's actions is sobering and it is to warn humanity not to go down that path. Help us to heed your warning. In Jesus' Name, Amen.

God had a gripe with Miriam. How dare she speak evil against Moses, God's chosen? True, Moses had his own faults and his past was not picture perfect, but Moses was acutely aware of that even before God appointed him to lead the Israelites. God's judgement against Miriam was quick; instantaneous leprosy. And it was the same Moses she had criticized who intervened for mercy on Miriam's behalf to God. Lest we think this account is for Old Testament times only, let us remember that God's character does not change. God still judges those who dare to come against God's chosen without consulting with God. If a leader or person is at fault, pray for them with Scripture as your guide and allow the Holy Spirit to give you instructions as to what you should do. God may send you to speak to them, God may send others to them or God may deal with the person directly, instantaneously or in God's perfect timing. Let us trust God in every situation and not take God's direct matters into our own hands.

© By Dr. Sheila Hayford.

January 18
It Made Sense After All!

Nehemiah Chapter 8, verse 8:
So they read in the book in the law of God distinctly, and gave the sense, and caused them to understand the reading.

Prayer: Dear God, help us to always trust you, especially during the "this does not make sense' times. We know you always have our best interests at heart. In Jesus' Name, Amen.

I never understood why some would sit outside on their front steps overlooking the streets when they could be inside their homes or outside at their back yards. Well, one day the Holy Spirit decided to give me some insight. There was a community parking garage building downtown and opposite that building was a block of row houses. On this particular day, the older men were sitting on their front steps, some in conversation. Suddenly, a flashy car with extremely loud music came to a screech and parked near the entrance to the parking garage. The loud music continued. The loud music and the guy driving, who looked to be in his twenties, seemed out of place. Then I heard one of the men on the front steps say, "Yo Bro! You're looking for somebody?" All the eyes of the men on the steps were fixed on the young man. The young man looked up, probably decided he would not take a chance on standing up against the older men and sped off. Suddenly I got it! The men on the front steps were the 'unofficial' neighborhood watch for their community. They were protecting their properties and families from intruders and those who might not have good intentions for their neighborhood. Sometimes in life, we may see or experience situations which seem out of place. They may have been unanticipated or unplanned. God has us in unfamiliar territory and we might wonder how it will turn out. Then we find out, those situations were sent by God to show us favor, protect us, prevent harm, to advance God's kingdom.

What did not make sense at the time it was happening made sense later. God wants us to always trust him. Will you?

© By Dr. Sheila Hayford.

January 19
The Rainbow

Revelation Chapter 9, verse 16:
Whenever the rainbow appears in the clouds, I will see it and remember the everlasting covenant between God and all living creatures of every kind on the earth."
Revelation Chapter 4, verse 3:
And he that sat was to look upon like a jasper and a sardine stone: and there was a rainbow round about the throne, in sight like unto an emerald.
Prayer: Our heavenly Father, how we love you! Your promises to us are more than we deserve and you prove yourself faithful and true every time. Thank you! In Jesus' Name, Amen.

One of my friends is an excellent driver. When you can calmly drive through busy Manhattan, in rush hour, the way you would drive in your neighborhood city, you are really good! And so when I had an important errand to run in New York, I asked her if she would drive. I would take care of the gas and the tolls and she was happy to do the driving, her schedule permitting. It did, so all three of us rode up; my friend, our mutual friend and myself. It was a smooth wonderful drive; hardly any traffic, nice weather and wonderful company. There was no rain when suddenly a huge rainbow appeared! It was so… beautiful! And then suddenly a second rainbow appeared! A double rainbow!! And the rainbow 'led' us as we drove. At one point we took the wrong exit and my friend asked if I could see the rainbow. I said "No!" and when we got back on track the rainbow reappeared. I felt like we were following the star that guided the wise men to baby Jesus! We arrived safely, my appointment was successful and we headed back. After enjoying a quick meal on our way back we were soon home. Mission accomplished with God's help! When I set out on the errand to New York, it was in response to a directive from God who made it clear that was the right time. And the rainbow was a sign reminding us of God's promises and God's faithfulness to his words. What has God promised you? God's promises will always be in line with his character and his words. Hold fast to the truths and promises of God's words. You can take God's words with you to New York and back!

© By Dr. Sheila Hayford.

January 20
Don't Make Your Enemy Your Idol

Mark Chapter 12, verses 30, 31:
And thou shalt love the Lord thy God with all thy heart, and with all thy soul, and with all thy mind, and with all thy strength: this is the first commandment. And the second is like, namely this, Thou shalt love thy neighbour as thyself. There is none other commandment greater than these.

Prayer: Dear God, your love commandment for God and for our fellow man is a tall order because such love does not always come easy in our human strength. Enable us by your Holy Spirit to excel in both. In Jesus' Name we pray, Amen.

Do not let your enemy become your idol? So one might ask, "What do you mean by that?" I mean: do not breathe and live out your life with your enemy as your primary focus or priority. I read where a woman set herself on fire because she hated President Trump so much. Think of this; someone was willing to hurt themselves or sacrifice their life because they hated their enemy. That is the same as someone sacrificing their life for the sake of their idol, the thing or person that is their ultimate focus in life. The Lord Jesus has given us commandments on what our priorities in life should be and we must be about doing that. Does that mean we overlook wrongdoing, whatever the source? No! It means that whatever another person's sins may be, we should also look to ourselves lest we fall into the same sin. Talk to God about whatever personal issue, situation or challenge you may be facing. Read the Word of God and allow the Holy Spirit to lead you in your actions. Remember, that everyone, including us and those who may be in the wrong, ultimately have to answer to God. Thus, if anyone persists in wrongdoing, their actions are primarily against God. You do your part loving God with all your heart, soul, mind, strength and loving your neighbor as yourself and let God take care of God's part.

© By Dr. Sheila Hayford.

January 21
Giftings

Matthew Chapter 25, verses 19-20:

After a long time the lord of those servants cometh, and reckoneth with them. And so he that had received five talents came and brought other five talents, saying, Lord, thou deliveredst unto me five talents: behold, I have gained beside them five talents more.

1 Corinthians Chapter 12, verses 4-6:

There are different kinds of gifts, but the same Spirit distributes them. There are different kinds of service, but the same Lord. There are different kinds of working, but in all of them and in everyone it is the same God at work. (NIV)

Prayer: Dear God, there is a difference between admiring another person's talents, gifts and abilities and being envious or jealous of their gifts. Help us to encourage each other. When we live our truest self in Christ, striving for perfection by the Holy Spirit's power, we will help answer our prayers that your will be done on this earth as it is in your heaven. In Jesus' Name. Amen.

Wouldn't it be boring if everyone did the same job? Not only that, the world would not be able to function. God planned it well by giving each individual specific abilities, gifts and talents. We need you and your abilities and gifts to be in existence and in service so you and your family as well as the greater community may find them beneficial. There is no one that can do what you do the way you do it and you can always improve on your giftings. You may even discover gifts you did not know you had. And humanity is the better for it. There is no need to keep up with the Jones, only the need to be yourself. Can striving to be a better person bring unnecessary pressure on yourself? Only if you allow it to be. Remember, God created you with a spirit, soul and physical body and all three areas of your life need to be taken care of in order to live wholly and fully. So cherish your gifts and abilities, work them and share them. God wants the world to be a better place because of you!

© By Dr. Sheila Hayford.

January 22
Who Are You Serving?

Colossians Chapter 3, verse 23:

And whatsoever ye do, do it heartily, as to the Lord, and not unto men;

Prayer: Dear God, it is an honor to position you as our first priority in life. Thank you for salvation through your Son Jesus Christ, through whom we have everything we need to live productively. Help us serve you lovingly and in so doing serve our fellow man with joy. In Jesus' Name, we pray. Amen.

Why do you do what you do? In your personal life, your home, your family, your job, your church and in your community? Of course, you may have several reasons but what is your primary reason? Is it to make you happy? Is it to make others happy? Is it to make God happy? It is possible to make you happy, others happy and God happy at the same time. It is also possible to make you happy, others happy but God unhappy by your actions. When someone makes God happy by doing for others, they and others may be unhappy. How so? It depends on if you are serving God with the right attitude and the right motives. God desires us to put his priorities first and for us to be happy doing so. Indeed, God's priorities for our lives will bring us the greatest fulfillment and satisfaction in life. Are we ready to serve God wholeheartedly?

© By Dr. Sheila Hayford.

January 23
Put Forth The Challenge

I Kings Chapter 18, verse 21, 24:

And Elijah came unto all the people, and said, How long halt ye between two opinions? if the Lord be God, follow him: but if Baal, then follow him. And the people answered him not a word. And call ye on the name of your gods, and I will call on the name of the Lord: and the God that answereth by fire, let him be God. And all the people answered and said, It is well spoken.

Matthew Chapter 6, verse 24:

No man can serve two masters: for either he will hate the one, and love the other; or else he will hold to the one, and despise the other. Ye cannot serve God and mammon.

Psalm 1 verse 6:

For the Lord knoweth the way of the righteous: but the way of the ungodly shall perish.

Prayer: Dear God; it is time out for us to take our service in your kingdom seriously. You have given us the good news of Jesus Christ to share and you will back up your Word. Enable us to do our part in humility and in submission to the leading of the Holy Spirit. In Jesus' Name we pray, Amen.

Sometimes there is no need to beat around the bush, so to speak. The prophet Elijah had had enough. The people were double minded; serving God when they felt like doing so and worshipping the false god Baal at the same time. And so the prophet Elijah issued a challenge on Mount Carmel against the four hundred and fifty prophets of Baal. In his challenge, whoever's God answered by fire, He is the true God. The One True God answered the prophet Elijah's challenge by fire and the prophets of Baal were eventually destroyed. The Lord Jesus tells us that a person cannot hold allegiance to two opposing masters at the same time. The time to sit by doing nothing and allow evil to flourish is past. Pray for the nation. Put forth the challenge to those who are concerned about the wellbeing of the nation, be it the spiritual challenge of prayer with fasting, evangelism at every level of society or that of being the hands and feet of the Lord Jesus in addressing the needs of society. It's time out for inaction! God's ministering and warrior angels are waiting for your call!

© By Dr. Sheila Hayford.

January 24
Pass it On!

Exodus Chapter 12, verse 26:
And it shall come to pass, when your children shall say unto you, What mean ye by this service?

Prayer: Dear God, thank you for the joys and responsibilities of teaching our generation and future generations what you have taught and entrusted us with. Help us to be found faithful. In Jesus' Name, Amen.

Most have heard of family recipes and family traditions. You know; Grandma's special cake tradition or Aunt's sweet potato pie recipe. Even Colonel Sanders' famous fried chicken recipe is passed down to future generations. Some of these recipes are shared, others are closely guarded. The Bible encourages us to teach our children and the generations after us the godly traditions we have and why we practice them. What will you say when a child asks you why you attend church services on Sundays? Or why your family prays before eating your meal? Children are naturally curious and your answer may shape their life for eternity. You can also start your godly parent tradition, what I refer to in my earlier Morning Glory book as the G.P.T. or Godly Parent Tradition. Pass it on!

© By Dr. Sheila Hayford.

January 25
A Time To Speak and A Time To Keep Silent

Genesis Chapter 24, verse 21:
Without saying a word, the man watched her closely to learn whether or not the Lord had made his journey successful. (NIV)
Ecclesiastes Chapter 3, verse 1:
To every thing there is a season, and a time to every purpose under the heaven:
Prayer: Dear Holy Spirit, enable me to speak when I ought to speak and to know when to be quiet for you do all things well. In Jesus' Name, Amen.

There is always the right time to speak. I know the many times I have wanted to make a remark during a conversation when the Holy Spirit would ask me to hold my peace. In every such instance I was glad when I obeyed God. The same concept applies when what you are saying is right on point. Speaking the right words at the wrong time is a mistake. When your spouse is upset from his day job (not with you, of course!) may not be the best time to discuss ways to resolve conflicts. So how do we know when the timing is right? The short answer is to depend on the Word of God and the Holy Spirit. The long answer is to use the abilities, experiences, resources, tools, people that God has given us in conjunction with the Holy Bible and the Holy Spirit as our guide. For you see, knowing when to speak and when to keep silent is a discipline and disciplines must be practiced to be perfected. Abraham's servant was on a mission for Abraham. He prayed to God for success and was specific in how he wanted God to respond to his request. And when the opportunity presented himself, he did not rush to speak, he watched closely. When Abraham's servant was convinced the timing was right, he spoke. God blessed him and his mission and he returned to Abraham with a successful outcome. There is indeed a time for everything under the sun!

© By Dr. Sheila Hayford.

January 26
A New Song

Psalm 96, verse 1:
O sing unto the Lord a new song: sing unto the Lord, all the earth.
Prayer: Praise the Lord God! For he is good and his mercy endures forever! We praise and we thank you, dear heavenly Father, for your goodness to us each day. Thank you for your wonderful creation, for your provision, your grace and most of all, for the gift of our Lord Jesus and the Holy Spirit. In Jesus' Name, Amen.

We know there is a time for everything under the sun and today it is time for a new song. How do we know that? It is because God has new mercies and loving kindness for us every day and we ought to sing and praise God for that. Gratitude is a choice; no one can force you to be grateful. God certainly will not force you to be grateful but He sure appreciates our songs of gratitude. Let us not be stingy towards God. Let all the earth praise God!

© By Dr. Sheila Hayford.

January 27
Fruitfulness

Genesis Chapter 13, verse 16:

And I will make thy seed as the dust of the earth: so that if a man can number the dust of the earth, then shall thy seed also be numbered.

Romans Chapter 4, verses 16-17:

Therefore, the promise comes by faith, so that it may be by grace and may be guaranteed to all Abraham's offspring - not only to those who are of the law but also to those who have the faith of Abraham. He is the father of us all. As it is written: "I have made you a father of many nations." He is our father in the sight of God, in whom he believed - the God who gives life to the dead and calls into being things that were not. (NIV)

Prayer: Dear God: I get excited when I reflect on the promises you have given us; promises for the present and for the hereafter. Help us to remember that some of your promises are conditional on our obedience to you. In Jesus' Name, Amen.

What a wonderful promise God gave to Abram at the time! Just look at the timing! In response to God's request, Abram, his wife, Sarai at the time and his household set out from their familiar surroundings on a journey with God into the unfamiliar. God did not ask Abram to take Lot with him but he did and now there was strife between Lot's household and Abram's household because the land was too small to accommodate both households. And so the households separated, with Abram giving Lot the first choice as to where to live. After Lot moved and Abram moved on, God gave Abram and Sarai this wonderful promise of children. They were going to be so fruitful, their descendants would be like the sand without number. True to his word, God gave them biological children and changed their names to Abraham and Sarah. Abraham, who is also called the Father of faith, has spiritual children, too numerous to number, who are all part of the family of God. Aren't you glad God in his mercy keeps his promises to us, even when like Abram we may mess up at times?

© By Dr. Sheila Hayford.

January 28
Favored

Luke Chapter 1, verses 19, 28, 38:

And the angel answering said unto him, I am Gabriel, that stand in the presence of God; and am sent to speak unto thee, and to shew thee these glad tidings.

And the angel came in unto her, and said, Hail, thou that art highly favoured, the Lord is with thee: blessed art thou among women.

And Mary said, Behold the handmaid of the Lord; be it unto me according to thy word. And the angel departed from her.

Prayer: Dear God; we thank you for favor through our Lord Jesus. It is a gift you freely give us for we could never earn it. May we be eager to receive your promises and quick to obey you. In Jesus' Name we pray, Amen.

The angel Gabriel was sent by God to bring good news directly to two people we read of in Luke Chapter 1; to Zacharias, the father of John the Baptist and to Mary, the mother of Jesus. Think about this! This is the angel who stands in God's presence, now on earth speaking God's promises to humankind. Let us look to see what how each of them responded. Zacharias doubted what the angel said and became dumb until the good news God said came to pass. Mary believed God, even though she was initially unsure of the details and ended with these faith-filled words to the angel: Behold the handmaid of the Lord; be it unto me according to thy word. God has given us everything good through our Lord and Savior Jesus Christ. When we believe the Lord Jesus and invite him into our heart to be our Lord and Savior, we have favor with our heavenly Father God because we come to God through Jesus' death on the cross as punishment for our sins. God's promises may be conditional on our faith and our obedience so although God's promises to us are yes through Jesus Christ, doubt and unbelief may cause some to miss out. Do you believe you are blessed and favored of God because of your faith and your acceptance and profession of salvation though the Lord Jesus? Yes, you, the blessed and highly favored one!

© By Dr. Sheila Hayford.

January 29
Shame For His Name

John Chapter 16, verse 33:

These things I have spoken unto you, that in me ye might have peace. In the world ye shall have tribulation: but be of good cheer; I have overcome the world.

Acts Chapter 5, verses 38-42:

Therefore, in the present case I advise you: Leave these men alone! Let them go! For if their purpose or activity is of human origin, it will fail. But if it is from God, you will not be able to stop these men; you will only find yourselves fighting against God." His speech persuaded them. They called the apostles in and had them flogged. Then they ordered them not to speak in the name of Jesus, and let them go. The apostles left the Sanhedrin, rejoicing because they had been counted worthy of suffering disgrace for the Name. Day after day, in the temple courts and from house to house, they never stopped teaching and proclaiming the good news that Jesus is the Messiah. (NIV)

Prayer: Dear God; persecution for our faith in any form can be challenging. You are the righteous Judge and we submit our lives to your care. So help us live for you in the power of the Holy Spirit. In Jesus' Name we pray. Amen.

All through the ages, we see persecution of Christians for their faith take various forms. In this Scripture, Jesus Christ's disciples were physically beaten for preaching and teaching about the Lord Jesus. Today, some are openly mocked and ridiculed for their faith, others are forbidden from discussing their faith in certain forums where other ideologies are openly permitted. Even worse, some are murdered as martyrs as they make the ultimate sacrifice for their faith with their lives. So, aren't we blessed and highly favored of God? We are, but the Lord Jesus did say our blessed and favored status would come with persecution because there are some who would rather wickedness and evil triumph, as opposed to sharing God's good news. There is a Day of Judgment coming when God will judge everyone on this earth according to how we lived here on earth. That is God's prerogative. Ours is to ask God daily for his wisdom, grace, guidance and the ministry of his holy angels as we live here on earth in the power of the Holy Spirit. So do not be fearful; be joyful in your Christian faith, even when you suffer persecution. God knows how to make it up to you in eternity.

© By Dr. Sheila Hayford.

January 30
Earth – Your Practice Run

Luke Chapter 19, verses 16-17, 20-26:
Then came the first, saying, Lord, thy pound hath gained ten pounds. And he said unto him, Well, thou good servant: because thou hast been faithful in a very little, have thou authority over ten cities. And another came, saying, Lord, behold, here is thy pound, which I have kept laid up in a napkin: For I feared thee, because thou art an austere man: thou takest up that thou layedst not down, and reapest that thou didst not sow. And he saith unto him, Out of thine own mouth will I judge thee, thou wicked servant. Thou knewest that I was an austere man, taking up that I laid not down, and reaping that I did not sow: Wherefore then gavest not thou my money into the bank, that at my coming I might have required mine own with usury? And he said unto them that stood by, Take from him the pound, and give it to him that hath ten pounds. (And they said unto him, Lord, he hath ten pounds.) For I say unto you, That unto every one which hath shall be given; and from him that hath not, even that he hath shall be taken away from him.

Prayer: Dear Lord Jesus: you have given us a lifetime lesson in this parable. Help us to take our life on this earth seriously, for it is a forerunner of our life in eternity. Thank you for sharing this with us ahead of time. Amen.

Sometimes we hear of someone asking for a promotion and we chuckle. Why? It is because they do not have a handle on their current assignment so we wonder if they can handle the extra responsibilities that would come with a promotion. Sometimes it is the reverse. The person who is promoted is not well qualified for their new position. In this life God is telling us in advance, "This earth is your practice run." We know how football teams send scouters to watch different athletes play on the field before they decide if they will offer them a position on their team. They may talk about how good their skills may be, but how do they actually play? In the parable above, God promoted the one who did something with what he had and brought profit to his boss. The one who badmouthed his boss and came up with excuses as to why he got nothing done, didn't just get fired, what he had was taken from him. God wants the best for you. He has entrusted you with creative abilities, giftings and talents because he wants to bless you, on this earth and for eternity. So do not despise or complain about what you have been endowed with by your Creator. Show the Creator and humanity what you can do on this earth practice run. There is a great cloud of heavenly witnesses cheering you on. Give life your best and get ready for God's heavenly promotion. May we be favored to say, "See you there!"

© By Dr. Sheila Hayford.

January 31
*** Let The Children Come

Mark Chapter 10, verses 13-14:
People were bringing little children to Jesus for him to place his hands on them, but the disciples rebuked them. When Jesus saw this, he

was indignant. He said to them, "Let the little children come to me, and do not hinder them, for the kingdom of God belongs to such as these. (NIV)

Prayer: Dear Lord Jesus: I look at your beautiful children and I am amazed. I see their little fingers and smiling faces and watch them grow. They come with enthusiasm for life, worry free, carefree, trusting their parents for their need. Their energy seems boundless, their creativity limitless. What happens in life that causes many adults to exchange these wonderful qualities for a life filled with fear, worry and regret? Help us to come to you as little children and trust you for every need. Forgive us where we allowed doubt, fear or worry to limit our potential and enable us to move forward, empowered by your Holy Spirit. In Your Name I pray. Amen.

While on a business trip I would meet these eight-year-old twin girls in the lobby from time to time. I am fascinated with twins and the miracle of life they represent and we would talk and laugh together. One day they came to the lobby with a young boy about their age who needed help connecting his mobile device to the Wi-Fi. One of the twins brought him to me. "That's my buddy", she told him as she introduced me, "we hang out together." I was old enough to be her mother! Honored and somewhat flattered, I smiled as he handed me his device to work on. Soon his Wi-Fi was working perfectly. I thought about our Lord Jesus Christ. Children were always comfortable with him. Indeed it was the Lord Jesus who said that we must come to him as children, in childlike trust, as we acknowledge our total dependence on him. Take the Lord Jesus at His Word and let the children come.

© By Dr. Sheila Hayford.

*** Excerpt from 2017 Edition of Morning Glory -365 Devotionals like no other! By Dr. Sheila Hayford. Used with permission

February 1
Bring the Sonshine With You

John Chapter 8, verse 12:

Then spake Jesus again unto them, saying, I am the light of the world: he that followeth me shall not walk in darkness, but shall have the light of life.

Matthew Chapter 5, verse 16:

Let your light so shine before men, that they may see your good works, and glorify your Father which is in heaven.

Prayer: Dear Lord Jesus; let us always bring you to bear on whatever issues or situations we face. We want to share your light. Amen.

The depravity we are seeing in society was unimaginable not so long ago. Sin has always been around since Adam and Eve. However, there used to be some things that were sacrosanct in society. Today you cannot turn on the television or read the news without hearing of horrible atrocities, abuse, profane rants, violence and the like. So what are we to do? Bring the Sonshine, the Lord Jesus Christ, with us. All that is needed for the influence of darkness to diminish is to apply the light. Shine the love of God, the wisdom of God, the character of God, the Word of God, prayer and the power of the Holy Spirit and things have to change. Change is either for better or for worse. In the Lord's Prayer we pray for God's will to be done on earth as it is in God's heaven. So bring the Sonshine with you!

© By Dr. Sheila Hayford.

February 2
God's Way – The Best Way!

Proverbs 14, verses 11, 12:

The house of the wicked shall be overthrown: but the tabernacle of the upright shall flourish. There is a way which seemeth right unto a man, but the end thereof are the ways of death.

Prayer: Dear Lord Jesus: God's Word says you are the Son of God and the only way to God. Help us not to be deceived by satan, sin or vain ideologies. God's way is always the best way and we willingly submit to your authority. Amen.

I was in highway traffic when the Holy Spirit asked me to move into the next lane. I hesitated and just then a stone from behind the truck in front of me hit and cracked my car's windshield. It didn't look like obeying God in such a "small" thing mattered but with the cracked windshield it was apparent God's way was the best way. Why does God say there is a way that seems right but whose end is death? It is because of the deceitfulness of satan and sin. Satan lied when he told Eve she would not die if she disobeyed God. In the end, Adam, Eve and all humanity discovered that Satan lied when death entered the human race. Thank God for Jesus. Jesus not only died for our sins, Jesus conquered death once and for all when he rose again. The Lord Jesus gives all who believe and receive him as Lord and Savior the gift of eternal life. And every one who receives the Lord Jesus has the seal of the Holy Spirit with the gift of the indwelling of the Holy Spirit. Any ideology contrary to God's Word may seem right but will lead to death. For God's way is always the best way!

© By Dr. Sheila Hayford.

February 3
Civility

James Chapter 1, verses 19-20:
My dear brothers and sisters, take note of this: Everyone should be quick to listen, slow to speak and slow to become angry, because human anger does not produce the righteousness that God desires. (NIV)

Romans Chapter 12, verse 18:

If it be possible, as much as lieth in you, live peaceably with all men.

Prayer: Dear God, sometimes it is easier to lash out in anger than to take the time to submit to the Holy Spirit's promptings but that is never worth it. So help us by the Holy Spirit to walk in love and to apply your wisdom. In Jesus' Name, we pray. Amen.

The lady made an irresponsible remark and my first reaction was to say to her: "Don't get smart with me!" The Holy Spirit said not to do that so I obeyed. I knew I was right and since there were three others close by who heard her "you don't need to do that..." remark, I felt the situation needed clarification. I decided to say something to her. Before I did, the Holy Spirit said, "just be careful!" I approached her and asked if she really said what she said and followed up with a few more questions. Taken aback, she squirmed and wiggled her words as she looked for an explanation and made it clear I did the right thing and that what she was suggesting was a short cut. It was a rational conversation. Now everyone in the vicinity was clear about the situation. Satisfied, I went back. I was glad I had obeyed God and thankful for the Holy Spirit's promptings.

It is easy to lash back at someone who has done the wrong thing. But what does that accomplish? Hard feelings, a sense of retaliation, carnal satisfaction, rationalization and/or more? While we do not have to sit by when someone says something that may be totally out of place, the way we speak matters; especially to God. When God asks us to walk in love, God makes it practical. In Romans Chapter 12, verse 18 we are encouraged live at peace with all men as far as it depends on us, considering our faith and our Christian principles. If someone decides to act foolishly, we can firmly speak the truth in love and follow God's instructions. Their actions are ultimately between them and God. And we can rest assured God will always have the final word!

© By Dr. Sheila Hayford.

February 4
You Are What You Think!

Hebrews Chapter 4, verse 12:

For the word of God is quick, and powerful, and sharper than any twoedged sword, piercing even to the dividing asunder of soul and spirit, and of the joints and marrow, and is a discerner of the thoughts and intents of the heart.

Proverbs Chapter 12, verse 5:

The thoughts of the righteous are right: but the counsels of the wicked are deceit.

Prayer: Dear Holy Spirit; how and what we think is how we live so enable our thoughts to be in line with God's words and God's will. In Jesus' Name we pray, Amen.

You are what you think? At first glance, this may appear to be an oversimplification. Upon reflection, it represents a deep spiritual truth. Your life is a display of your thoughts. Some, out of fear, cowardice, 'political correctness' or some other reason do not say what they actually believe in their heart or they give lip service to what they do not adhere to; in this case they have made the thoughtful decision to keep silent or to lie. Your beliefs shape your thoughts which in turn direct your actions. To change for the better, we must have our priorities right; spiritually, in our soul and physically, in that order. Is your spiritual relationship with the Lord Jesus right? Then, allow the Holy Spirit to lead and teach you. As you renew your mind with the Word of God and agree with the will of God, your beliefs will show in your thoughts and your actions will show God's transformation at work in you.

© By Dr. Sheila Hayford.

February 5
The Trumpet Sound

1 Thessalonians Chapter 4, verses 13-17:

But I would not have you to be ignorant, brethren, concerning them which are asleep, that ye sorrow not, even as others which have no hope. For if we believe that Jesus died and rose again, even so them also which sleep in Jesus will God bring with him. For this we say unto you by the word of the Lord, that we which are alive and remain unto the coming of the Lord shall not prevent them which are asleep. For the Lord himself shall descend from heaven with a shout, with the voice of the archangel, and with the trump of God: and the dead in Christ shall rise first: Then we which are alive and remain shall be caught up together with them in the clouds, to meet the Lord in the air: and so shall we ever be with the Lord.

Prayer: Dear Lord Jesus; you are coming again soon. Help us to be ready. Amen.

Sometimes when we talk about the Second Coming of the Lord Jesus to earth, it seems so out of place. As it was in the days of Noah, many are going about their business preoccupied with the cares and concerns of the world, with little or no thought about their eternal destiny. The Bible teaches us about this important event so there is no excuse for ignorance or apathy. For the trumpet will indeed sound, and the Lord Jesus will come back to earth again. The Lord Jesus is coming to take those who have received him as Lord and Savior on this earth, past and present, with him. At this Second Coming, the Lord Jesus is going back with an entourage; those believers who died in faith will be resurrected first and be with him and those believers who are alive at that time will be caught up with the Lord Jesus in the air. It is going to be one amazing sight! Are we ready?

© By Dr. Sheila Hayford.

February 6
Jesus – The Embodiment of Life

John Chapter 11, verses 25, 26:

Jesus said to her, "I am the resurrection and the life. The one who believes in me will live, even though they die; and whoever lives by believing in me will never die. Do you believe this?" (NIV)

Prayer: Yes, Lord Jesus; we believe and we trust you. Amen.

Everything associated with the Lord Jesus is associated with life. The Lord Jesus is the Bread of Life, the Water of Life, the Wisdom of God, the Word of God, the Resurrection and the Life. Help us, Lord, to apply godly wisdom as we live responsibly here and in the hereafter.

© By Dr. Sheila Hayford.

Tax & Income Planning
---

*Tax Planning
*Income Planning
*Estate Planning
*Investment Planning

Although each planning category is separate, they impact each other. Understanding how all of these planning pieces fit together, and what investments to use is key to a well-designed plan.

William L. Curry
JD, RFC, ChFC, CLU
Registered Representative
bill@WealthWisdomGroup.com

<u>Located At:</u>
701 Foulk Road, Suite 2G   Phone: (302) 651-9191
Wilmington, DE 19803   FAX: (302) 651-9173

William L. Curry is a registered representative with and securities are offered through Berthel Fisher & Company Financial Services, Inc. (**BFCFS**).
Member FINRA/SIPC. Advisory services offered through **BFC Planning, Inc.**
Wealth Wisdom Group, Inc. is not affiliated with **BFCFS/BFC Planning, Inc.**
Our firm does not provide legal or tax advice. Be sure to consult with your own legal and tax advisors before taking any action that may have tax implications.

February 7
Emboldened

Deuteronomy Chapter 6, verse 17:

Be sure to keep the commands of the Lord your God and the stipulations and decrees he has given you.

Prayer: Dear God; there is no substitute for obedience and we may never get the same opportunity twice. Help us to be diligent in obeying you. In the Name of your Son Jesus Christ, our perfect model of obedience to you, we pray. Amen.

It was the day of the church picnic and I noticed a stranger in attendance. I had greeted her as I went inside the church building and the Holy Spirit said to invite her to sit at my table. When I got outside, I went up to her. Pointing to my table, I asked her to join us. She asked if it was in the shade and said she needed to have her feet up. Our table was almost full and the empty seats were not in the shade. The lady behind me heard our conversation and invited her to sit with them. In obeying the Holy Spirit to extend an invitation to a stranger, another person was emboldened to do the same. We may never know whose actions are dependent on our obedience to God; God does. Just obey God!

© By Dr. Sheila Hayford.

February 8
Thankful

1 Thessalonians Chapter 5, verse 17:

In every thing give thanks: for this is the will of God in Christ Jesus concerning you.

Prayer: Dear God: we always have reason to be thankful because the Lord Jesus has given humanity the gift of salvation to all who will receive him. Thank you for this beautiful earth, for the gift of life and for everything you have given us through our Lord and Savior Jesus Christ. In Jesus Name, Amen.

I have a preference for warm compared to cold weather. Although I love to look at the beautiful snow right after it is freshly fallen, I do not like to drive in it. On the other hand, an acquaintance just loves the snow. In fact, she likes to be called "Snowy." Some do not like rainy weather. They would describe a rainy day as a "miserable" day. However, without the rain crops would not grow, the farmers would be out of food and work and society as a whole could not function. God, in his mercy, has given each of us more than we deserve to enjoy. We should be thankful for life, family, friends, the weather, free air, food, provision, work, and the list goes on… I have made the decision not to base my thankfulness on my circumstances, but on my God, who allows, directs and changes my circumstances. When I magnify God with my thankfulness, I am joyful and my circumstances have no choice but to respond to my God. Of course, we need to do our part for the betterment of humanity and help bring about positive change where needed. In other words, being thankful does not mean we shirk our responsibilities. When we trust God and know God is for us, we can't help but thank God. Hallelujah!

© By Dr. Sheila Hayford.

February 9
Back In The Family

Luke Chapter 15, verses 10, 21-24:
Likewise, I say unto you, there is joy in the presence of the angels of God over one sinner that repenteth. And the son said unto him, Father, I have sinned against heaven, and in thy sight, and am no more worthy to be called thy son. But the father said to his servants, Bring forth the best robe, and put it on him; and put a ring on his hand, and shoes on his feet: And bring hither the fatted calf, and kill it; and let us eat, and be merry:

For this my son was dead, and is alive again; he was lost, and is found. And they began to be merry.

Prayer; Dear God; help us to extend your love, compassion and mercy to others, even as we receive from you. In Jesus' Name, Amen.

Everybody makes mistakes, some more consequential than others. What is interesting is how society chooses to respond to those mistakes. Some years back it was "three strikes and you're out" which lead to the warehousing of several individuals in jails. Today, those with the same problems are no longer considered a menace to society but sick individuals in need of medical and mental treatment. While personal responsibility for one's actions is appropriate, individuals who have shown remorse for their actions and have moved on should be welcomed back into society. God our heavenly Father is not looking for an opportunity to cast a person away; God is looking for an opportunity to welcome a person back. You see, God created Adam and Eve and the human race for fellowship with God. God would come down in the cool of the day and hang out with Adam and Eve. But when Adam and Eve disobeyed God, God had to punish sin and Adam and Eve lost fellowship with God. However, God did not give up on humanity. God sent his Son, the Lord Jesus, to take the punishment for the sins of humanity and restore humanity to a right relationship with God. Salvation through Jesus is free but you have to receive him. For those who do, there is a 'Welcome Back' party with God's angels rejoicing in heaven, as these individuals are reborn, this time into the family of God. We all need God's compassion and forgiveness so let us extend God's compassion and forgiveness to others as they strive to move ahead in life.

© By Dr. Sheila Hayford.

February 10
The Elder Brother

Luke Chapter 15, verses 31-32:

'My son,' the father said, 'you are always with me, and everything I have is yours. But we had to celebrate and be glad, because this brother of yours was dead and is alive again; he was lost and is found.' NIV)

I John Chapter 4, verse 20:

If a man say, I love God, and hateth his brother, he is a liar: for he that loveth not his brother whom he hath seen, how can he love God whom he hath not seen?

Prayer: Dear God; your love for humanity is unconditional. How dare we, who receive so much love from you continuously, fail at times, to extend your love to others? Forgive us when we act selfishly or outside of your love character. In Jesus' Name we pray, Amen.

It is somewhat surprising that the elder brother in this parable was sulking like a toddler instead of being a part of the celebration when the prodigal son in the parable returned home. His father was happy, the servants were busy with the preparations for the welcome party and the elder brother would not even go in to meet his sibling. And lest the elder brother get all the blame, consider what happens in some religious circles when the son returns home. It was a crying shame to see the initial response when hip hop rapper Kanye West decided he would go all out with music relating to his faith in Jesus Christ. Some of the 'elder' Christian brothers began to question his authenticity, putting themselves in the place of God; others expected him to preach and speak as if he had walked with God in his faith journey for decades. Worse still, some began to mock his Sunday services. Appalling! Nevertheless, there are many elder brothers who are exemplary, in and out of the spotlight. It did my heart good to see Pastor Joel invite his fellow brother in the faith, Kanye West, to Lakewood Church. The joy radiating from Pastor Joel and Kanye West in conversation reflected God's glory and was a wonderful example of the elder brother's love. **When the prodigal son comes home, welcome him!** Pray for him, teach him and most importantly, disciple him in the truth of the Word of God. Why disciple him? So he will know truth, discern truth, live truth and teach truth. If you cannot love your brother whom you can see, how can you say you love God?

© By Dr. Sheila Hayford.

February 11
For The Least of These

Matthew Chapter 25, verses 34-41:
Then shall the King say unto them on his right hand, Come, ye blessed of my Father, inherit the kingdom prepared for you from the foundation of the world: For I was an hungred, and ye gave me meat: I was thirsty, and ye gave me drink: I was a stranger, and ye took me in: Naked, and ye clothed me: I was sick, and ye visited me: I was in prison, and ye came unto me. Then shall the righteous answer him, saying, Lord, when saw we thee an hungred, and fed thee? or thirsty, and gave thee drink? When saw we thee a stranger, and took thee in? or naked, and clothed thee? Or when saw we thee sick, or in prison, and came unto thee? And the King shall answer and say unto them, Verily I say unto you, Inasmuch as ye have done it unto one of the least of these my brethren, ye have done it unto me. Then shall he say also unto them on the left hand, Depart from me, ye cursed, into everlasting fire, prepared for the devil and his angels:

Prayer: Dear Lord Jesus; taking care of the weak and suffering is sometimes a thankless act, in society and, in some cases, from the recipients. However, it is never a thankless act to you. Help us to serve you with joy as we serve others. Amen.

Technology is rapidly advancing and society is moving ahead, yet many seem to be left behind. Those left behind may be working paycheck to paycheck and not be able to make ends meet, they may be homeless, they may have physical or personal issues that impact their ability to function well, they may be orphaned, widowed or refugees. Who advocates for them? You see, when people cannot or choose not to vote or do not have much influence in society, people tend to discount what it is they have to contribute or say. Not so with God. God is always concerned about the downtrodden. In fact, some of the promises the Lord Jesus makes is in relation to those who minister to the poor and downtrodden and he couples these promises with warnings to those who would despise and neglect them. The Lord Jesus is the righteous judge so let us do our part in helping those who cannot help themselves; not just with handouts but with meaningful solutions. They are very dear to God's heart.

© By Dr. Sheila Hayford.

February 12
Paved with Apathy

Matthew Chapter 24, verse12:

Because of the increase of wickedness, the love of most will grow cold, (NIV)

Prayer: Dear God, help us to speak when we ought to speak out. In Jesus' Name, Amen.

Doing nothing in the face of gross evil is tantamount to sanctioning the evil atrocity. History bears witness to the atrocities of the Holocaust and Slavery in that they persisted for far too long. God wants us to take a stand. You see, the war between good and evil is already going on. Hell was originally designed for the devil and the angels who followed satan. Satan was the one who lured Adam and Eve into following him and thus humanity became subject to God's punishment. However, the Lord Jesus came and took back satan's hold over humanity by living a sinless life, dying on the cross for the sins of humanity and overcoming satan, sin and death for all time. Apathy to this finished work of the Lord Jesus is tantamount to rejection of salvation through the Lord Jesus. In other words, some roads to hell may be paved with apathy. Humanity has everything to gain eternally with salvation through the Lord Jesus. Satan and those who follow satan have everything to lose for eternity. Do not allow apathy to get in your way!

© By Dr. Sheila Hayford.

February 13
The Value of A Soul

Proverbs Chapter 3, verses 21-23:

My son, let not them depart from thine eyes: keep sound wisdom and discretion: So shall they be life unto thy soul, and grace to thy neck. Then shalt thou walk in thy way safely, and thy foot shall not stumble.

Proverbs Chapter 11, verse 30:

The fruit of the righteous is a tree of life; and he that winneth souls is wise.

Prayer; Dear God, thank you for the value you have placed on every soul. We only need to look to your Son, Jesus Christ to see how much you love and value each soul. Praise be to your Name! Through Jesus Christ our Lord. Amen.

It was a Saturday morning and I planned to do some work in the morning. The clock alarm sounded, I turned it off and woke up later than I wanted to. At first, I was upset because I felt the Holy Spirit could have awakened me earlier. Wait a minute! God did wake me up; I was the one who turned the alarm off and was responsible for my actions. I quickly had a change of attitude, repented to God and decided I would run a few errands and do some one on one personal evangelism instead. My first two errands went well. As I got ready to go to my next errand, I noticed a young boy with an older looking gentleman. I had a coloring sheet and some Christian stickers with me so I asked the gentleman if I could give those to his son. He told me the little boy was his grandson and he graciously accepted the gift as he browsed though. He was so happy with the gift that I gave him Christian literature. This time he was elated and wanted to know more. So we began talking about spiritual things. Turns out he was visiting from Tanzania with his wife and would be leaving the United States in less than two weeks. The Holy Spirit nudged me to lead him in the prayer of salvation. I asked him if he was a born again Christian and explained what I meant. He said he attended church but had been too busy for that commitment. I asked him if he wanted to pray the prayer of salvation right then. He said, 'Yes!" and so I led him in prayer. After the prayer he was overjoyed! I gave him a prayer line, some Christian resources and he mentioned a Bible believing church fellowship close by his daughter's home where they were staying. He was very grateful and thankful. Wow! The value of a soul! God in His wisdom already had this precious gentleman in mind when the Holy Spirit re-worked my initial plans. Glory to God!

© By Dr. Sheila Hayford.

February 14
Love - Ly

1 Corinthians Chapter 13, verses 4, 5, 6, 7, 13:

Love is patient, love is kind. It does not envy, it does not boast, it is not proud. It does not dishonor others, it is not self-seeking, it is not easily angered, it keeps no record of wrongs. Love does not delight in evil but rejoices with the truth. It always protects, always trusts, always hopes, always perseveres.

And now these three remain: faith, hope and love. But the greatest of these is love. (NIV)

Prayer: Dear God; you are love in its fullest and so we can only love to the fullest with your grace, strength and power. Help us to live love-ly as we demonstrate your love characteristics and to share our love knowledge of you with others. In Jesus' Name we pray, Amen.

The characteristics of love that we read here are a tall order for any human. Especially so on this day that love is celebrated worldwide. We all know society would be a more civil and better place if we practice love for one another; love for self, family, friends, neighbors, strangers, government, God's creation. We must make the decision to love God's way, understanding that God's love is unconditional love. Loving a person does not mean you agree with any wrong they may be doing. Loving a person does not mean you do not apply correction or discipline if needed. Loving a person does not mean you overlook sin. Loving a person means your ultimate goal is for their best, even if they knowingly choose otherwise. God loves us and yet God gives everyone the free will to accept or reject His Son, the Lord Jesus, and thus face the consequences of their own decisions. As we celebrate love today and each day, let us ask God for grace and power to fully love for love never fails.

© By Dr. Sheila Hayford

February 15
The Safest Place

Psalm 91, verse 2:
I will say of the Lord, He is my refuge and my fortress: my God; in him will I trust.

Prayer: Dear God, thank you that Jesus Christ is our solid foundation and in you is our safe place. In Jesus' Name, Amen.

The safest place for any born again believer is in the will of God. When you receive the Lord Jesus into your life as Lord and Savior you become a part of God's family. The Holy Spirit guarantees your position in Christ in God by dwelling in you at the time of your salvation. So your eternal destination is secure. However, you still have your free will and God respects that. Will you will obey God and live according to the will, plans and purpose of God revealed in the Holy Bible? Will you follow God wholeheartedly? There are consequences to our actions; obedience to God pleases God and brings God's rewards from God, disobedience to God is a set up for God's judgment. As I grew in my Christian walk, I realized that if I was not where God wanted me to be, I was missing out on the blessings of where God wanted me to be, and God was not obligated to protect what He had not sanctioned. Thus, I strive to walk in the will of God. Do I fail at times? Yes! That is why the Lord Jesus came; to take away our past, present and future sin when we confess and repent of our sins. Therefore in Christ, we are not condemned. When we truly repent and ask God for forgiveness through the Lord Jesus, we are free to move on and allow the Holy Spirit to work us back into God's plans. Don't ask God to sanction your mess. Ask God to teach you, lead and direct and lead you and enable you to apply God's wisdom. Go ahead, obey God and be safe!

© By Dr. Sheila Hayford.

February 16
That Was Funny!

Genesis Chapter 21, verse 6:
And Sarah said, God hath made me to laugh, so that all that hear will laugh with me.
Prayer: Dear God; we thank you for the gift of laughter. We thank you that you laugh with us as we share our joy. In Jesus' Name, Amen.

I was listening to the radio and the host asked the callers to say something silly they had done. Well, this lady called. She was scheduled to attend a company meeting and her boss had given her instructions on how to get there. He told her how many traffic lights she would go through to get there. So she started her journey. Everything seemed okay but the next thing she knew she was in another state! Frantically, she called her boss and told him she was lost. He asked her a few questions. Suddenly it dawned on her that she had only been counting the red stop traffic lights. When the lights were green she just drove through without counting them. That was funny! God knows that we will have challenges and tests in life, and that these come with the potential to cause stress. So in God's infinite wisdom God has wired humankind to appreciate humor; good, clean, humor. Sarah was so full of joy and laughter because God had made her glad. Notice Sarah did not keep her laughter to herself; she shared it and no doubt brought joy and laughter to others. Share your joy and laughter!

© By Dr. Sheila Hayford.

Tap, Ballet, Lyrical, Jazz, Hip-Hop, Acrobatics, Cheer Dance, and More.

Dance Delaware is a family friendly & professional dance studio that provides a positive atmosphere where students of all ages and levels can grow and strive to be the dancer of their dreams. Come join us, and become part of the Dance Delaware Family.

302-998-1222
DanceDelaware Studios
www.dancedelaware.com
2005 Concord Pike, Suite 204 Wilmington Delaware 19803
(located above IHOP)

Instagram: dancedelaware_studios
Facebook: https://www.facebook.com/DanceDelaware/

February 17
Simon Biles - Excellence on Display

Daniel Chapter 6, verse 3:

Then this Daniel was preferred above the presidents and princes, because an excellent spirit was in him; and the king thought to set him over the whole realm.

Prayer: Dear God; Thank you for the abilities, gifts and talents you have given us. May we diligent use and develop them for your glory. In Jesus' Name, Amen.

Simone Biles amazes me. How can she do what she does in Gymnastics and make it look so effortless? At the 2019 Gymnastics World Championships, she won five gold medals to become the most decorated gymnast in the history of the World Championship games with a total of 25 medals. She excelled in gymnastics early in life and at 22 years of age has already won 25 World medals including 19 Gold World medals and has two gymnastic moves named after her. What really amazes me, is how she consistently displays her excellent spirit, an excellent attitude and excellent gymnastic performances in spite of the obstacles she faces. Her beginnings in life were difficult. Her mother was addicted to illegal drugs, her dad left the family before she was born, she was in foster care before she was raised by her grandparents, Ron and Nellie, who later adopted her. In spite of sexual abuse by her former U.S. gymnastics team doctor, Simone still loves and excels in gymnastics. So how does Simone do all this? Simone credits her abilities, her successes and her life to God and is very vocal in her faith. God is an excellent God who excels in everything He does, Shouldn't we, as God's creation, strive to be and do the same?

© By Dr. Sheila Hayford.

February 18
President Abraham Lincoln – A Life of Service

Matthew Chapter 5, verse 16:
Let your light so shine before men, that they may see your good works, and glorify your Father which is in heaven.

Prayer: Dear God, we pray that you will restore your Word and your influence in society for we need your solid foundation in the way we live; mindful of the eternity that awaits us on the other side of this earth. In Jesus' Name, Amen.

February is the month we celebrate U.S. Presidents, so it is an honor to remember one of my favorite American Presidents, the 16th President, President Abraham Lincoln. President Abraham Lincoln was a man of faith, an example of extraordinary perseverance and a man of great service. We are thankful for his famous Emancipation Proclamation that made forever free those slaves within the Confederacy in 1863 and for his Proclamation as the last Thursday in November as a Day of Thanksgiving and Praise to our benevolent Father who dwelleth in the Heavens in 1863. President Lincoln had challenging and humble beginnings. His mother passed away when he was ten years of age, he lived and worked on a farm during his upbringing, did a lot of self-education, became a lawyer, a politician and an excellent president. President Lincoln was fully aware of his responsibilities towards God and his service to his country, not just on earth but for eternity. Indeed, President Lincoln once said, "Surely God would not have created such a being as man, with an ability to grasp the infinite, to exist only for a day! No, no, man was made for immortality." In the words of President Lincoln, "I like to see a man proud of the place in which he lives. I like to see a man live so that his place will be proud of him." To President Lincoln I say, the world is a much better place because of your life and your contributions to humanity and your legacy still lives on. May God say the same about us!

© By Dr. Sheila Hayford.

February 19
Giving

Luke Chapter 6, verse 38:
Give, and it shall be given unto you; good measure, pressed down, and shaken together, and running over, shall men give into your bosom.

For with the same measure that ye mete withal it shall be measured to you again.

Prayer: Heavenly Father, we thank you for the gift of our Lord Jesus. Help us as we serve you in our giving. In Jesus' Name, Amen.

Giving is a part of living. How so? Parents give birth to a child and everything else after that involves giving and receiving. God birthed humanity and everything afterwards involves giving and receiving. Wow! When God birthed Adam and Eve God **gave** them specific instructions, they **received** those instructions and humanity had to deal with what they did with what they received. God is the source of all the good things we receive us and God does not want us to be selfish. Yes, be good to yourself, but also do good to your family, your community and wherever God places you. When you give good, expect a harvest of good. What if you give good but receive evil in return? Ask God how you should proceed, obey God and leave the results to God.

© By Dr. Sheila Hayford

February 20
Goals: Pressing On

Philippians Chapter 3, verses 12-14:

Not that I have already obtained all this, or have already arrived at my goal, but I press on to take hold of that for which Christ Jesus took hold of me. Brothers and sisters, I do not consider myself yet to have taken hold of it. But one thing I do: Forgetting what is behind and straining toward what is ahead, I press on toward the goal to win the prize for which God has called me heavenward in Christ Jesus. (NIV)

Prayer: Dear Lord Jesus, help us to continue to press on. Amen.

Press on; allowing God to help you accomplish your goals.

© By Dr. Sheila Hayford

U.S. Tax Pros

INTEGRITY, PROFESSIONALISM, COMMITMENT
Year Round Tax, Accounting and Business Support!

- ✓ **TAX SERVICES**
- ✓ **ACCOUNTING SERVICES**
- ✓ **BUSINESS CONSULTING**
- ✓ **TRUST MANAGEMENT**
- ✓ **FREE CONSULTATION**.

Contact Us Today! Telephone: (484) 821-7904
www.ustaxpros.us

February 21
Wealth

Psalm 112, verse 3:
Wealth and riches shall be in his house: and his righteousness endureth for ever.

Deuteronomy Chapter 8, verse 18:
But thou shalt remember the Lord thy God: for it is he that giveth thee power to get wealth, that he may establish his covenant which he sware unto thy fathers, as it is this day.

Why is it that some have a problem when Christians begin to talk about money? Many have no problem when their mortgage company asks them to pay for their home loan, or when Macy's asks them to pay for their store purchase. However, some feel it is out of place for a Christian to talk about money. What is more important is God's take on wealth. First, we have to understand that wealth is more than money. True wealth involves prosperity in every area of your life. A person may have a wealth of money but be poor in health. Or conversely. A person may have a wealth of good counsel or a wealth of bad counsel. A person may be wealthy in their relationship to God through the righteousness that comes through the Lord Jesus or they may be spiritually poor towards God. What is important is acknowledging where you are and placing God, the giver of all good gifts, as your priority in life. The kind of wealth you have and what you do with it is important. If you are spiritually poor, you may be filled by applying what the word of God says about salvation through the Lord Jesus Christ. If you are financially challenged, you may have your finances improved by seeking and applying wise financial counsel. If you are in need of physical health, you may apply good healthy habits, seek medical advice where needed and heed the words of the great Physician, the Lord Jesus Christ. What is your need? God needs you to be truly wealthy. Why? It is so God's righteous plans and promises for you and humanity will be established.

© By Dr. Sheila Hayford.

February 22
Fearless

John Chapter 6, verse 20:
But he said to them, "It is I; don't be afraid." (NIV)
Prayer: Dear Lord Jesus: I so love your boldness. It is because you know your true identity in God. Help us to walk in faith in you and not in anxiety, worry or fearfulness. Amen.

Jesus Christ is **fearless**. In other words, there is never any fear in what Jesus does, what Jesus says or who Jesus is. Why? It is because fear and faith in God are antagonistic to each other. If a person is fearful or doubtful about what they should do or say, it is more likely the person will not move forward in what they ought to do. The Lord Jesus knows that in this world there are circumstances and people who may try to rob you of your joy, your drive to move forward and may try to invoke fear, intimidation or anxiety in you. Thus, the Lord Jesus gives this promise ahead of time. Jesus was walking on the sea when the disciples saw him. In other words, the Lord Jesus was doing what was humanly impossible to mankind. Instead of being filled with amazement at what God could do, the disciples were filled with fear! Why? Did they think he might drown, forgetting the Lord Jesus is God? Were they afraid because of the circumstances they had encountered? Whatever the reason, they heeded these words of the Lord Jesus, "don't be afraid" and received him into their ship. When they did so, they immediately reached their destination. With the Lord Jesus in their boat they arrived at their intended destination faster than they could have done otherwise and in spite of the initial contrary situation. What is causing you anxiety, fear or worry? The Lord Jesus is telling you not to fear, but to have faith in him and to let him direct you and work out what God knows needs to be done on your behalf. Take the Lord Jesus at his word. Your faith in God will determine your outcome.

© By Dr. Sheila Hayford.

February 23
You are Who God Says You Are

John Chapter 5, verse 32:
There is another that beareth witness of me; and I know that the witness which he witnesseth of me is true.

Prayer: Dear God; we believe what you say about us. Help us, by the power of the Holy Spirit, to act and speak accordingly. In Jesus' Name. Amen.

The Lord Jesus knows the hearts of all and he knew there were many who claimed to recognize Moses as a prophet of God but who were speaking and plotting evil against the Lord Jesus. Did that cause the Lord Jesus worry or anxiety? No! The Lord Jesus got it right because he knew what God said about him. If a person agrees with what God says about the Lord Jesus, that is fine. If a person disagrees with what God says about the Lord Jesus, that does not change what God says about him. What is the Lord Jesus teaching us here? First, that you must know and believe what God says about you because God's word is true. Then you must agree in word and deed with what God says about you. For if what God says about you is good, even if others say otherwise, you're good!

© By Dr. Sheila Hayford.

February 24
Thanksgiving

John Chapter 6, verses 9-12:
There is a lad here, which hath five barley loaves, and two small fishes: but what are they among so many? And Jesus said, Make the men sit down. Now there was much grass in the place. So the men sat down, in number about five thousand. And Jesus took the loaves; and when he had given thanks, he distributed to the disciples, and the disciples to them that were set down; and likewise of the fishes as much as they would. When they were filled, he said unto his disciples, Gather up the fragments that remain, that nothing be lost.

Prayer: Dear God; thank you for our Lord and Savior Jesus Christ. Thank you for his teaching and for his perfect example. May our thanks always precede our requests for your miracles. In Jesus Name. Amen.

Thanksgiving is the precedent to your miracle. Really? Yes! It seemed like an impossible situation. Five loaves and two fishes to feed about five thousand men! Not impossible for God. However, there is a way things have to be done to make sure the miracle happens. The Lord Jesus demonstrates to us the way it should be done. First, you have to know what the need is and what the desired outcome of the miracle is. Then you have to remain calm in the situation. The Lord Jesus asked that the men be seated. The Lord Jesus then took the loaves, representing the situation, and **gave thanks.** Thanks, of course, to God but also I am sure he gave thanks to the little boy who had donated his meal so that many could be fed. Afterwards, Jesus began to distribute the food and the miracle flowed first to the disciples, followed by those to whom the miracle was needed and there was enough food for everyone to be satisfied. The miracle of the multiplication of five loaves and two fishes fed five thousand men with some left over. Now is the time to put this lesson into practice. We all have situations where we need God's miraculous intervention. Give thanks first!

© By Dr. Sheila Hayford.

February 25
Guaranteed!

Isaiah Chapter 14, verse 27:
For the Lord Almighty has purposed, and who can thwart him? His hand is stretched out, and who can turn it back? (NIV)

Prayer: Dear God; it is so reassuring that you offer the perfect guarantees. We bless you and we thank you. In Jesus' Name. Amen.

Have you ever bought an appliance or an item that was guaranteed by the manufacturer? It may have been guaranteed for a year, five years or even for a lifetime. However, with any manufacturer's guarantee, you will usually notice a disclaimer with that warranty which states that the warranty may be limited, null and void under certain conditions, or if the warranty does not live up to the guarantee your appliance or item may be repaired, replaced or your money refunded, at the manufacturer's option. Not so with our perfect God. If God guaranteed it, there is nothing or no one that can stop God. So how do you know what God has guaranteed for you? You have to read and study the Word of God and talk with God in prayer to find out. And then hold fast to God's unchanging words!

© By Dr. Sheila Hayford.

February 26
God's Good Plans

Ephesians Chapter 2, verse 10:

For we are his workmanship, created in Christ Jesus unto good works, which God hath before ordained that we should walk in them.

Prayer: Dear God, you amaze us! Thank you for all the good works you have planned for us. It is an honor and a joy to serve you. May we always remember that with you, we are overcomers. In Jesus' Name, Amen.

How reassuring to know that even before we were born, God had planned our future and that includes good works. Through his Son, our Lord and Savior, Jesus Christ, not only are we are born into God's kingdom, we are given everything we need to live a life filled with purpose. You see, if you were not absolutely necessary in God's creative plans you would not be here. There are somethings only you can do for God. There is only one you, so only you can praise and serve God the way you do. And that brings God joy as God admires his workmanship in you. So go ahead, continue your good works and make God happy. We may not be perfect in this earthly life but we have a perfect God and when the Lord Jesus Christ comes to receive us in eternity to come, we will be made perfect in Christ. Let's celebrate God's good plans!

© By Dr. Sheila Hayford

February 27
As Clean As You Want It To Be

John Chapter 15, verse 3:

Now ye are clean through the word which I have spoken unto you.

Prayer: Dear Lord Jesus, thank you for your cleansing power. We receive you and your words to and for us. Amen.

I was multitasking while I was cooking some rice (on the stove top, not with the rice cooker!) and when I finally got to checking it the bottom of the rice was burnt! It was so burnt the bottom was hard to clean. I scrubbed the bottom using my go to "as seen on tv" kitchen cleaner to no avail and so after doing the best I could cleaning the pot, I placed the pot on the shelf. Less than a couple of weeks later, I decided to cook four different dishes at the same time and needed to use that pot. I knew I needed God's intervention to fully clean the bottom of the pot, which I should have asked for much earlier. Thank God for God being patient with me. I prayed seriously while reminding God that I was fully aware of my need and began to scrub the pan. The stuck burnt portions just fell off!!! The more I scrubbed, the cleaner the pot looked until I began to realize if I continued scrubbing it would look better than new. There may have been circumstances or situations in the past where you got burnt, so to speak. You decided to put that situation on the shelf and thought that was just the way it was. Then the Lord Jesus says, not only are you forgiven, you have been made clean by Jesus' words. In other words, you are now a new creation in God. You can be as clean as you want to be. You do not need to let your past determine your future. The more you allow the Word of God to cleanse you, the better you look. As clean as you want to be!

© By Dr. Sheila Hayford.

February 28
A Joyful Noise

Psalm 100:
Make a joyful noise unto the Lord, all ye lands. Serve the Lord with gladness: come before his presence with singing. Know ye that the Lord he is God: it is he that hath made us, and not we ourselves; we are his people, and the sheep of his pasture. Enter into his gates with thanksgiving, and into his courts with praise: be thankful unto him, and

bless his name. For the Lord is good; his mercy is everlasting; and his truth endureth to all generations.

Prayer: Dear God; we cannot keep silent as we praise you, thank you and bless your glorious Name. In Jesus' Name, we pray, Amen.

What a beautiful Psalm; so short and yet so poignant. Have you seen someone in church trying to stop a child who is loudly praising God? Usually the child begins to shout all the more! There is a time to make some noise and praising, thanking and worshipping God with a joyful noise tops them all. Listen; God is always good, his mercy towards us is forever, his truth lasts through all generations. Hallelujah! SHOUT!

© By Dr. Sheila Hayford.

February 29
The Mirage

Isaiah Chapter 35, verses 3,4:
Strengthen the feeble hands, steady the knees that give way; say to those with fearful hearts, "Be strong, do not fear; your God will come, he will come with vengeance; with divine retribution he will come to save you."

Prayer: Dear God, we entrust ourselves to your care and to your divine providence. In Jesus' Name. Amen.

In life, we sometimes face what looks like a mirage. Have you ever seen what appeared to be a sheet of water on the road but you found out when you got there that there was no water? So what is a mirage? It is something that appears real but is not in fact. You see a successful person and it looks like he or she got where they are in life overnight. That is a mirage because you do not see all the sweat, toil and sometimes pain, they put into their achievements. You see a couple married for fifty years and is looks like they never had an argument their entire marriage. That is a mirage because they kept their arguments private and worked hard to commit to their relationship, even when they felt like quitting. I have so much respect for Will Smith and Jada Pinkett-Smith, especially their commitment to each other in spite of the challenges. Will shared the time his wife cried for forty straight days during their marriage and he knew then his marriage was in trouble. They did not quit, they stayed strong and committed to their marriage. When life's circumstances try to discourage you from pressing forward in Christ, remember what God says about you in His Word and recognize those situations for the mirages they are. God says to you, "Be strong, do not fear; your God will come with vengeance; with divine retribution he will come to save you." What God says is no mirage!

© By Dr. Sheila Hayford.

March 1
To Your Neighbor Be True

Leviticus Chapter 6, verses 1-5a:

The Lord said to Moses: "If anyone sins and is unfaithful to the Lord by deceiving a neighbor about something entrusted to them or left in their care or about something stolen, or if they cheat their neighbor, or if they find lost property and lie about it, or if they swear falsely about any such sin that people may commit - when they sin in any of these ways and realize their guilt, they must return what they have stolen or taken by extortion, or what was entrusted to them, or the lost property they found, or whatever it was they swore falsely about. (NIV)

I Samuel Chapter 15, verses 10-11, 13, 14, 16, 26:

Then the word of the Lord came to Samuel: "I regret that I have made Saul king, because he has turned away from me and has not carried out my instructions." Samuel was angry, and he cried out to the Lord all that night. When Samuel reached him, Saul said, "The Lord bless you! I have carried out the Lord's instructions." But Samuel said, "What then is this bleating of sheep in my ears? What is this lowing of cattle that I hear?" "Enough!" Samuel said to Saul. "Let me tell you what the Lord said to me last night." But Samuel said to him, "I will not go back with you. You have rejected the word of the Lord, and the Lord has rejected you as king over Israel!" (NIV)

Prayer: Dear God; thank you for making serving you practical and simple. Help us to serve you in sincerity and in truth. In Jesus' Name we pray, Amen.

I find it interesting and comforting that God cares about what some would consider the mundane things of life, or to use their terminology, "that's no big deal." Look at the examples given here, someone entrusted to keep something for a person did not return it and then lied about it. Did they get off the hook? Not with God. God gave King Saul specific instructions. King Saul carried out only a part of God's instructions and then lied to the man of God when King Saul said he had done what God told him to do. The animals he kept became a curse to him, bleating in the ears of God. Did King Saul get away with it? No! With that act, God took the kingship away from King Saul and King David was chosen by God to be the new King. Was God's punishment instantaneous? God's judgement was and it became obvious in God's time. Better to return the property to its rightful owner than to remain cursed of God.

© By Dr. Sheila Hayford.

March 2
Injustice? Speaking God's Truth To Power

Amos Chapter 5, verse 10, 12, 14:
There are those who hate the one who upholds justice in court and detest the one who tells the truth. For I know how many are your offenses and how great your sins. There are those who oppress the innocent and take bribes and deprive the poor of justice in the courts. Seek good, not evil, that you may live. Then the Lord God Almighty will be with you, just as you say he is. (NIV)

James Chapter 2, verses 2-4:

Suppose a man comes into your meeting wearing a gold ring and fine clothes, and a poor man in filthy old clothes also comes in. If you show special attention to the man wearing fine clothes and say, "Here's a good seat for you," but say to the poor man, "You stand there" or "Sit on the floor by my feet," have you not discriminated among yourselves and become judges with evil thoughts? (NIV)

Prayer: Dear God; you hate injustice and so should we. Help us always stand for what is right. In Jesus' Name, Amen.

We say we live in a democratic society where all people are created equal. Then we read of the famous billionaire involved in horrific sex trafficking crimes and virtually getting away with it for several years. Injustice in society? That is a reality also. Money and power should not be the primary determinant of how a person is treated, whether it be in society, in the courts or in the church. So what does God, the Ultimate Authority in all matters, have to say about injustice? First, that God sees all. Some may hide their actions from men some of the time or all of the time but their actions are never hidden from God. Next, God will judge and punish unrighteousness and those who abuse their position and power, especially when they unjustly deal with the poor or those who speak against their evil actions. Finally, God gives everyone the opportunity to repent of evil and do right by God as long as they are living on this earth. God's intention in Scripture is to warn humankind not to go down the wrong path because God wants you to live. Yes, God would rather you chose life through his free gift, his Son Jesus Christ. Seek God and seek good!

© By Dr. Sheila Hayford.

March 3
You. Stand. Forever.

Revelation Chapter 19, verse 1:

And after these things I heard a great voice of much people in heaven, saying, Alleluia; Salvation, and glory, and honour, and power, unto the Lord our God:

Hebrews Chapter 1, verses 1-3:

God, who at sundry times and in divers manners spake in time past unto the fathers by the prophets, Hath in these last days spoken unto us by his Son, whom he hath appointed heir of all things, by whom also he made the worlds; Who being the brightness of his glory, and the express image of his person, and upholding all things by the word of his power, when he had by himself purged our sins, sat down on the right hand of the Majesty on high:

Prayer: Dear Lord Jesus; authority and power belongs to you. You have conquered sin, satan and death and you live and reign forever. Hallelujah! Amen.

It is important to acknowledge the Lord Jesus as the holy Son of God, to whom God has appointed authority and power forever. It is even more important to acknowledge and receive the Lord Jesus Christ as your **personal** Lord and Savior. Your eternal destiny depends on that one choice. The Lord Jesus Christ stands forever. Dear Lord Jesus, we stand with you!

© By Dr. Sheila Hayford.

March 4
The Appointed Time

Habakkuk Chapter 2, verse3:

For the vision is yet for an appointed time, but at the end it shall speak, and not lie: though it tarry, wait for it; because it will surely come, it will not tarry.

Prayer: Dear heavenly Father, help us not to become impatient with your appointed times in our life and for humanity. In Jesus' Name. Amen.

As we read Scripture, we see times that God has set aside for different events; a time for the Lord Jesus to come into this world to save humanity, a time for the Lord Jesus to die on the cross and rise from the dead and there is a set time for the Lord Jesus to come back again as promised. What about your personal appointed times? Like the Lord Jesus, God had a time for you to be born and brought you to this earth full of purpose. So what is your purpose? Your natural abilities and talents will give you a clue as to what God's purpose and plans for you are on this earth. However, God has much more to reveal to you concerning his plans and purpose for your life. Study God's Word and get into right relationship with God through Jesus Christ. Pray and write down the vision, goals and plans God gives you. Work out the appointed times of your vision with God as you put a plan into action to achieve the goals of your vision. As you begin to execute your vision, allow God to lead you and tweak your plans so they are always relevant. And what should you do if the vision seems to take a long time in coming to fruition? Re-evaluate the vision and make sure it is God given. If God said it and you do your part, the vision is for the appointed time so wait for it. God has a due date for your appointed time and it will show up!

© By Dr. Sheila Hayford.

March 5
I Am Glad I Prayed

2 Chronicles Chapter 7, verse 15:
Now my eyes will be open and my ears attentive to the prayers offered in this place. (NIV)

Prayer: My heavenly Father; thank you for the joy of answered prayer. In Jesus' Name, Amen.

I love to cook and I cook most of the time without recipes. In other words, no two of my food dishes are exactly the same. I know what I want to create and just go about cooking it. And it works most of the time. However, there are certain dishes that I specifically pray about when I want to get it just right. And so it was, I had guests coming and I needed the food to be just "perfect!" I prayed and God heard and answered my prayer. The food was great and everyone had a great time! I thanked God and said to myself, "I am glad I prayed." Are there some things you need God to do for you? If God is concerned about my cooking and about making sure the birds have food to eat, your concerns are very important to God. Right now is a great time to have a conversation with God!

© By Dr. Sheila Hayford.

March 6
Worship - The Missing Ingredient

Matthew Chapter 15, verse 25, 28:
Then came she and worshipped him, saying, Lord, help me. Then Jesus answered and said unto her, O woman, great is thy faith: be it unto thee even as thou wilt. And her daughter was made whole from that very hour.

Philippians Chapter 2, verse 11:
And that every tongue should confess that Jesus Christ is Lord, to the glory of God the Father.

Prayer: Dear God, we acknowledge you as God and as Lord in every aspect of life. May we always remember you are our God first, and our worship is due you. In Jesus' Name, Amen.

The woman mentioned in this Scripture reading needed help. Her daughter was in need of Jesus' healing and deliverance. However, the Lord Jesus was on assignment after ministering earlier to the multitudes and Jesus' disciples sought to send her away because her cries were a distraction. Nevertheless, look at what the woman did. She worshipped the Lord Jesus. That got the Lord Jesus' attention. After a short dialogue with her, the woman received her request from the Lord Jesus and her daughter was completely healed. Some want God to do things for them but they don't want to serve God. They might ask God why God did not spare them from the flood and then continue cursing God in the same sentence. That is not only rude, that is irreverent. They would not talk to their boss that way; how much more to God? God wants to help you, but he is your God first. God is happy to have a conversation with you, but you must show God some respect. Are you experiencing all God has for you? Does it seems like God does not always respond to your prayers? Worship God; that may be your missing ingredient for success.

© By Dr. Sheila Hayford.

Laurece West

Gospel Singing and Speaking
Sound amazing, stay healthy,
move listeners,
and present powerfully,
with confidence to sing or speak
God's magnificence!

Laurece West: Singer. Speaker. Voice Coach.
Laurece West Studios
www.laureceweststudios.com
laurece@laureceweststudios.com
Tel: 919.383.4876

March 7
By Faith

Hebrews Chapter 11, verses 32-36:

what more shall I say? I do not have time to tell about Gideon, Barak, Samson and Jephthah, about David and Samuel and the prophets, who through faith conquered kingdoms, administered justice, and gained what was promised; who shut the mouths of lions, quenched the fury of the flames, and escaped the edge of the sword; whose weakness was turned to strength; and who became powerful in battle and routed foreign armies. Women received back their dead, raised to life again. There were others who were tortured, refusing to be released so that they might gain an even better resurrection. Some faced jeers and flogging, and even chains and imprisonment.

1 Peter Chapter 1, verse 7:

These have come so that the proven genuineness of your faith - of greater worth than gold, which perishes even though refined by fire - may result in praise, glory and honor when Jesus Christ is revealed.

Prayer: Dear God, thank you for your miraculous interventions in our lives as we exercise our faith and walk with you. In Jesus' Name, Amen.

This "By faith" chapter is ongoing; through generations of humanity. No wonder the Apostle Paul could not write down all the testimonies of those whose faith brought about God's intervention in miraculous ways, sometimes unexpected according to conventional human wisdom. Some "By Faith" faced persecution for their faith in the Lord Jesus Christ, even to the point of death. Tests and challenges are a part of the Christian faith journey, they come to test the genuineness of your faith. Faith comes from God, and as we read, hear and study Scripture, the Holy Spirit helps our faith grow. When we experience faith victories, others are also encouraged and God is lifted up in our conversations. What is your "By faith" story?

March 8
Servant Leadership

Nehemiah Chapter 8, verses 8-10:

They read from the Book of the Law of God, making it clear and giving the meaning so that the people understood what was being read. Then Nehemiah the governor, Ezra the priest and teacher of the Law, and the Levites who were instructing the people said to them all, "This day is holy to the Lord your God. Do not mourn or weep." For all the people had been weeping as they listened to the words of the Law. Nehemiah said, "Go and enjoy choice food and sweet drinks, and send some to those who have nothing prepared. This day is holy to our Lord. Do not grieve, for the joy of the Lord is your strength." (NIV)

Prayer; Dear God; thank you for the good news of salvation through the Lord Jesus Christ. Help us, as Ezra did, to share this good news simply so many will understand and respond. In the Name of Jesus we pray, Amen.

How beautiful! Nehemiah, the Governor and Ezra the Priest and Teacher collaborating jointly to plainly instruct the people on the Words of Scripture. At first the people began to weep, no doubt sorry for the sins they had committed against God. Nehemiah, knowing God's heart, explained that God's desire was not for them to die. What God wanted of the people then is what God wants for us today; confession, repentance and turning away from sin as we live in submission to God. Thus, the gospel of salvation in Jesus Christ is good news; to be believed, received and celebrated. For the joy of the Lord is our strength!

March 9
Another Perspective

James Chapter 1, verses 15, 16:
Then when lust hath conceived, it bringeth forth sin: and sin, when it is finished, bringeth forth death. Do not err, my beloved brethren.

Prayer: Dear God; sin is never worthwhile. Help us to consider your eternal perspective in our decision making and make the right choices. In Jesus' Name. Amen.

It was the start of the work week and there was road construction almost everywhere. This detour was out of the way and long. Road workers, some holding signs, others directing traffic seemed hard at work. One guy blurted, "That is the easiest job in the world!" and pointed to the road workers. The other guy replied, "I think that is the hardest job in the world." He went on to explain; those road workers had to be standing on their feet most of the time during their eight or twelve hour shifts, work outdoors in all kinds of weather conditions and by the time he was done, the first guy had changed his mind. The devil likes to portray sin and temptation as pleasurable. Immediately, the Holy Bible replies with God's perspective. God is a holy and just God who judges and punishes sin. God's wages or payday for sin is death, and that death in hell is eternal. Receiving God's free gift of salvation through the Lord Jesus comes with the gift of eternal life and the indwelling of the Holy Spirit. Suddenly, sin and temptation are no longer attractive. So go ahead; invite the Lord Jesus to be your Lord and Savior. When you are tempted to sin, remember God's take on the matter and ask God to help you make the correct decision. If you sin, be quick to confess your sins to God, asking for forgiveness and since the Lord Jesus took your punishment for sin on the cross, God will forgive you. It's winning time when you are on God's side!

© By Dr. Sheila Hayford.

March 10
Endurance

Hebrews Chapter 12, verse 1:
Wherefore seeing we also are compassed about with so great a cloud of witnesses, let us lay aside every weight, and the sin which doth so easily beset us, and let us run with patience the race that is set before us,

Matthew Chapter 24, verse 13:
But he that shall endure unto the end, the same shall be saved.

Prayer: Dear Holy Spirit, we are depending on you to help us finish our race strong. Help us, by your power, not to be sidetracked by distractions. In Jesus' Name, Amen.

Life is a race. However, it is not a sprint designed for the fastest runner. It is a marathon, and life's winners are those who put aside hindrances and distractions and become overcomers. In other words, despite how you start, your rewards from God will depend on how you finish. Wow! As with any race, there are spectators watching. In this verse it talks about those born again believers who have completed their race here on earth watching us run our race. They are cheering us on because they know it will be worthwhile when we live and reign with our Lord Jesus Christ forever.

© By Dr. Sheila Hayford.

March 11
A Child's Curiosity

Isaiah Chapter 55, verses 6, 7:
Seek ye the Lord while he may be found, call ye upon him while he is near: Let the wicked forsake his way, and the unrighteous man his thoughts: and let him return unto the Lord, and he will have mercy upon him; and to our God, for he will abundantly pardon.

Prayer: Dear God, we call on you today. Thank you that you are never too busy and always have a watchful eye for what is best for your creation. In Jesus' Name, Amen.

It was a relatively cool day and the child was out playing under her mother's watchful eyes. She looked to be about three or four years of age. She had her coat on, her beanie cap on and was dressed for the weather. As she played she passed by a rope, the rope brushed by her cap and her cap fell to the ground. Most grown-ups would have shaken the dust off the cap and put it back on. Not this girl. She picked up her cap, went back to the rope and folded her cap on the rope until it stayed put on the rope. She then stood by the rope and began to shake the rope to see at what level of pressure her cap would fall! A short while later her mother asked her to put her cap back on and placed the cap on her child's head. So the little girl began chasing the pigeons. She was soon bored and went back to the rope. She wondered what would happen if she tried to use the rope as a swing. This time she sat on the rope and moved forwards and backwards. The front end of the rope started to lean towards her. By this time the mother had had enough of her daughter's antics. She beckoned the child to her side and the child had to end her adventure. The child's curiosity reminded me of the prophet Moses. When Moses saw the bush burning but not being destroyed, Moses' curiosity caused him to draw close to the bush to find out why that was so. When Moses got near the burning bush, Moses had a powerful encounter with God. Was Moses the first one to see that bush scenario? Probably not! Some who saw it may have started running away from the bush in fear. Others may have told their fellow men to observe the bush from a distance. When God asks us to seek Him in these verses, God is talking about our posture. Are we desiring to know God in a more personal way? Do we yearn to find out what God says to humanity in the Holy Bible? Are we spending time in conversation with God? We are living in days of grace before the Second Coming of our Lord and Savior Jesus Christ in order that all who call upon the Lord Jesus, repenting and turning from sin and inviting the Lord Jesus to be their Lord and Savior will receive God's forgiveness and salvation through Jesus Christ. God's posture, desire or will towards and for humanity is for all to come into his family through his Son, Jesus Christ. Thus, God sent the Lord Jesus to take the punishment for the sins of humanity for all time. God is nearer than you may think, call on Him today!

© By Dr. Sheila Hayford.

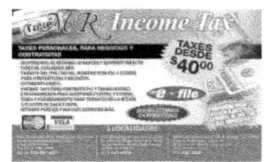

MR. INCOME TAX

Personal & Business Taxes; Great service at the best price!

Individual Tax preparation starting at $80***

*** Preparation for single taxpayers with up to 3 W2 forms

OPEN YEAR ROUND

We offer the following services:

- Tax preparation for any year, any state
- Business Taxes for LLC, S-Corp, C-Corp and Partnerships
- 1099 forms for Contractors
- Audits (Federal and NC)
- Accounting for small businesses
- Free estimates and consultation (1st 5 min.)
- "Notary Public and much more!"

4008 Capital Blvd Suite 104-B, Raleigh, NC 27604
Tel: (919) 526-4829
Hours: Jan - Apr: every day 10am to 9pm;
May - Dec: Mon-Fri 11am to 7pm or by appointment.

March 12
Beyond The Clouds

Acts Chapter 1, verse 11:

Which also said, Ye men of Galilee, why stand ye gazing up into heaven? this same Jesus, which is taken up from you into heaven, shall so come in like manner as ye have seen him go into heaven.

Prayer: Dear Lord Jesus, what is man that you show us such great favor? We are in awe of your love. Amen.

I looked up and saw thick grey clouds and what appeared to be painted blue swatches interspersed in-between. The Holy Spirit told me the blue was the clear blue skies. However, at the time I was focused on the clouds and wondered if there was a manufacturing plant nearby spewing out blue smoke. As we went further, more blue swatches appeared over a much wider area and I figured it could not be a manufacturing plant. As we went even further, there was a break in the clouds and just as the Holy Spirit had said, the beautiful blue skies were evident. Immediately, to the right in the corner of the adjacent cloud was the image of the face of Jesus. Yes, the image you see in pictures depicting Jesus Christ, but this time it was up, close and personal. I was overwhelmed! As I gazed at the face of the Lord Jesus in awe, all I could do was sigh, Mmm, Mmm, Mmm...! After a while, the image disappeared. When we look at the dark clouds of evil that seem to be looming in the affairs of humanity, one might tend to focus on those clouds instead of on the clear blue skies God has provided in Jesus Christ. For through the Lord Jesus, the Holy Spirit gives us the breakthroughs and empowerment we need to please God and to be successful in life. This same Lord Jesus is coming back again. Rejoice! The Lord Jesus Christ is coming again through the clouds and with great power!

© By Dr. Sheila Hayford.

March 13
Guard Your Faith

Numbers Chapter 26, verse 65:
For the Lord had said of them, They shall surely die in the wilderness. And there was not left a man of them, save Caleb the son of Jephunneh, and Joshua the son of Nun.

Jude Chapter 1, verses 3-5, 24-25:

Beloved, when I gave all diligence to write unto you of the common salvation, it was needful for me to write unto you, and exhort you that ye should earnestly contend for the faith which was once delivered unto the saints. For there are certain men crept in unawares, who were before of old ordained to this condemnation, ungodly men, turning the grace of our God into lasciviousness, and denying the only Lord God, and our Lord Jesus Christ. I will therefore put you in remembrance, though ye once knew this, how that the Lord, having saved the people out of the land of Egypt, afterward destroyed them that believed not. Now unto him that is able to keep you from falling, and to present you faultless before the presence of his glory with exceeding joy, To the only wise God our Saviour, be glory and majesty, dominion and power, both now and ever. Amen.

Prayer: Dear Lord Jesus; help us to guard the faith that you have entrusted to us and to hold onto the truth of your Word. God's grace is not an excuse to sin so help us reject false doctrines. Amen.

In the Scripture reading this month, we discussed the importance of endurance; that is, adherence to the Christian faith. In the verses above, the Apostle Jude strongly encouraged the believers to stand hold onto the truths of God's words and not be caught up in erroneous teaching by those who used the grace of God as an excuse to engage in sinful acts. Jude gives the example of those God brought out of Egypt who did not make it to Canaan, which was their intended destination. Why? It was because of their persistent, unrepentant sins against God and their ingratitude, thus despising of the grace of God. Except for Joshua and Caleb, the rest of them died in the wilderness. The devil is not happy about the fact that we will be living and reigning with the Lord Jesus, especially when the devil has such a horrible future in hell. So do not be caught off guard. God the Holy Spirit will keep us from falling, as we submit our lives to God and yield to the promptings and work of the Holy Spirit. Have no fear, in God we win! © By Dr. Sheila Hayford.

March 14
Better Than Reserved

Luke Chapter 7, verses 11-15:

Soon afterward, Jesus went to a town called Nain, and his disciples and a large crowd went along with him. As he approached the town gate, a dead person was being carried out - the only son of his mother, and she was a widow. And a large crowd from the town was with her. When the Lord saw her, his heart went out to her and he said, "Don't cry." Then he went up and touched the bier they were carrying him on, and the bearers stood still. He said, "Young man, I say to you, get up!" The dead man sat up and began to talk, and Jesus gave him back to his mother. (NIV)

Prayer: Dear Lord Jesus, we thank you for your heart of compassion and for your prayers of intercession to God on our behalf. We call on you and receive from you in faith. Blessed be your holy Name. Hallelujah! Amen.

I was making reservations for my trip and there was an offer to purchase what appeared to be preferred seating for an additional "reserved" seating price. I decide to forego that additional expense. When I arrived, the seat in which I sat was on the other side of the "reserved seats." I looked and those seats appeared to be cramped with less leg room. I still had the other amenities they had, a large table to do my work if I wanted to, secure cup holders, and more importantly, much more legroom than those seats. I thought to myself, "This is better than reserved seating!" A woman in one of those "reserved" seats complained about the legroom, tried to move into the other reserved seat which was already taken and finally moved out of the reserved seating area altogether into a regular seat, even though she had paid the extra price! The widow in the verses above had not been informed that the Lord Jesus, his disciples and a large crowd were coming to her area. She just "happened" to be there. Her need was great as she had lost her only son. The Lord Jesus had compassion on her and restored her son back to life.

She must have been more than elated and probably thought, "Wow! The outcome was much better than expected." You see, you do not have to wait until Sunday to go to church nor wait for your friend to come from work to pray for you in order to receive from God. As long as you have a need, you have the opportunity to be a recipient of God's compassion and God's miracles. Cry unto God and receive!

© By Dr. Sheila Hayford.

March 15
Do You Know How Lovely You Look?

Psalm 139, verse 14:

I will praise thee; for I am fearfully and wonderfully made: marvellous are thy works; and that my soul knoweth right well.

Prayer: Dear God, we praise and thank you for your human creation is amazing! It is amazing how you created the human organs, each working in perfect detail; how you have the senses defined; how you give us a soul that will endure throughout eternity; and foremost, the spirit of life you give us in Jesus Christ. We thank you, In Jesus name. Amen.

It was at the church service and we had a short time of fellowship afterwards. One of the ladies came to me and gave me a compliment about my dress. I thanked her and then she told me she had asked her friend if I knew how lovely I looked. Nice encouraging words! I am comfortable in who God made me because each person is uniquely and specifically wonderfully created by God. Remember, each human being was worth sending the Lord Jesus to earth to die for the sins of humanity. And so I share this compliment with you: Do you know how lovely you look? There are some who will find fault with just about everything; why is the coffee so hot or too cold? Why did you show up for work so early or so late? You should not have on that shade of lipstick when that other color looked better on you! If you are not careful, you could start doubting and second guessing yourself. Even worse, you could refuse to move forward and try new things because you have been told you do not have what someone thinks it takes. We are to be celebrated as a part of God's wonderful works. Celebrate God and celebrate you! Do you know just how lovely you look?

© By Dr. Sheila Hayford.

March 16
We Made It Together: Once!

Matthew Chapter 14, verses 28, 29:

And Peter answered him and said, Lord, if it be thou, bid me come unto thee on the water. And he said, Come. And when Peter was come down out of the ship, he walked on the water, to go to Jesus.

Prayer: Dear God; I am so grateful you give to us the spirit of adventure as we enjoy your beautiful creation. Thank you. In Jesus' Name, Amen.

When I travel I love to explore the special sites and see the local culture. I am also intrigued by waterfalls. On this trip, we had the opportunity to visit the local waterfall up close and decided to go for it. We were dressed for the occasion, very excited and the weather was gorgeous. We had been given the chance to climb to the top of this gorgeous waterfall! There were others with us, everyone was happy and the atmosphere was great. Sure, there were obstacles as we went up. However, we laughed, encouraged each other, each of us went up comfortably at our own pace and, most importantly, <u>we made it together to the top of the waterfall; ONCE!</u> I thoroughly enjoyed it and had an experience of a lifetime! Would I do it again? I am not planning to. Would I trade that experience? Never! Peter saw the Lord Jesus doing the impossible by walking on water, and wanted to do the same. The Lord Jesus invited Peter, his disciple, to come to him walking on the water, and Peter walked on the water to go to Jesus. **Yes, Peter defied**

gravity and walked on water! Some who read these verses put Peter down and end by saying Peter began to sink when Peter looked around and saw the boisterous water. However, most of those putting Peter down have never walked on water. In fact, the Apostle Peter is part of the history of the Bible because he did something that I do not think has ever been done, even if it was for just a short time. Many times, God calls us to do impossible tasks in our human strength, but achievable with God. If we fix our eyes on the circumstances, we might never start to do God's bidding. If we focus on God, God's Word and God's ability to bring us to a successful completion in spite of any challenges, we will succeed. So get it done with God; you might get that opportunity ONCE!

© By Dr. Sheila Hayford.

March 17
After God Said, God Saw

Genesis Chapter 1, verses 1, 2, 3, 4, 20-21:

In the beginning God created the heaven and the earth. And the earth was without form, and void; and darkness was upon the face of the deep. And the Spirit of God moved upon the face of the waters. And God said, Let there be light: and there was light. And God saw the light, that it was good: and God divided the light from the darkness. And God said, Let the waters bring forth abundantly the moving creature that hath life, and fowl that may fly above the earth in the open firmament of heaven. And God created great whales, and every living creature that moveth, which the waters brought forth abundantly, after their kind, and every winged fowl after his kind: and God saw that it was good.

Prayer: Dear God; thank you for teaching us the creative power of our words. May we apply the lessons you teach us in the way you instruct us. In Jesus' Name, Amen.

Wow! God's Opening Statement! When you write an important speech or an essay, be it a Commencement Address, a Presidential

Debate, A Legal Argument or something else, you want to get the listener or the reader's attention with something you consider paramount to your discussion. God's letter or address to humankind is the Holy Bible and Genesis is the first book in the Bible. So, in the first four verses, God gives us His opening statements which are of paramount importance in God's discussions with humanity. First, God lets us know that God is the Creator of heaven and earth. None of us would be alive on this earth if it were not for this fact. And as the Creator, what was the means by which God created his amazing creations? First God said. In other words, God spoke what it was that he wanted done. God wanted light and so God spoke light. God wanted to populate the oceans and the seas and so God spoke. And then God saw what God spoke. It is interesting that in the creation of light in the earth, God spoke and the light appeared right away. In the creation of the creatures of the ocean and the fowl that would fly above them, God spoke, then God did some work, then God saw. What is the paramount principle God is teaching humankind here? It is this; Words have creative power so speak what you want to see created. In other words, work with your spoken end result in mind. When God spoke, God saw. When we speak, we see!

© By Dr. Sheila Hayford.

March 18
Which Version Are You?

Romans Chapter 12, verse 2:

And be not conformed to this world: but be ye transformed by the renewing of your mind, that ye may prove what is that good, and acceptable, and perfect, will of God.

Prayer: Dear God, transformation through your Word is a required discipline of a follower of Jesus Christ and is not always easy. Enable us to genuinely desire change and to allow the Holy Spirit to work in us what you desire in and of us. In Jesus' Name, Amen.

In Christ change is possible and transformation is required. I accepted the Lord Jesus as my Lord and Savior in my teenage years and considered myself to be a "mature" Christian. I studied God's Word and prayed but did not want my relationship with God to become "status quo." So I prayed that in reading and studying God's word, I would be transformed. God took me up on that prayer. I noticed I was acutely aware of things like not extending God's love and compassion to my fellow man. The truth spoken can hurt and it can cut and God's intention is for a person to make a positive change when truth is spoken. I thought I had forgiveness 'down packed' but God showed me I held a grudge against someone not because they had wronged me but because they had wronged a casual acquaintance. Even though I never said anything negative about the person, I had to repent because in my mind at the time I held a grudge against the person. I was getting frustrated as I realized genuine transformation was not an easy process. Then the Holy Spirit reminded me that was why Christ came. When we sin in thought, word or deed we are to repent, receive God's forgiveness though the Lord Jesus and move on. I began to enjoy small victories, shall we say, my gentler 2.0 version; still direct in what I said but with a better attitude, love and empathy. Do you desire change? By that I mean, change that will make you look more like Christ when God sees you? Remember, change is not only possible, it is inevitable. A person is either changing for the better and moving forward with God, or stuck in their status quo and stagnating in their Christian journey. Ask God for the change you desire and allow God to take you on.

© By Dr. Sheila Hayford.

March 19
Defending Her Faith

1 Timothy Chapter 3, verse 13:
Those who have served well gain an excellent standing and great assurance in their faith in Christ Jesus.

Prayer: Dear God, we thank you for godly examples of men, women and children from all works of life who are not ashamed to share their faith. Thank you for our greatest example, the Lord Jesus Christ. Amen.

There are a lot of people I respect and admire and Queen Elizabeth, the longest reigning British monarch, is one of them. Over the years, she has made various references to her faith. In 2014 she said, "For me, the life of Jesus Christ, the Prince of Peace, whose birth we celebrate today, is an inspiration and an anchor in my life. A role model of reconciliation and forgiveness, he stretched out his hands in love, acceptance and healing. Christ's example has taught me to seek to respect and value all people, of whatever faith or none." What an inspiration!

The Queen serves her country well, no doubt has challenges just as every human does and yet allows her faith to anchor her life. We all need the Lord Jesus to be the anchor in our lives. Take hold of the Lord Jesus today!

© By Dr. Sheila Hayford.

March 20
Your Witness

Mark Chapter 16, verse 15:
He said to them, "Go into all the world and preach the gospel to all creation. (NIV)

1 John Chapter 1, verse 3:
That which we have seen and heard declare we unto you, that ye also may have fellowship with us: and truly our fellowship is with the Father, and with his Son Jesus Christ.

Prayer: Dear Lord Jesus; in order to be a witness for you we must speak up! You were not ashamed to die the horrific death on the cross for our sins and the sins of all humanity and we cannot keep such good news to ourselves. So help us, dear Holy Spirit. In Jesus' Name. Amen.

What is does it mean to be a witness for Jesus Christ? The disciples of the Lord Jesus heard his words, believed and received the Lord Jesus' as their Lord and Savior. They lived by faith in God and in the power of the Holy Spirit. They also shared their relationship with the Lord Jesus, God's Word and God's plan of salvation with others. That is being a witness for Christ. As disciples of the Lord Jesus, we are commanded by our Lord Jesus to share the good news of salvation. It is not the work of a chosen few, it is the work of **every** disciple of the Lord Jesus. Let's do our part with God's help and leave God's part to God.

© By Dr. Sheila Hayford.

March 21
Your Greatest Challenge

Galatians Chapter 5, verses 22-26:

But the fruit of the Spirit is love, joy, peace, forbearance, kindness, goodness, faithfulness, gentleness and self-control. Against such things there is no law. Those who belong to Christ Jesus have crucified the flesh with its passions and desires. Since we live by the Spirit, let us keep in step with the Spirit. Let us not become conceited, provoking and envying each other. (NIV)

Prayer: Dear Lord Jesus, you are our greatest example. In the midst of your busy earthly schedule, you made time to spend with our heavenly Father, you spent time alone in prayer and reflection and taught us, by your example, a life yielded to God. Thank you! Amen.

Your greatest challenge is you! Not your boss, your adversaries, your in-laws or out-laws, not even the devil. How can you say not even the devil, when we know the devil is the originator of the sins of humanity? It is because God has given everyone the gift of free will. That is, the choice to align with the originator of all things good or the originator of all things evil. So choosing God and a life yielded to God is a choice and conversely, so is choosing to reject God.

As human beings, we all need salvation through the Lord Jesus Christ who bore the punishment of all human sin for all time. Accepting the Lord Jesus as personal Lord and Savior comes with the gift of the Holy Spirit and is a personal decision, that is, a personal choice. The indwelling Holy Spirit teaches us, instructs us and also shows us areas we need to work on or change in order to please God. Thus, our greatest challenge becomes working on ourselves, with God's help.

Yes, we by all means need to work to help and empower others responsibly. However, we should not neglect our first priority and our primary focus, which should be living for God and pleasing God. So we should each do our part in changing the world by first working with God on "me"!

© By Dr. Sheila Hayford.

March 22
Loving Your Child God's Way

Proverbs Chapter 3, verses 11-12:
My son, despise not the chastening of the Lord; neither be weary of his correction: For whom the Lord loveth he correcteth; even as a father the son in whom he delighteth.

Prayer: Dear God, discipline does not always come easy to children and adults alike. Help us to apply correction with your heart of love. In Jesus' Name, Amen.

Doesn't every parent love their child? At first glance, one might wonder why anyone would ask that person. Aren't parents supposed to love their children? They are but, unfortunately, we read of abuse and neglect of children by their parents. The word of God goes much deeper. God loves his children, so he corrects us. As born again believers we have the indwelling Holy Spirit to help us live for God and when we confess and repent of our sins, God forgives us. However, in spite of God's forgiveness, God may allow a person to experience the unpleasant consequences of their actions. When we read of parents offering bribes to get their children accepted into prestigious schools for which their child may not be qualified or suited for, you have to agree with God that neither the parent nor the person receiving the bribe is showing true love for the child. Loving a child the way God says involves teaching the child right from wrong because you want that child to succeed in life. It means correcting a child and applying discipline when they do wrong. It means teaching and training a child to honor and respect God, their parents and others. Otherwise, a parent may be setting a child up for unrealistic life expectations which may harm the child in the end.

When God corrects his children out of love, he does it for our betterment. We must do no less!

© By Dr. Sheila Hayford.

March 23
God Has The Right

Psalm 6, verses 1-3, 9:
Lord, do not rebuke me in your anger or discipline me in your wrath. Have mercy on me, Lord, for I am faint; heal me, Lord, for my bones are in agony. My soul is in deep anguish. How long, Lord, how long? The Lord has heard my cry for mercy; the Lord accepts my prayer. (NIV)

Isaiah Chapter 54, verses 7-8:
For a small moment have I forsaken thee; but with great mercies will I gather thee. In a little wrath I hid my face from thee for a moment; but with everlasting kindness will I have mercy on thee, saith the Lord thy Redeemer.

Prayer: Dear God; we submit ourselves to your authority. In Jesus' Name, Amen.

God's Word encourages us not to despise or become weary when God corrects us. God is always a God of love. However, as a holy God, God warns humanity about the unpleasant consequences of sin. In the

Scripture reading today, the psalmist became faint in body and weary in his soul as a result of God's correction and discipline and wondered how long God's correction would last. He realized, however, that God is still merciful and when he humbled himself before God and asked for God's mercy, God accepted his prayer. Are you committed to doing what God requires of you? God knows and sees your anguish over sin, and knows your heart. Allow the Holy Spirit to work with you. Afterwards, you will thank God for loving you enough to show you who you really are and enabling you to become a better person in Christ. God's discipline may not be pleasant in the short term, but the hope is that it will be worthwhile. So do not despise correction, nor become weary. If human parents will remind a child that the parent's correction is for their child's good, how much more does God?

© By Dr. Sheila Hayford.

March 24
Work At It

Genesis Chapter 2, verse 15:
And the Lord God took the man, and put him into the garden of Eden to dress it and to keep it.
Prayer: Dear God, help us to do the work for which you created us. In Jesus' Name, Amen.

Isn't it interesting that right after God created Adam, the first human being, God gave Adam work to do? God placed Adam in the beautiful garden of Eden but did not expect Adam to just sit down and enjoy the benefits of the garden without doing anything towards the upkeep of the garden. There were plants for food that needed cultivation and harvesting and there were beautiful trees that required maintenance. Isn't it also interesting that God gave Adam work to do before God provided Adam with Eve, Adam's wife? If Adam did not take good care of the garden of Eden, how was he going to take good care of his wife and family? Just like Adam, God brought each of us into this world with gifts, talents and abilities. These gifts, talents and abilities are different for each individual and unique to the individual. God expects us to work with what God has given us and produce a return on God's investment in us. Yours may be to work in a profession or a trade, another's may be to work their business, another's may be continuously invent and produce new products, others provide innovative ideas but we all are expected to work for the glory of God. Don't sit on your gift to God and to humanity, work at it. For when your purpose in God's plan of creation is being fulfilled in every aspect of your life, including in your spiritual life, you will experience your greatest and truest joy.

© By Dr. Sheila Hayford.

March 25
Whose Responsibility?

Deuteronomy Chapter 10, verse 18:
He doth execute the judgment of the fatherless and widow, and loveth the stranger, in giving him food and raiment.

Esther Chapter 2, verse 7:
Mordecai had a cousin named Hadassah, whom he had brought up because she had neither father nor mother. This young woman, who was also known as Esther, had a lovely figure and was beautiful. Mordecai had taken her as his own daughter when her father and mother died. (NIV)

Prayer: Dear heavenly Father, thank you for giving us responsibility for sharing what you have given us stewardship over with others, consistent with your commands and principles. Our first priority is to you. So help us in the power of God the Holy Spirit to live for you and extend your love, compassion, respect and responsibility towards God and man in our daily living. In Jesus name, Amen.

Whose responsibility is it to take care of the fatherless, the widow, the children or even the stranger? Every society has grappled with this question over the years and especially in this day and age when the political climate has become so polarized. Hadassah, who later on became Queen Esther, started off with a major challenge, having lost both her parents. Her Uncle Mordecai stepped up, took her in and raised her as his daughter. History will always be grateful to Queen Esther for saving the lives of her people and to Mordecai for giving Esther the chance she needed to show off what God can be do when a person is given the chance. In the case of those who have family, it is logical to expect their family to step up to their responsibility; although this is not always to case nor is not always possible. However, when it comes to taking care of strangers, one tends to hear a lot of different opinions. So what does God say about it? First, God respects the dignity of all mankind and so no stranger should be abused or ill-treated just because they are strangers. In the Bible, we are told that God's angels sometimes show up on this earth in the form of strangers. How about strangers who are immigrants? And what if they are illegal immigrants? Does God have a responsibility to let into God's heaven everyone who wants to be there, whether or not they complied with God's rule requiring a person to receive his Son, the Lord Jesus as Lord and Savior? Those who follow God's rule will have their name written in God's book of life with all the privileges therein. In other words, does a society have a responsibility to provide for those who have broken their laws? It depends on the laws. Should those who are able bodied but cannot work because they are in a country illegally become the burden of those citizens or legal immigrants who are working hard and obeying the rules? For Christians whose first allegiance is to God, one must ask whether the laws are consistent with God's laws as revealed in Scripture. Remember, God is the Righteous Judge and the One who has the final authority. In the end, each of us has to ultimately answer to God for our individual actions. Do right by God, do right by you and your family and do right by your fellow man.

© By Dr. Sheila Hayford.

March 26
God's Kingdom Or Your Kingdom?

Matthew Chapter 18, verses 1-4:

At the same time came the disciples unto Jesus, saying, Who is the greatest in the kingdom of heaven? And Jesus called a little child unto him, and set him in the midst of them, And said, Verily I say unto you, Except ye be converted, and become as little children, ye shall not enter into the kingdom of heaven. Whosoever therefore shall humble himself as this little child, the same is greatest in the kingdom of heaven.

Matthew Chapter 20, verses 20-21, 23:

Then came to him the mother of Zebedees children with her sons, worshipping him, and desiring a certain thing of him. And he said unto her, What wilt thou? She saith unto him, Grant that these my two sons may sit, the one on thy right hand, and the other on the left, in thy kingdom. And he saith unto them, Ye shall drink indeed of my cup, and be baptized with the baptism that I am baptized with: but to sit on my right hand, and on my left, is not mine to give, but it shall be given to them for whom it is prepared of my Father.

Prayer: Dear God: Our personal agenda should never substitute for your greater agenda. Help us to each recognize who you have called us to be and what you would have us do to advance your kingdom. And then let us serve you joyfully and in humility. In Jesus' Name, Amen.

God's kingdom or your kingdom? Why the question? It is because your beliefs dictate your leadership style. Is your priority advancing God's kingdom or is your priority advancing your kingdom in any aspect of life; whether it be financially, in family and other relationships, in business, and/or in spiritual ministry? If a person is seeking to advance God's kingdom, they will view their role as one of training, mentoring and empowering the individuals under their authority to pursue all God has for each individual, using their unique gifts and abilities for the betterment of society. If a person is seeking to advance their personal kingdom, they will try to prevent individuals under their authority from responding to God's direct initiatives, sometimes using manipulation, threats and Scripture misrepresentations to try to advance their personal agenda. The Lord Jesus did not come to advance his personal agenda on earth, the Lord Jesus came to advance God's plans for humanity. Yes, God rewarded the Lord Jesus and gave the Lord Jesus an awesome kingdom, and yes, God will reward us for we will live and reign with our Lord Jesus forever. However, our service to and for God must always be God initiated. Did you hear God? What did God say? Go do it!

© By Dr. Sheila Hayford.

March 27
No Competition

Matthew Chapter 22, verses 29-30:

Jesus answered and said unto them, Ye do err, not knowing the scriptures, nor the power of God. For in the resurrection they neither marry, nor are given in marriage, but are as the angels of God in heaven.

Prayer: Dear Lord Jesus; we are yours, all yours! It is a joy, and not a grudge, to honor and to serve you. We bless you, we praise you and we thank you. Amen.

The Lord Jesus was asked what some might have thought was a trick question. If a person remarried; in the resurrection, whose wife would she be? The Lord Jesus used that question to make things clear. In the resurrection, when the church who is the bride of Christ is reunited with our bridegroom, the Lord Jesus Christ, there will be *"No Competition!"* In other words, the Lord Jesus will have *"No Competition!"* You see, the question presumed that earthly marriage relationships between husband and wife would continue in heaven. "Oh, No!" the Lord Jesus is saying, "there will be no earthly marriage relationships continuing in heaven; anyone who thinks or says otherwise is in error." This is cause for great celebration as the church of born again believers, the Lord Jesus' bride, celebrate at the marriage feast of the bridegroom, our Lord and Savior Jesus Christ. Glory! Glory! Hallelujah, Praise and thanks be to our bridegroom, the King of Kings and Lord of Lords, Jesus Christ!

© By Dr. Sheila Hayford.

March 28
I've Got You!

John Chapter 6, verses 38-40:

For I came down from heaven, not to do mine own will, but the will of him that sent me. And this is the Father's will which hath sent me, that of all which he hath given me I should lose nothing, but should raise it up again at the last day. And this is the will of him that sent me, that every one which seeth the Son, and believeth on him, may have everlasting life: and I will raise him up at the last day.

John Chapter 10, verse 29:

My Father, which gave them me, is greater than all; and no man is able to pluck them out of my Father's hand.

Prayer: Dear Lord Jesus; You are so worth knowing, so worth believing on and so worth living for, here on earth and for eternity. Amen.

It had been one of those precious moments spending time with our Lord Jesus. I have been on my Christian journey for some years now and in conversation with the Lord Jesus, I thanked God for his keeping power. To which the Lord Jesus replied, "I've got you!" As in signed, sealed and delivered. We are signed for, sealed and delivered by our Lord Jesus Christ. You see, the Lord Jesus has every one who receives him as Lord and Savior signed for and placed in the Lamb's book of life through his death on the cross when he bore the punishment for our sins, sealed by the indwelling Holy Spirit as a gift from Jesus Christ, and resurrected at the Second Coming of the Lord Jesus to be with our heavenly Father and His Son, Jesus Christ for eternity. How reassuring!

Nothing can separate us from God's love and none can pluck us out of God's hands. Powerful hands indeed!

© By Dr. Sheila Hayford.

March 29
Don't Fight A Losing Battle

Acts Chapter 26, verses 10-16:

Which thing I also did in Jerusalem: and many of the saints did I shut up in prison, having received authority from the chief priests; and when they were put to death, I gave my voice against them. And I punished them oft in every synagogue, and compelled them to blaspheme; and being exceedingly mad against them, I persecuted them even unto strange cities. Whereupon as I went to Damascus with authority and commission from the chief priests, At midday, O king, I saw in the way a light from heaven, above the brightness of the sun, shining round about me and them which journeyed with me. And when we were all fallen to the earth, I heard a voice speaking unto me, and saying in the Hebrew tongue, Saul, Saul, why persecutest thou me? it is hard for thee to kick against the pricks. And I said, Who art thou, Lord? And he said, I am Jesus whom thou persecutest. But rise, and stand upon thy feet: for I have appeared unto thee for this purpose, to make thee a minister and a witness both of these things which thou hast seen, and of those things in the which I will appear unto thee;

Prayer: Dear God, our desire is to work with you and for you. So help us, by the power of the Holy Spirit. In Jesus' Name, Amen.

No one can fight God and win. A person may try to fight God, but will ultimately lose. Saul, whose name was later changed to Paul, started out fighting God. And Saul thought he was doing God a service by persecuting the Christians. So what happened? God knocked Saul down in the match at Damascus. Saul was still fighting God in that match and did not realize God going to win in a knock-out. Saul fell down, and when Saul came to, could not see but heard the Lord Jesus speaking to him. Saul asked questions and the Lord Jesus introduced himself. Saul was converted, had his name changed to Paul and the scales of ignorance, doubt, unbelief, rebellion, and pride fell from his eyes. Saul had fought God in persecuting God's children and now the Lord Jesus told Saul who became Paul the believer that Paul would now experience and suffer persecution for Christ's sake. Paul ended up becoming an Apostle of the Lord Jesus whom God used to write several books of the Holy Bible. What are the lessons we learn from Paul? First, how we treat other people, especially God's children, matters to God. Secondly, some of the situations we face in life are the result of or the consequences of our actions. Next, despite where you have been or where you are, God is not intimidated by our questions. And finally, no matter what anyone may think, God can use anyone to advance God's kingdom beyond their wildest imaginations.

© By Dr. Sheila Hayford.

March 30
Why Study

Romans Chapter 10, verses 13-14:

For whosoever shall call upon the name of the Lord shall be saved. How then shall they call on him in whom they have not believed? and how shall they believe in him of whom they have not heard? and how shall they hear without a preacher?

Acts Chapter 17, verse 11:

Now the Berean Jews were of more noble character than those in Thessalonica, for they received the message with great eagerness and examined the Scriptures every day to see if what Paul said was true. (NIV)

Prayer: Dear Lord God, I love reading your Word. It is always relevant, always full of truth and always inspired by your goodwill for humanity. Teach us, by the Holy Spirit, as we study your Word and enable us to be good stewards of the truths you entrust us to share. In Jesus' Name, Amen.

Sometimes we study certain subjects or topics because we have no choice but to study them. If you want to work in a particular field, you may have to study certain subjects in college. And you have to pass the tests associated with your course of study. If you work in a specialized field you may have to study certain topics and take related tests. However, when it comes to studying the Bible, some just rely on their Pastor or teacher to do the studying and fail to do any personal Bible study. In the example above, the Bereans were commended for studying the Bible for themselves to make sure what had been preached to them was consistent with what God said in Scripture. Thus, it is important to study Scripture so a person can discern error, either error in incorrectly quoted Scripture or in the interpretation of Scripture. A more important reason would be to spend personal time with God. If you love a person, wouldn't you want to spend quality time with the person? In Romans Chapter 10, verse 14, the question is asked as to how a person can believe in the Lord Jesus if they have never heard about the Lord Jesus. So we need to study Scripture so we can accurately share Scripture with others and invite others to receive the Lord Jesus as their personal Lord and Savior. Of course, there are many other reasons to study Scripture but God wants us to at least start studying Scripture with these in mind. Will we?

© By Dr. Sheila Hayford.

March 31
What If?

Matthew Chapter 11, verse 28:
Come unto me, all ye that labour and are heavy laden, and I will give you rest.

Prayer: Dear Lord Jesus: I give you my life and choose to cast all my cares and concerns on you. Fill me with your peace as I rest assured in you. Amen.

When I travel, I tend to over pack. "What if I need this or I need that but did not bring it with me?" I rationalize. Most of the time I don't use half of what I take with me! An acquaintance who also does a lot of travelling tells me I need to learn how to pack. You only need so and so… she says and then you mix and match. Sounds easy! The Lord Jesus knew that as we live this earthly life there may be circumstances that may try to wear us down or try to hinder or discourage us and become "excess baggage" in our life's journey. As one who lived a perfectly focused life on this earth, our Lord and Savior Jesus Christ invites us to come to him with whatever heavy burden, concerns, situations or worries we might have. God cares for us and when we cast our concerns on Him, we allow God to work on us as well as on the circumstances. In return, we receive the peace of God, knowing that God is well able to take care of any circumstance better than we could on our own. What if we took God at His Word?

© By Dr. Sheila Hayford.

April 1
You Blessed You!

1 Peter Chapter 4, verses 9, 10:
Offer hospitality to one another without grumbling. Each of you should use whatever gift you have received to serve others, as faithful stewards of God's grace in its various forms. (NIV)

Prayer: Dear God; may I be a faithful steward of the gifts you have trusted me with. In Jesus' Name, Amen.

I was minding my business when a stranger did a kind deed. I thanked her and told her God would bless her. Later that afternoon, God asked me to bless her. I thought, "I have already told her God would bless her; who greater than God to bless her?" I decided to obey God and blessed her. Immediately after I did that, the Holy Spirit said to me, "You blessed you!" "How so?" I wondered. God's reply, "When you blessed her out of obedience to me, I blessed you as a reward for your obedience." Wow! We know that obedience to God's will and God's ways are not always celebrated. Some may mock or ridicule you, still others may try to intimidate you for doing what God said you should do or what God teaches in the Bible. Some may even be persecuted because of their obedience to God. At the end of this earthly life, it is what God says about you that will count for eternity. So go ahead, obey God and let God bless you!

© By Dr. Sheila Hayford.

April 2
Think About This!

Genesis Chapter 50, verse 20:
You intended to harm me, but God intended it for good to accomplish what is now being done, the saving of many lives.

Philippians Chapter 4, verse 13:
I can do all things through Christ which strengtheneth me.

Prayer: Dear God, thank you for turning into good whatever evil satan had hoped to accomplish in our lives, in the Name of Jesus and by the power of the Holy Spirit. Amen.

Think about this! Why would anyone pay someone to harm them? We read about the harmful effects of nicotine and the many diseases associated with cigarette smoking and yet many, including professing Christians, end up paying tobacco manufacturers, cigarette advertisers and tax collectors good money by purchasing the cigarettes. Some might say they just cannot help themselves, but is that really true? We can do all things through Jesus Christ, by the power of God at work in and through us. However, we must first be willing or desirous of the change that is necessary. God has much work to be done and God needs all hands on board. Whatever change you desire, talk with God about it. Then take steps with God to bring about the desired change. Change usually requires time because change is usually a process. In other words, change does not usually come easily. When your change comes, may you say, like Joseph in the book of Genesis, satan intended to use others to harm you but God turned things around for your good and in the process saved many lives. Glory to God!

© By Dr. Sheila Hayford.

April 3
Delegated Authority

Luke Chapter 7, verse 8:

So Jesus went with them. He was not far from the house when the centurion sent friends to say to him: "Lord, don't trouble yourself, for I do not deserve to have you come under my roof. That is why I did not even consider myself worthy to come to you. But say the word, and my servant will be healed. For I myself am a man under authority, with soldiers under me. I tell this one, 'Go,' and he goes; and that one, 'Come,' and he comes. I say to my servant, 'Do this,' and he does it." (NIV)

John Chapter 14, verses 13-14:

And whatsoever ye shall ask in my name, that will I do, that the Father may be glorified in the Son. If ye shall ask any thing in my name, I will do it.

Prayer: Dear Lord Jesus; help us work with the delegated authority you have given us. Amen.

You have delegated authority. One might ask, "what do you mean by that?" The centurion in these verses had probably 80 to 100 soldiers under his authority and as one under authority himself he understood delegated authority. We know that in every company, there are leaders and managers who have authority over those assigned to them. What about those of us who are Christians? The truth is this: As a born again believer and disciple of our Lord Jesus Christ, the Lord Jesus has given us delegated authority to do the works God has for us to do. We must not presume to do everything God wants us to do in our own strength. We need the Word of God, the Will of God, the Wisdom of God, the Name of Jesus, the Holy Spirit and God's holy angels to accomplish the tasks set before us. God does not want us to be intimidated or overwhelmed when we consider the work we must do, God wants us to be assured that he has given us the delegated authority to be able to accomplish the task with the resources God provides. Thank God!

© By Dr. Sheila Hayford.

April 4
Pork; To Eat or Not To Eat!

Acts Chapter 10, verses 9-15:

About noon the following day as they were on their journey and approaching the city, Peter went up on the roof to pray. He became hungry and wanted something to eat, and while the meal was being prepared, he fell into a trance. He saw heaven opened and something like a large sheet being let down to earth by its four corners. It contained all kinds of four-footed animals, as well as reptiles and birds. Then a voice told him, "Get up, Peter. Kill and eat." "Surely not, Lord!" Peter replied. "I have never eaten anything impure or unclean." The voice spoke to him a second time, "Do not call anything impure that God has made clean." (NIV)

Romans Chapter 4, verses 1, 2, 3:

Accept the one whose faith is weak, without quarreling over disputable matters. One person's faith allows them to eat anything, but another, whose faith is weak, eats only vegetables. The one who eats everything must not treat with contempt the one who does not, and the one who does not eat everything must not judge the one who does, for God has accepted them. (NIV)

Prayer: Dear God; thank you for the freedom you give us to eat what we choose out of the myriad of foods you have given us. In Jesus' Name, Amen.

The gentleman was in a spiritual discussion and this time the discussion was about eating pork. With an almost self-righteous attitude he proclaimed, "I do not eat anything unclean!" Well, that discussion about pork has been going on for centuries. I used to say I would eat anything, until I heard about some foods which were considered delicacies in some places, then I changed that to I would eat almost anything but **prefer** not to eat such and such. In the Old Testament, pork was considered unclean. The Lord Jesus, in the salvation of humanity through his death on the cross, burial and resurrection, changed that and now any food that is blessed in the name of Jesus, regardless of the food or the source may be eaten and enjoyed without condemnation. When the Apostle Peter told the Lord God he had never eaten anything unclean, God told him not to call unclean what God had cleansed. So what if someone says he cannot in good conscience eat pork or some other food because it was sacrificed to idols or for some other reason? The Bible makes it clear; do not force such a person to violate their conscience, and neither should that person adversely judge those who are happy and enjoy eating whatever. Back to the question. Pork; to eat or not to eat? The answer? It depends on your conscience. If your conscience is clear, enjoy. If eating pork would offend your conscience, eat something else. Rise and eat!

© By Dr. Sheila Hayford.

April 5
What Is The Reason For Your Hope?

1 Peter Chapter 3, verse 15:

But in your hearts revere Christ as Lord. Always be prepared to give an answer to everyone who asks you to give the reason for the hope that you have. But do this with gentleness and respect, (NIV)

Prayer: Dear Holy Spirit, lead us as we share our faith with others. In Jesus' Name, Amen.

If you went into a class and the teacher did not seem to know much about the subject they were teaching, you might walk out of that class. So why would it be different if someone asked a person about their Christian faith. If they could not explain their relationship with the Lord Jesus Christ, God our heavenly Father and the Holy Spirit, the person asking the question might not think much of their faith. Being prepared to share your faith does not mean you have memorized the exact verses of specific Scriptures, even though with frequent use you might have. It means you can explain why every human being has need of a Savior, who the Lord Jesus is to you, how to pray and invite the Lord Jesus to be a person's Lord and Savior and the eternal benefits of living with and for the Lord Jesus. You may not have all the answers to everybody's questions about your Christian faith, but in humility and respect, you can make time for further discussions or Bible study to find out what the Bible says about the topics at hand. Start preparing today!

© By Dr. Sheila Hayford.

April 6
What Time Is It?

1 Chronicles Chapter 12, verse 32:

And of the children of Issachar, which were men that had understanding of the times, to know what Israel ought to do; the heads of them were two hundred; and all their brethren were at their commandment.

Prayer: Dear Lord Jesus; we are looking forward to your Second Coming and do not want to be derelict in our responsibilities to you and to our fellow man. Let us be serious and intentional in sharing your wonderful message of salvation and trust you with the outcomes. Amen.

What time is it? We ask this question all the time. Or so it seems; especially when the train is running late, an event is about to start soon or the event is late in getting started. In other words, many times we ask this question because of a perceived lateness. And so God is asking us, "What time is it?" The children of Issachar were descendants of Leah and Jacob. [Jacob's name was later changed by God to Israel.] These descendants not only had understanding of the times; that vital information was necessary in order to know what Israel as a people ought to do. Today, confusion and chaos seem rampant in society, worldwide there are areas of famine, destruction, corruption and the like. What times are these? And what ought we as Christians to do? First, we have to understand that the Lord Jesus said in the last days on earth before his Second Coming, evil would be multiplied, so we must understand the <u>times we are living in are the last days</u>. At the same time, the Lord Jesus told us the work that we need to do as Christians is plentiful and more helpers are needed. So now is time to be serious about our heavenly Father's business and share the good news of salvation so many will come to know the Lord Jesus Christ as their Lord and Savior. The Lord Jesus does not want us to slack in our service to God and humanity. The eternal destination of countless individuals is at stake; lives are depending on you. Wake up!

© By Dr. Sheila Hayford.

April 7
How Do You Respond?

Mark Chapter 14, verses 3-8:
And being in Bethany in the house of Simon the leper, as he sat at meat, there came a woman having an alabaster box of ointment of spikenard very precious; and she brake the box, and poured it on his

head. And there were some that had indignation within themselves, and said, Why was this waste of the ointment made? For it might have been sold for more than three hundred pence, and have been given to the poor. And they murmured against her. And Jesus said, Let her alone; why trouble ye her? she hath wrought a good work on me. For ye have the poor with you always, and whensoever ye will ye may do them good: but me ye have not always. She hath done what she could: she is come aforehand to anoint my body to the burying.

Prayer: Dear Lord Jesus; thank you for loving us enough to take the taunts and abuses of mortal men, knowing how much our salvation through your death on the cross, burial and resurrection would make our heavenly Father glad. It is a privilege to be a part of your family. Amen.

It was a simple act. The woman poured expensive spikenard all over the Lord Jesus as her form of worship. The Lord Jesus was very impressed with her and gave her such a recommendation that we are still reading about her today. Some who saw that same act were furious with her; complaining she had wasted the spikenard, saying she could have sold the spikenard and used that money to feed the poor. Who were they to tell her how to worship God when their hearts were so far from God? Judas Iscariot was so upset that he went to the chief priests and offered to betray his Master, the Lord Jesus, and was promised money from the chief priests. In other words, some could not discern the beautiful action this woman did in preparing the Lord Jesus for his burial when he was about to be hang on the cross and crucified for the sins of all humanity. Jesus' adversaries thought they were killing the Lord Jesus but could not discern that God was going to use that same act of the Lord Jesus dying on the cross to pay the price for the sins of all humankind for all time. How do you respond to what you see with your natural eyes? Always observe life through the eyes of God and see every individual, every action and every circumstance with God's perspective in mind.

© By Dr. Sheila Hayford.

April 8
In A Hurry? Where To?

Proverbs Chapter 3, verses 1, 2, 21-23:

My son, forget not my law; but let thine heart keep my commandments: For length of days, and long life, and peace, shall they add to thee. My son, let not them depart from thine eyes: keep sound wisdom and discretion: So shall they be life unto thy soul, and grace to thy neck. Then shalt thou walk in thy way safely, and thy foot shall not stumble.

Luke Chapter 6, verse 9:

Then said Jesus unto them, I will ask you one thing; Is it lawful on the sabbath days to do good, or to do evil? to save life, or to destroy it?

Prayer: Dear God; help us value our life and the lives of others for each life is a gift from you. In Jesus' Name, Amen.

I was about to cross the Pedestrian crosswalk when I noticed this oncoming car speeding, bent on whizzing by. I decided to wait and let the car pass by, not wanting to take the chance that the driver would slow down in time. After he drove by, I proceeded to cross the street. I was still on the crosswalk when I heard a loud noise. The driver had run right into the back of the car in front of the speeding vehicle! In retrospect, I was at that stop to prevent the driver from getting into that accident but that driver seemed to be in a hurry to get to what would cause harm to the car and the driver. Sometimes it seems like people are in so much of a hurry. The more important consideration should be, "Where are you in a hurry to?" Is it worth driving recklessly when a person's life is at stake? Is it worth harming your body with toxins that can lead to an early death when your eternal future in heaven or hell is not certain? Is it worth indulging in the pleasures of sin for a short moment and living a lifetime of misery as a consequence? Wouldn't it be better to spend time with God and allow God to order your steps?

© By Dr. Sheila Hayford.

April 9
It Keeps Getting Better!

Colossians Chapter 1, verses 10-14:

so that you may live a life worthy of the Lord and please him in every way: bearing fruit in every good work, growing in the knowledge of God, being strengthened with all power according to his glorious might so that you may have great endurance and patience, and giving joyful thanks to the Father, who has qualified you to share in the inheritance of his holy people in the kingdom of light. For he has rescued us from the dominion of darkness and brought us into the kingdom of the Son he loves, in whom we have redemption, the forgiveness of sins.

Prayer: Dear Holy Spirit, thank you for living in us and enabling us to grow in our Christian faith and in our relationships with God and with our fellow man. Help us not to be easily frustrated, but to hold on to the Word of God, knowing that by your power, our Christian faith journey will indeed get better with time. Amen.

Have you had to learn a new skill for work or in order to advance your career? In the beginning, it was probably difficult. In your initial frustrations, you may have even wondered why you made the choice to learn that skill in the first place. With practice you got better at that skill and with time, it came easy. So easy you were asked to teach and train others in that skill. So it is with our Christian faith. When you receive the Lord Jesus as Savior and Lord by faith, there are skills that you have to learn in order to grow in your relationship with God. These include Prayer, Bible Reading and Bible Study, hearing and understanding what the Holy Spirit is speaking to you and sharing fellowship and Holy Communion at church services. At first, it may be a challenge. The language in the Bible may be unfamiliar, you may not understand everything you read in the Bible and you will need others to help you. With time your faith grows as you understand the Bible better, you have conversations with God in prayer more frequently and the next thing you know, you are sharing your faith with others and inviting them to have a personal relationship with the Lord Jesus. So do not get discouraged when the beginning of your Christian walk seems difficult; It Does Get Better!

© By Dr. Sheila Hayford.

April 10
God's Reversal

Esther Chapter 9, verses 1, 21-22:
Now in the twelfth month, that is, the month Adar, on the thirteenth day of the same, when the king's commandment and his decree drew near to be put in execution, in the day that the enemies of the Jews hoped to have power over them, (though it was turned to the contrary, that the Jews had rule over them that hated them;)To stablish this among them, that they should keep the fourteenth day of the month Adar, and the fifteenth day of the same, yearly, As the days wherein the Jews rested from their enemies, and the month which was turned unto them from sorrow to joy, and from mourning into a good day: that they should make them days of feasting and joy, and of sending portions one to another, and gifts to the poor.

Prayer: Dear God, thank you for your divine miraculous interventions in our lives in response to our prayers with fasting. You give us reasons to celebrate and so we praise and thank you. May your kingdom be advanced in our lives and in our communities. In Jesus' Name. Amen.

Wicked Haman! Haman hated the Jewish people so much that he plotted and orchestrated an evil plan to destroy all the Jews, including Esther, who was the wife of King Ahasuerus at the time. Haman even got King Ahasuerus to agree with Haman's evil plan because the King thought Haman had the King's best interests at heart. Mordecai who had raised Queen Esther as his child when she was orphaned asked Queen

Esther to intervene. Queen Esther, in turn, called a fast and prayed, asked others to pray and fast with her and her maidens and went into the king's presence without being called, an act punishable by death if Esther did not find favor with the king. As a result of God's divine reversal, the evil that Haman wished on the Jewish people fell upon Haman and Haman's ten sons and instead of being destroyed, the Jews triumphed in battle against their enemies. It was to commemorate this miraculous act of God, the bravery of Queen Esther, and to celebrate their victory as a people and their protection as a nation by God that the festival of Purim was established. What do you need God to divinely reverse in your life? Learn from the example of Queen Esther. Even when it seemed her fate was sealed with the king's ink she did not give up and as a result, Queen Esther and the people of Israel were delivered from what looked like certain destruction. We are blessed that through our Lord Jesus Christ we are able to experience God's divine reversals on our behalf. God <u>can</u> bring good out of what satan had meant for harm. We should pray and fast individually and with others and listen to what God instructs us to do through the Holy Spirit. Then we must obey God's instructions and watch God's hand at work in our situations. Let God work all things for our good.

© By Dr. Sheila Hayford.

April 11
JESUS - The Passover Lamb

Exodus Chapter 12, verses 21-23:
Then Moses summoned all the elders of Israel and said to them, "Go at once and select the animals for your families and slaughter the Passover lamb. Take a bunch of hyssop, dip it into the blood in the basin and put some of the blood on the top and on both sides of the doorframe. None of you shall go out of the door of your house until morning. When the Lord goes through the land to strike down the Egyptians, he will see the blood on the top and sides of the doorframe and will pass over that

doorway, and he will not permit the destroyer to enter your houses and strike you down. (NIV)

1 Corinthians Chapter 5, verse 7:

Get rid of the old yeast, so that you may be a new unleavened batch - as you really are. For Christ, our Passover lamb, has been sacrificed. (NIV)

Prayer: Dear Lord Jesus; we are eternally grateful to you, our Passover Lamb. Thank you for submitting to the will of our heavenly Father on our behalf. May we, in turn, yield and submit to your Lordship. Amen.

King Pharaoh was determined not to let the people of Israel leave Egypt when the prophet Moses gave him God's directive to release the people of Israel from bondage to go and worship God. And when King Pharaoh persisted in his rebellion, God finally had enough! The God initiated Passover would bring King Pharaoh in submission to God's will and the people of Israel would be delivered from bondage. So God commanded the Israelites to select and slaughter a Passover lamb and place the blood of that lamb on the door frames of their houses. When God's sent destroyer saw that blood, that house would be passed over and not destroyed by the deadly plague. Immediately following that plague, King Pharaoh sent for the prophet Moses and Moses' brother Aaron. King Pharaoh then gave them permission to leave Egypt with the people of Israel and with all their flocks, herds and possessions. This Passover event foreshadowed what would happen at the cross of Calvary where the Lord Jesus would die openly as punishment for the sins of all humanity. Just as God allowed King Pharaoh to exercise free will, so God gives each person the free will to accept or reject the death of Jesus Christ for sin on their behalf personally. For those who repent of and confess their sin, accept the Lord Jesus' death on the cross for their sins personally and invite the Lord Jesus into their heart and life as their personal Lord and Savior, God looks at the finished work of the blood of Jesus and cleanses and forgives the individual of all their sin. In other words, when God sees the blood of Jesus appropriated by an individual, God **passes over** that individual's sins because Jesus took the punishment for their sins and paid their sin debt in full. Hallelujah! Accept the Lord Jesus today and be born again into God's family!

© By Dr. Sheila Hayford.

April 12
A Sham Trial

Luke Chapter 23: 13-26, 33-34:

And Pilate, when he had called together the chief priests and the rulers and the people, Said unto them, Ye have brought this man unto me, as one that perverteth the people: and, behold, I, having examined him before you, have found no fault in this man touching those things whereof ye accuse him: No, nor yet Herod: for I sent you to him; and, lo, nothing worthy of death is done unto him. I will therefore chastise him, and release him. (For of necessity he must release one unto them at the feast.) And they cried out all at once, saying, Away with this man, and release unto us Barabbas: (Who for a certain sedition made in the city, and for murder, was cast into prison.) Pilate therefore, willing to release Jesus, spake again to them. But they cried, saying, Crucify him, crucify him. And he said unto them the third time, Why, what evil hath he done? I have found no cause of death in him: I will therefore chastise him, and let him go. And they were instant with loud voices, requiring that he might be crucified. And the voices of them and of the chief priests prevailed. And Pilate gave sentence that it should be as they required. And he released unto them him that for sedition and murder was cast into prison, whom they had desired; but he delivered Jesus to their will. And as they led him away, they laid hold upon one Simon, a Cyrenian, coming out of the country, and on him they laid the cross, that he might bear it after Jesus. And when they were come to the place, which is called Calvary, there they crucified him, and the malefactors, one on the right hand, and the other on the left. Then said Jesus, Father, forgive them; for they know not what they do. And they parted his raiment, and cast lots.

Prayer: Dear Lord Jesus; I know I am a sinner. Thank you for dying on the cross, shedding your blood for my sins and for rising again from the dead. I confess and repent of my sins, sins for things I did wrong and sins for things I failed to do and I ask for your forgiveness. I invite you into my heart as my personal Lord and Savior and receive your gift of eternal life. Fill me with the Holy Spirit and help me live for you. I am now saved! Hallelujah! Amen.

It is astounding that at the trial of Jesus, Pilate, who said he found Jesus to be innocent of what the chief priests, rulers and the mob were accusing Jesus of and who said three times that he found nothing to show that the Jesus had done anything that merited crucifixion, should hand over Jesus to be crucified in such a horrible death. What a sham! Why bother to have the trial if the results were already fixed? If Pilate was going to cave in to the requests of the chief priests and those asking for the death of Jesus, he should have made that clear from the beginning and let everyone see who Pilate was at his core. You see, Pilate would do anything to save his position, even if it meant using false witnesses and giving in to the mob, knowing that the mob who were loud in their spewing of hatred were wrong. By contrast, observe the calmness of Jesus. Not only did Jesus take the punishment for our sins, he prayed for God to forgive the evildoers for their actions because they did not fully understand the implications of their actions. So how could Jesus remain so calm? It was because Jesus knew God our heavenly Father, knew who he was and his mission and knew the benefits for God and humanity from their actions far outweighed any short term suffering. The devil thought he was getting rid of an innocent man, Jesus, without realizing that the evil act of crucifying the innocent Jesus was the very way God would use Jesus to bear the sins of humanity for all time, thus defeating sin, satan and death and that the Lord Jesus would be raised up with all power. Hallelujah! If perchance, you have not accepted the finished work of the Lord Jesus in dying for the sins of humankind on your behalf, you can become a part of God's family now. Confess and repent of your sins in prayer and invite the Lord Jesus into your heart and life by praying the prayer of salvation above. You will receive eternal life and the indwelling of the Holy Spirit as the Lord Jesus' gift to you and you will then become a child of God with God as your heavenly Father. Now that you have prayed the prayer of salvation, it is important to talk with God in prayer daily, read the Bible, meet and learn God's Word and partake of Holy Communion with other born again believers at church services. For you see, <u>Good Friday ended up being Good for mankind but bad for the devil!</u> Thanks be to God!

© By Dr. Sheila Hayford.

April 13
It Is Written

John Chapter 19: 31-37, 41-42:

The Jews therefore, because it was the preparation, that the bodies should not remain upon the cross on the sabbath day, (for that sabbath day was an high day,) besought Pilate that their legs might be broken, and that they might be taken away. Then came the soldiers, and brake the legs of the first, and of the other which was crucified with him. But when they came to Jesus, and saw that he was dead already, they brake not his legs: But one of the soldiers with a spear pierced his side, and forthwith came there out blood and water. And he that saw it bare record, and his record is true: and he knoweth that he saith true, that ye might believe. For these things were done, that the scripture should be fulfilled, A bone of him shall not be broken. And again another scripture saith, They shall look on him whom they pierced. Now in the place where he was crucified there was a garden; and in the garden a new sepulchre, wherein was never man yet laid. There laid they Jesus therefore because of the Jews' preparation day; for the sepulchre was nigh at hand.

John Chapter 4, verse 10:

Then saith Jesus unto him, Get thee hence, Satan: for it is written, Thou shalt worship the Lord thy God, and him only shalt thou serve.

Prayer: Dear God; everything you say is so, because you always have the last word. Help us to live our lives according to your 'It is written' declarations concerning us. In Jesus' Name. Amen.

It is written! Remember these words of the Lord Jesus Christ. How true! As we read these Scripture verses about the Lord Jesus and his crucifixion we see the fulfillment of God's words revealed to man in the Holy Bible in detail. What God said happened then, and what God says about the present and the future will surely come to pass. What are some of the 'It is written' statements God has said about you? In the book of Matthew Chapter 4, verse 4 we read of Jesus, "But he answered and said, It is written, Man shall not live by bread alone, but by every word that proceedeth out of the mouth of God." In other words, we should live our lives based on what God says about us. So as we reflect on God's love for us, Jesus' sacrifice on our behalf and the Holy Spirit's presence in us, let us take comfort in the fact that God will always have the last word.

© By Dr. Sheila Hayford.

April 14
He Is Risen

Mark Chapter 16: 1-7:

And when the sabbath was past, Mary Magdalene, and Mary the mother of James, and Salome, had bought sweet spices, that they might come and anoint him. And very early in the morning the first day of the week, they came unto the sepulchre at the rising of the sun. And they said among themselves, Who shall roll us away the stone from the door of the sepulchre? And when they looked, they saw that the stone was rolled away: for it was very great. And entering into the sepulchre, they saw a young man sitting on the right side, clothed in a long white garment; and they were affrighted. And he saith unto them, Be not affrighted: Ye seek Jesus of Nazareth, which was crucified: he is risen; he is not here: behold the place where they laid him. But go your way, tell his disciples and Peter that he goeth before you into Galilee: there shall ye see him, as he said unto you.

Prayer: Dear Lord Jesus: You give us so much joy! What a celebration! Satan tried but failed to keep you down, for through you sin is conquered, satan is forever defeated and death has no hold. Thank you. Amen.

Have you heard the good news? What? Jesus Christ the Lord is Risen Indeed! Hall…e…lu….ja…h! We should be so excited that we cannot keep this good news to ourselves. The Lord Jesus Christ did a great work for all humanity when he died for our sins on the cross of Calvary and to our great joy the Lord Jesus is risen victorious with all power, seated at the right hand of authority of God our heavenly Father. Be bold, don't be afraid. Go; share the good news of salvation and tell others the Lord Jesus Christ is Risen! Do not forget to add the fact that the Lord Jesus is coming back again! What a celebration that will be!

© By Dr. Sheila Hayford.

April 15
Sent!

John Chapter 20: 20-21:
After he said this, he showed them his hands and side. The disciples were overjoyed when they saw the Lord. Again Jesus said, "Peace be with you! As the Father has sent me, I am sending you." (NIV)

Matthew Chapter 28, verses 18-20:
Then Jesus came to them and said, "All authority in heaven and on earth has been given to me. Therefore go and make disciples of all nations, baptizing them in the name of the Father and of the Son and of

the Holy Spirit, and teaching them to obey everything I have commanded you. And surely I am with you always, to the very end of the age." (NIV)

Prayer: Dear Lord Jesus, thank you for entrusting us with sharing the good news of salvation and with doing the work you have assigned to us. May it be said of us, "You Sent and we Went!" in faithfulness to you. Amen.

We have been sent! By whom? By our Lord and Savior Jesus Christ. And what our instructions? They are clearly defined in the verses above. The Lord Jesus promises to be with us and the Holy Spirit will empower us as we obey him. Will we go?

© By Dr. Sheila Hayford.

April 16
Healed

Acts Chapter 3: 11-16:

And as the lame man which was healed held Peter and John, all the people ran together unto them in the porch that is called Solomon's, greatly wondering. And when Peter saw it, he answered unto the people, Ye men of Israel, why marvel ye at this? or why look ye so earnestly on us, as though by our own power or holiness we had made this man to walk? The God of Abraham, and of Isaac, and of Jacob, the God of our fathers, hath glorified his Son Jesus; whom ye delivered up, and denied him in the presence of Pilate, when he was determined to let him go. But ye denied the Holy One and the Just, and desired a murderer to be granted unto you; And killed the Prince of life, whom God hath raised from the dead; whereof we are witnesses. And his name through faith in his name hath made this man strong, whom ye see and know: yea, the faith which is by him hath given him this perfect soundness in the presence of you all.

Prayer: Dear God, there is salvation in the Name of Jesus and none other! There is healing, deliverance, protection in the Name of Jesus.

Glory! There is eternal life in the Name of Jesus. Yes! And in the Name of Jesus, our Lord and Savior, we are part of your beloved family, sealed by the Holy Spirit. Thanks and praise be yours forever! Amen.

Look at the boldness of the Apostle Peter! The Apostle Peter laid out the case for his and our Lord and Savior, Jesus Christ. Those who wondered how it was that the lame man was healed were given their answer. The Name of the same Lord Jesus, who died on the cross of Calvary and rose again, healed the lame man. We have delegated authority given to us by the Lord Jesus to pray for the sick, the lame and those with infirmities in the Name of Jesus Christ and see God's power at work in those who believe. Be healed in the Name of Jesus!

© By Dr. Sheila Hayford.

April 17
Read. Hear. Apply.

Revelation Chapter 1, verse 3:
Blessed is he that readeth, and they that hear the words of this prophecy, and keep those things which are written therein: for the time is at hand.

Prayer: Our heavenly Father, help us read, hear and apply what you teach us in your Holy Word the way you would have us do. In Jesus' Name, Amen.

If you wanted to become a Plumber but couldn't read, although you had the desire to become one, you probably would not become one if you could not read the courses, measurements as well as the specifications for a career as a Plumber. However, knowing how to read would not be enough to qualify you as a Plumber. You would need someone to explain to you and show you what the words you read meant. In other words, you would have to hear what it was that you needed to do as a Plumber in class or as a trainee or apprentice of a Plumber. Finally you had to be able to study and apply what you had been taught in order to see your goal come to fruition. It is the same in our Christian life. When we read the Bible, we must hear with our spiritual ears what God is saying to us and then apply action with corresponding works in the way God expects of us. Each of us is on this earth on God's time so let us be who God has called us to be and get things done in the time God gives us.

Read. Hear. Apply!

© By Dr. Sheila Hayford.

April 18
Don't Fall For Evil

Genesis Chapter 3, verses 1-6:
Now the serpent was more subtil than any beast of the field which the Lord God had made. And he said unto the woman, Yea, hath God said, Ye shall not eat of every tree of the garden? And the woman said unto the serpent, We may eat of the fruit of the trees of the garden: But of the fruit of the tree which is in the midst of the garden, God hath said, Ye shall not eat of it, neither shall ye touch it, lest ye die. And the serpent said unto the woman, Ye shall not surely die: For God doth know that in the day ye eat thereof, then your eyes shall be opened, and ye shall be as gods, knowing good and evil. And when the woman saw that the tree was good for food, and that it was pleasant to the eyes, and a tree to be desired to make one wise, she took of the fruit thereof, and did eat, and gave also unto her husband with her; and he did eat.

Prayer: Dear God, help us not to fall into sin, nor allow others to lure us into sin, for you enable us to stand with our Lord Jesus, in the power of the Holy Spirit. Amen.

The Fall of Eve, and subsequently Adam, when they both yielded to the lies of satan and ate of the fruit God had told them not to eat, was not just a fall from a sinless human nature, it was a fall for evil. If misery loves company, it stands to reason that the goal of some would be to get other people to fall into the same mistakes, trap or sin they fell into, as harsh as that may sound. Why would someone who is familiar with the evils of prostitution lure other women into prostitution and sex trafficking? Why would a person who knows what is right tempt someone to fall into the temptations that person fell into, instead of seeking help for themselves? And, more importantly, why would anyone allow another person to let them fall into sin? Eve was the one who disobeyed God. So why did Adam allow Eve to cause him to sin against God? Maybe Eve told Adam that if he didn't eat the forbidden fruit with her, that meant he did not love her. Or maybe it was Adam who told Eve he was not going to leave her, no matter what God had said. Either way, that was not reason enough for Adam to disobey God. Now, by choosing the words of satan and falling for evil instead of obeying the instructions God gave, they were both condemned to hell! And so it would have remained if the Lord Jesus Christ had not come and taken on himself the punishment for the sins of Eve, Adam and all humanity. Each one of us will individually give an account to God. We cannot look to the left or right on that day looking for someone to blame, especially when God through the Lord Jesus and the Holy Spirit has given us what we need to be overcomers in life. Stand with God; don't fall for satan!

© By Dr. Sheila Hayford.

April 19
Keep Your Crown!

Revelation Chapter 3, verses 11, 12:
Behold, I come quickly: hold that fast which thou hast, that no man take thy crown. Him that overcometh will I make a pillar in the temple of my God, and he shall go no more out: and I will write upon him the name of my God, and the name of the city of my God, which is new Jerusalem, which cometh down out of heaven from my God: and I will write upon him my new name.

Prayer: Dear heavenly Father, we value our God given crowns. Help us not to allow anyone or anything to distract us from our call and service to you. In Jesus' Name, Amen.

Powerful revelations indeed! Is it possible to lose your God given crown? If so, how? You see, when we receive God's free gift of salvation, we have to work out our sanctification; that is, the process by which the Word of God transforms our lives to become more of the persons God intends for us to be. It is not easy and that is why we have God the Holy Spirit to help us. As we live our lives under the watchful eyes of God our heavenly Father, God is preparing many rewards for us, including different crowns. So how is it possible for a person to lose their crown? By taking their eyes off the prize. When you do well by God, that may make some persons unhappy. Thus, some may try to discourage you from living for God or try to make you stop serving God altogether. If you take your eyes off God's prize, you might focus on those unhappy persons and lose your crown. In the final analysis, you are responsible for what is worth keeping and what is worth losing. The Lord Jesus does not want you to lose your God given crown!

© By Dr. Sheila Hayford.

April 20
Hear; Hear!

John Chapter 10, verse 27:
My sheep hear my voice, and I know them, and they follow me:
Prayer: Dear Lord Jesus; I am so glad I belong to you! Thank you for saving me. Amen.

These words have special meaning for me because these were the words given to me at my Confirmation Service. At that time I did not understand what they meant and wondered why I did not hear something like 'God loves you' at the time! Of course, God always loves each of us! After I received the Lord Jesus into my heart and life as Savior and Lord, I began to appreciate these words and become even more grateful for them every day. How so? It is because of the assurance God gives us. God knows those persons who are is. In other words, one does not have to focus on the opinions of men to know if God approves of you when you can talk with God directly and study God's word. You must understand that God gives a person godly counsel through people as well so be careful not to reject God given counsel in your deliberations. Not only does God know us, God says we <u>hear God's voice.</u> Yes, we are able to recognize or discern God's voice just as a child can recognize the voice of his or parent. In other words, by the power of the Holy Spirit, we do not reject God's truth or fall for false ideologies. Furthermore, we are not only hearers, but doers of what God requires of us, by the grace of God. If we sin, we can confess our sins to God and to man, repent of sin, ask and receive God's forgiveness because the Lord Jesus has taken the punishment for our sins. God intends for us to move forward in our Christian journey. Hear! Hear what God has to say. And then, trust God to help you do God's bidding.

© By Dr. Sheila Hayford.

April 21
Love Has A Lot to Do With It

John Chapter 14, verse 15:

If ye love me, keep my commandments.

Luke Chapter 18, verses 18, 19: And a certain ruler asked him, saying, Good Master, what shall I do to inherit eternal life? And Jesus said unto him, Why callest thou me good? none is good, save one, that is, God.

Prayer: Dear Lord Jesus; we say we love you. Help us show our love for you by keeping your commandments. Amen.

It is interesting how the Lord Jesus spoke about love in this verse. The Lord Jesus associated love for him with the keeping of God's commandments. In other words, if a person says they love Jesus, and then go about doing everything the Lord Jesus told them not to do, it would be logical to wonder if that person really loved Jesus. Is the Lord Jesus saying that only perfect people love Jesus? No! As the Lord Jesus told the ruler, only God is inherently good. We know the Lord Jesus came to die for the sins of humanity because there was no perfect human being to be found. What the Lord Jesus is saying is this: if a person loves Jesus, that person will not delight in sinning against God. The indwelling Holy Spirit is the one who enables a Christian believer to live for God. What if a born again believer and follower of the Lord Jesus sins? That person will be sorry when they sin, confess and receive forgiveness of sin and will strive by God's power to be in good relationship with God.

© By Dr. Sheila Hayford.

April 22
And Bless Me Also

Exodus Chapter 12, verses 31-32:

And he called for Moses and Aaron by night, and said, Rise up, and get you forth from among my people, both ye and the children of Israel; and go, serve the LORD, as ye have said. Also take your flocks and your herds, as ye have said, and be gone; and bless me also.

1 Chronicles Chapter 4, verse 10:

And Jabez called on the God of Israel, saying, Oh that thou wouldest bless me indeed, and enlarge my coast, and that thine hand might be with me, and that thou wouldest keep me from evil, that it may not grieve me! And God granted him that which he requested.

Prayer; Dear God, it is sometimes amusing that some who reject your Word want to be participants in your blessing. Have mercy on us all, in Jesus' Name, Amen.

It would astound me that in the days of Jesus, some of the religious leaders failed to recognize the authority of the Lord Jesus whereas demons responded to the Lord Jesus in fear and trembling as the Lord Jesus cast them out. Even satan recognized the Lord Jesus. In modern times, I have seen some who do not care to live for God but want to participate in the blessings of God. There is nothing wrong in seeking God's blessings, as many of us do. However, would you think it right if a person insulted another person and then asked them for a huge favor? The person who was insulted might wonder what the person was thinking. Pharaoh adamantly refused to obey God and allow the prophet Moses and the people of Israel to leave, even when God sent plague after plague through the prophet Moses to get Pharaoh to change his mind. Finally, when God sent that last plague that caused Pharaoh to decide to let the prophet Moses, the people of Israel together with their flocks, herds and possessions leave Egypt, Pharaoh asked the prophet Moses to bless him. However, we know that Pharaoh was not truly repentant before God because soon afterwards Pharaoh changed his mind and Pharaoh and his army chased the prophet Moses and the people of Israel as they crossed the Red Sea. God had the waters rush back, killing Pharaoh and all Pharaoh's army. Jabez prayed in humility for God's blessing and Jabez received God's favor and God's blessing. So while it is okay to seek God's blessing, humble yourself before God and make sure you are in right relationship with God. Receive God's Son, Jesus Christ, as your personal Lord and Savior for God's blessings to humanity are yes through our Lord Jesus Christ.

© By Dr. Sheila Hayford.

April 23
Hidden Treasure

Psalm 119, verse 11:
Thy word have I hid in mine heart, that I might not sin against thee.

Matthew Chapter 13, verse 44:

The kingdom of heaven is like treasure hidden in a field. When a man found it, he hid it again, and then in his joy went and sold all he had and bought that field. (NIV)

Matthew Chapter 6, verse 21:

For where your treasure is, there will your heart be also.

Prayer: Dear God; you are our treasure. We hide your words in our hearts. Help us show you and the world how much we value you. In Jesus' Name, Amen.

What you spend your money on is an indicator of what you value. If you value your family you will take good care of them. By that I do not mean you will buy your children all the latest gadgets and toys their hearts may desire. I mean you will take the responsibility of meeting their needs seriously. God describes the kingdom of heaven in this parable as hidden treasure. In other words, sometimes a person stumbles on hidden treasure. The person in the parable did not set out to find something, but found something of such value that the person was willing to sell all he had to purchase that property. How do we value the Word of God? Is God's word worth spending time studying? Is God's Word worth allotting time on Sundays to fellowship with and learn from fellow believers? Is God's Word worth sharing with others? You decide; and then act accordingly!

© By Dr. Sheila Hayford.

April 24
God Knows Your Name

Psalm 147, verses 3-5: He healeth the broken in heart, and bindeth up their wounds. He telleth the number of the stars; he calleth them all by their names. Great is our Lord, and of great power: his understanding is infinite.

1 Samuel Chapter 3, verse 10:

And the Lord came, and stood, and called as at other times, Samuel, Samuel. Then Samuel answered, Speak; for thy servant heareth.

Prayer: Dear God; thank you for speaking to us personally, in the way only you as our God can. Speak to us now, and help us to obey you. In Jesus' Name. Amen.

You mean God knows my name? Yes, what makes you wonder? You see, sometimes when a person is going through a difficult time, they may think that God has forgotten them. They may not realize that, like Job, their challenging situation may be their test to prove they are for God, not against God. Sometimes, a person may despair in thinking their situation is hopeless. God wants us to know that if he knows the numbers of the infinitely appearing stars and calls each of those stars by their names, God not only knows our names, God calls each of us by our names. The prophet Samuel was expecting to hear from God, so when God called Samuel, Samuel was ready to hear from God. God is near to the broken hearted, ready to heal and ready to mend. God's power, might and understanding are infinitely more than we could fathom as human beings. So call on God with whatever situation you may be facing and expect God to call your name in response. In God's way and in God's timing God will come through for you.

© By Dr. Sheila Hayford.

April 25
The Power of Example

Psalm 78, verses 3-5:
things we have heard and known, things our ancestors have told us. We will not hide them from their descendants; we will tell the next generation the praiseworthy deeds of the Lord, his power, and the wonders he has done. He decreed statutes for Jacob and established the law in Israel, which he commanded our ancestors to teach their children, (NIV)

Prayer: Dear God, we love showing off our God! Enable us, by the Holy Spirit's power, to be role models and godly examples to our peers, our children and generations to come. In Jesus' Name, Amen.

As we show our sons and daughters by example, the joys and challenges of the work that we do, let us be mindful of showing our children by our example, the power of our God. For faith in God is what has enabled us to achieve what many who lived in ages past thought could never be accomplished and enabled us to remain anchored in spite of the tests we endured. Yes, we love to talk about our work and we sure love to talk about our God!

© By Dr. Sheila Hayford.

April 26
Be Authentic!

Genesis Chapter 42, verses 18-20: And Joseph said unto them the third day, This do, and live; for I fear God: If ye be true men, let one of your brethren be bound in the house of your prison: go ye, carry corn for the famine of your houses: But bring your youngest brother unto me; so shall your words be verified, and ye shall not die. And they did so.

Prayer: All knowing God our heavenly Father, we know you hate hypocrisy and pride. Help us to be authentic in our relationship with you and our relationships with others. In Jesus' Name, Amen.

Joseph wanted to test the authenticity of the words of his brothers since they had previously sold him into slavery and then lied to their father who now thought that his son, Joseph, was dead. And so he gave them a hard test, hard because the brothers were not sure how their father would respond. Nevertheless, his brothers were torn between a rock and a hard place as they needed the food and so they did what Joseph asked them to do. Cowardice is unbecoming and God hates hypocrisy and pride. God wants us to be authentic. Admit your faults, weaknesses, mistakes, sins. You are human and so are your fellow humankind. That is why the Lord Jesus came to bear the punishment for our sins. If you sin, don't stay defeated. Invite the Lord Jesus into your life, repent of your sin and ask God to enable you to change for the better. You must, however, be willing to do what it takes for your change. Share your struggles, victories, challenges and advice when appropriate so others know that with God's grace they can also make it in life. In other words, be and do "the authentic you" as you change for the better!

© By Dr. Sheila Hayford.

April 27
Pride

Proverbs Chapter 16, verse 18:
Pride goeth before destruction, and an haughty spirit before a fall.
Prayer: Dear God; help us to recognize pride in all its subtle forms. We humble ourselves before you and ask for your grace and mercy. In Jesus' Name, Amen.

One of the best ways of being authentic is to first acknowledge who you are. Remember, the real you is who you are in Christ. However, in our humanity, each person has challenges and issues we need to work on. One of the more subtle challenges is pride. Pride is more than an emotion. It begins with a thought. A person who is proud is haughty or arrogant and fails to acknowledge God as Lord in their life. A person can have a sense of pride when they accomplish their goals or attain certain positions and that could be healthy. There is also a form of pride which can make a person feel that they are spiritually, morally, financially, educationally or racially superior to another person and which causes them to look down on, demean or mistreat another person based on their sometimes misguided opinions. So why does God hate pride? It is because pride puts a person in the driver's seat and fails to acknowledge God as the Creator of life and the Creator of all the creative abilities and talents endowed by God on the person. In other words, no man can exist on this earth without God. So while God hates pride, God is readily available to the humble, those who acknowledge their need for God. If God brought you here, God can keep you while you're here. And depending on how you live on this earth, God will accept or reject you when you leave this earth. Pride initiated satan's downfall and now satan will spend eternity in hell. Don't let pride set you up for a fall, humble yourself before God and let God lift you up. Acknowledge God as your source of life and give God glory.

© By Dr. Sheila Hayford.

April 28
Satisfaction

Isaiah Chapter 53, verse 11:
He shall see of the travail of his soul, and shall be satisfied: by his knowledge shall my righteous servant justify many; for he shall bear their iniquities.

Prayer; Dear Lord Jesus, we love you! Thank you for not giving up on humankind when Adam and Eve disobeyed God and for bringing us back into God's family. We are eternally grateful! Amen.

Sometimes, when we observe injustice and suffering and what those who try to change that have to go through, one might wonder if it was worth what they had to go through. One of my personal heroes, President Nelson Mandela was one who took it upon himself to fight apartheid in South Africa. Sure, he had others join him in the fight but he bore the brunt of the persecution and suffering for his cause. We would see people holding "Free Mandela" pictures of a youthful Nelson Mandela as they marched in anti-apartheid protests, while he was kept all those years in prison. I tuned in to watch his release from prison on television and Nelson Mandela looked so frail as he walked out. Was it worth it? Yes!! When he went to prison, Nelson Mandela was willing to die for the freedom of all the races in South Africa. After he left prison, President Nelson Mandela became the President of the same nation. What a turnaround! Only God! As we celebrate Easter and reflect on all the injustice and suffering the Lord Jesus endured to purchase humankind's redemption, one might wonder if it was worth it. Yes, it was!! When the Lord Jesus looks at his suffering and then sees all of us he has redeemed for all time into the family of God joyfully serving God, overcoming sin in the power of the Holy Spirit and gifted to the Lord Jesus as his future bride, the Lord Jesus is SATISFIED! And that makes my heart glad! When we look at our present tests and trials, if ever there was a question as to whether they were worth it, consider the eternal rewards awaiting us and may our souls be satisfied, too!

© By Dr. Sheila Hayford.

April 29
Lacking Nothing

2 Peter Chapter 1, verse 3:

According as his divine power hath given unto us all things that pertain unto life and godliness, through the knowledge of him that hath called us to glory and virtue:

Psalm 84, verse 11:

For the Lord God is a sun and shield: the Lord will give grace and glory: no good thing will he withhold from them that walk uprightly.

Prayer: Dear God, you are truly a good God and you want all that is best for us. Help us to move from lack to lacking nothing good in Christ in God. In Jesus' Name, Amen.

Think about what is implied in this verse. If God has given us everything we need that pertains to life and godliness, then we should lack nothing that we need for living on this earth and living godly. So if we experience lack in any area that pertains to life and godliness it is not God's fault. Which means that if we lack anything we have to examine ourselves and these verses more closely. As we do, we find out that the secret of lacking nothing good is found through the knowledge of God, who desires good for us. As we experience right standing with God though his Son, Jesus Christ, know God, know and understand God's ways, hear God's voice and obey God's instructions, God will give us grace, be our source and strong defense and we will move from lack to lacking nothing good. Amen.

© By Dr. Sheila Hayford.

April 30
Grace For Each Day

1 Corinthians Chapter 15, verse 10:

But by the grace of God I am what I am: and his grace which was bestowed upon me was not in vain; but I laboured more abundantly than they all: yet not I, but the grace of God which was with me.

Prayer: Dear God, give us your grace this day to accomplish the tasks that must be done today and help us not procrastinate. In Jesus' Name, Amen.

With the understanding of the times we live in comes the recognition that we are living in days of grace. However, day<u>s</u> of grace may cause a person to think they have a lot of days to accomplish their goals. That, in turn, may lead to procrastination. Each day is a gift from God and God gives us the grace we need to be and to do each day. Just like God gives us new mercies each day and provides for our daily bread, so there are certain graces for specific times. If you miss that grace then you might not get that opportunity again. So let us not take God's grace for granted and let us encourage others not to take God's grace for granted. God gives all alive on this earth the opportunity to receive Jesus Christ as their Lord and Savior <u>today</u>.

© By Dr. Sheila Hayford.

May 1
Home Décor

John Chapter 14, verse 2:

In my Father's house are many mansions: if it were not so, I would have told you. I go to prepare a place for you.

Revelation Chapter 21, verses 15-22:

And he that talked with me had a golden reed to measure the city, and the gates thereof, and the wall thereof. And the city lieth foursquare, and the length is as large as the breadth: and he measured the city with the reed, twelve thousand furlongs. The length and the breadth and the height of it are equal. And he measured the wall thereof, an hundred and forty and four cubits, according to the measure of a man, that is, of the angel. And the building of the wall of it was of jasper: and the city was pure gold, like unto clear glass. And the foundations of the wall of the city were garnished with all manner of precious stones. The first foundation was jasper; the second, sapphire; the third, a chalcedony; the fourth, an emerald; The fifth, sardonyx; the sixth, sardius; the seventh, chrysolyte; the eighth, beryl; the ninth, a topaz; the tenth, a chrysoprasus; the eleventh, a jacinth; the twelfth, an amethyst. And the twelve gates were twelve pearls: every several gate was of one pearl: and the street of the city was pure gold, as it were transparent glass. And I saw no temple therein: for the Lord God Almighty and the Lamb are the temple of it.

Prayer: Dear heavenly Father; I do want one of your gorgeous heavenly mansions. Even more, I want more of you. Help me in my desire to be transformed by your Word. In Jesus' Name, Amen.

Mansions; they are so beautiful! I know the hard work that goes into one; building, maintaining, upkeep, home décor and more… It looks great, you enjoy it but it does take work. And yet, it is somewhat surprising that many will put so much time and effort into their earthly mansions and no thought into their heavenly mansions or even to the thought of having a heavenly mansion. Especially when you consider the fact that the mansions here on earth are temporal. Reading the wondrous beauty and detail of the heavenly city described in the book of Revelation is awe inspiring. What are we doing here on earth in preparation for our heavenly mansion? How will our mansions be adorned? As a believer, God the Holy Spirit indwells you. We must ask God what changes we need to make on this earth as we prepare for our Lord Jesus' Second Coming and then make those changes. It will be wonderfully worthwhile when we each move into our new home, I mean, into our God designed mansion!

© By Dr. Sheila Hayford.

May 2
Bliss; The Joy Of Answered Prayer

Daniel Chapter 2, verse 23:

I thank and praise you, God of my ancestors: You have given me wisdom and power, you have made known to me what we asked of you, you have made known to us the dream of the king."

Prayer: Dear God; we thank and praise you for the joy of answered prayer! May we share your goodness with others. In Jesus' Name, Amen.

I know the joys of answered prayer! I shared some of my joys in Morning Glory - 365 devotionals like no other! The wonderful thing is that the answers to my prayers are ongoing. This year has been a wonderful year of celebrations, celebrations in answer to prayer. I am sure God has done many good things for you. Like Daniel, did you praise and thank God for the answers to your prayers? Or did you take those answers for granted? Did you encourage someone by sharing your good news with them? You see, sharing your testimony could make the difference between life and death in another person's life. Some things are too good to keep solely for ourselves. Share God's goodness!

© By Dr. Sheila Hayford.

May 3
Friendships - The Gift Goes On ... !

John Chapter 15, verses 15-16:

I no longer call you servants, because a servant does not know his master's business. Instead, I have called you friends, for everything that I learned from my Father I have made known to you. You did not choose me, but I chose you and appointed you so that you might go and bear fruit - fruit that will last - and so that whatever you ask in my name the Father will give you.

Prayer: Our heavenly Father, We thank you for the gift of our loyal friend, our Lord and Savior, Jesus Christ. As we celebrate Loyalty Day, we are especially thankful and grateful for our generational friendships, given by you as gifts to be shared. To you be all praise and glory! In Jesus' Name. Amen.

May 1 is Loyalty Day in the United States so this week is a wonderful time to reflect on friendships. I was honored, privileged and blessed to share in the goodwill and to personally congratulate our Family Advisor, Counselor, Friend, Father in the Faith, Statesman and Exceptional Role Model on his 100th birthday year. Amazing! He knew my parents before they were married, before I even came to be on this earth. Growing up we shared special family events together, he was the Keynote and Commencement Speaker at various school and social events, handed me awards in school, I looked up to him in his successful professional life as a distinguished physician and later in academia and as an extraordinary husband and father.

The beautiful thing is our Family Friendship is generational, continuing in the children and descendants. I followed in his footsteps into the medical field and his daughter followed my dad's profession and we the daughters try to visit each other when we are in town. Most of all, as children, grandchildren, and families we each have our individual personal relationship with the Lord Jesus Christ. Priceless! Treasure and value your God ordained relationships. Genuine friendships are gifts to be shared as only you can, with God's help. Yes, there are detractors out there and there are some who have not proved loyal to their fellow man. Remember, friends are chosen, so choose wisely. Our Lord and Savior, Jesus Christ, chose us to be his friends. Are we faithful friends, loyal and committed to our Lord Jesus Christ? Do we spend time with our Lord? Do we introduce him to our family, friends and even to strangers? Does our life reflect the disciplines of our friend, the Lord Jesus Christ? On this Loyalty Day, celebrate family and friends, especially those priceless meaningful relationships. And let us celebrate our bestest friend, King of kings and Lord of lords, Jesus Christ!

© By Dr. Sheila Hayford.

May 4
It's Springtime

Matthew Chapter 24, verse 32:

Now learn a parable of the fig tree; When his branch is yet tender, and putteth forth leaves, ye know that summer is nigh:

Prayer: Dear God; we are anticipating many wonderful things this spring season. Help us in our decision making as we decide what we need to let go of, what needs to be pruned and what we must keep. In Jesus' Name, Amen.

Springtime is here! The children are eager to go outside to play and we are cleaning out the closets to make room for the new. Spring time is indicative of new life; new leaves, new flowers, new clothes for the warmer weather and more... Clutter has to go! What clutter has to be removed from your life? Spring is also a time of planting, cultivating, maintaining, pruning, protecting and preparing for a hoped for harvest. This month we will discuss the spiritual disciplines we must maintain, the soul changes we need to make to renew our mind with the Word of God, the fruit of the Spirit that we need to cultivate with the Holy Spirit's power and the hoped for harvest for we want to hear God's "Well Done!

Thou good and faithful servant." And so as we do our home spring cleaning, take time today to write your spiritual spring cleaning "to do" list. Place your list where you will see it every day this month. Then ask God the Holy Spirit to help you begin the implementation of that list today!

© By Dr. Sheila Hayford.

May 5
Peace; At Any Cost?

Romans Chapter 12, verse 18:
If it be possible, as much as lieth in you, live peaceably with all men.
Acts Chapter 4, verses 19-20:
But Peter and John answered and said unto them, Whether it be right in the sight of God to hearken unto you more than unto God, judge ye. For we cannot but speak the things which we have seen and heard.

Prayer: Dear Holy Spirit, help us to walk in peace with God first, and then let us extend your peace as appropriate without compromising our Christian faith. In Jesus' Name, Amen.

Tis not an easy world that we live in. Just ask any Christian! It seems there is so much evil; hatred, political divisions, denominational strife over preferences, violence and the like. In the midst of this we are called by the Prince of Peace, our Lord and Savior Jesus Christ, to manifest peace as a fruit of the Holy Spirit who indwells us. What are we to do? The answer is found in the verses for today. You see, satan wants to tempt us with evil, strife, hatred, intolerance, Anti-Semitism, Racism and all kinds of …isms, for satan is the author of confusion. The Holy Spirit wants us to live with the peace we have in Christ extended to others as fruit. Does that, therefore, mean peace at any cost? The answer is 'No!' when a person is confronted with a situation where they are asked to compromise or to speak or act contrary to their Christian faith. Peter and John, disciples of our Lord Jesus, were asked not to speak or teach about their Lord Jesus. And they responded appropriately by refusing to compromise and by continuing to speak up for God for they realized that it was more important for them to please God than to disobey God. And so as we cultivate this fruit of peace, let us allow the Holy Spirit to help us bring glory to God by our actions.

© By Dr. Sheila Hayford.

May 6
The Faith Fruit

Hebrews Chapter 11, verse 6:
But without faith it is impossible to please him: for he that cometh to God must believe that he is, and that he is a rewarder of them that diligently seek him.

Romans Chapter 10, verse 17:
So then faith cometh by hearing, and hearing by the word of God.

Prayer: Dear God; thank you for your answers to our prayers. There is nothing too hard for you so help us to trust you at all times and not doubt. In Jesus' Name, Amen.

Faith is a fruit of the Holy Spirit which means it must be cultivated and developed. God gives every person a measure of faith. It is then up to us, with God's power and grace, to develop and exercise our faith. So how do we grow in faith? Faith grows as we hear and read God's Word, the Holy Bible. Faith also grows as we exercise our faith and see God answer our prayers. That encourages and emboldens us to have faith in God for answers to prayers for us and for others. Our faith also increases when we see evidence of God's miracles and hear testimonies of the wonderful interventions of God. So this month, take God at his Word. Believe God to do for you what you ask him in accordance with His Word. Start or maintain your Prayer Journal. Date it with the date you prayed to God with your request and the day it was answered. I have had some prayers answered even before I finished praying and I have had a prayer take twenty years to be answered. It was ALL GOOD! So pray and give God time. Then discern God's answer. Is it yes, wait or no? As you exercise your faith, continue to read and hear Scriptures that address your need and continue to move forward with God in every area of your life. Exercise your faith fruit!

© By Dr. Sheila Hayford.

May 7
For Goodness Sake

Galatians Chapter 5, verse 22:

But the fruit of the Spirit is love, joy, peace, longsuffering, gentleness, goodness, faith,

Proverbs Chapter 3, verses 27, 28:

Withhold not good from them to whom it is due, when it is in the power of thine hand to do it.

Say not unto thy neighbour, Go, and come again, and to morrow I will give; when thou hast it by thee.

Prayer: Dear Holy Spirit: Please lead, guide and direct us as we extend God's goodness to others. In Jesus' Name. Amen.

We all know good when we see it. Did you also know that goodness is fruit of the Holy Spirit? Since God is a good God, one would expect his children to manifest that character trait. So since we must do good, whom should we do good to? There is an answer for that in Scripture! Do good when it is due to whomever when you are able to do it. Do not procrastinate in doing good, do not do good primarily to be seen or for show, do not be coerced into doing good, do good primarily for God. The Holy Spirit will lead you and direct you as you maintain your relationship with the Holy Spirit and will help you please God in the manifestation of this good fruit.

© By Dr. Sheila Hayford.

May 8
Meekness And Temperance

Galatians Chapter 5, verses 23, 25:

Meekness, temperance: against such there is no law. If we live in the Spirit, let us also walk in the Spirit.

Prayer: Dear Holy Spirit: temperance is a part of self-control so empower us to exercise both in our relationships with others and in our individual self- discipline. In Jesus' Name, Amen.

What is temperance? I define temperance as the ability to exercise self-control in word, thought or deed. Temperance is a fruit of the Holy Spirit. If a person is exercising temperance they will not go overboard in what would ordinarily be permissible in Christ in God. Eating is necessary and permissible. Indeed, we have a myriad of foods to choose to eat but, at the same time, gluttony is avoided by exercising temperance. So why does the Word of God have meekness and temperance together as fruit of the Holy Spirit? I define meekness as strength with humility; and sometimes it takes meekness to exercise self-control when it comes to a person's actions. Just because one is right does not mean that person has the right to lash out at another person right away. Just because you are stronger than the bully in school does not mean you should fight or beat up the bully. Meekness and temperance are also taught. As we train children and others in the Word of God we should also place emphasis on meekness and temperance in our day to day living. As we grow in our relationship with God, meekness and temperance tend to come a little easier. What once frustrated you no longer bothers you. But remember, when you pass one test, God has another test for you in order to keep promoting you so do not rest on your laurels. Grow by God's grace and in meekness and temperance.

© By Dr. Sheila Hayford.

May 9
Fellowship

Acts Chapter 2, verse 42:
And they continued stedfastly in the apostles' doctrine and fellowship, and in breaking of bread, and in prayers.

Prayer: Dear God; it is wonderful that as Christians we can come together with fellow believers in love to worship you corporately and to encourage and share with our sisters and brothers in Christ. Continue to teach, direct and guide us as we study Scripture, brake bread and pray, in the power of the Holy Spirit. In Jesus' Name, Amen.

Sometimes, in my discussions I will meet someone who claims to be a Christian and as the conversation progresses, I ask if they fellowship with other believers. That person will sometimes respond by saying that they do not attend church services or participate in a local church. When asked why, the reasons are varied; God knows their heart, they are upset with some "hypocrites" in the church, they have a grudge against a Pastor, they experienced a church hurt or some other reason. The question then becomes, "Is it healthy for a Christian to stay away from fellowship with other Christians?" In our verses today, the early disciples continued to fellowship together; studying God's Word, in Holy Communion, in meals and in prayer. In other words, church fellowship is a discipline of the Christian believer that must be practiced or exercised. It is a spiritually healthy Christian discipline! My testimony is that I had a personal relationship with God in my teenage years and I do not know where I would be in my Christian walk if I had not had those early years of Bible study, prayer and fellowship with fellow believers. It was great positive peer pressure and it emboldened us in our stand for God. If perhaps you have given up on church fellowship, the Holy Spirit is inviting you to change your way of thinking. Allow the Holy Spirit to lead you and direct you to the one that is right for you.

© By Dr. Sheila Hayford.

May 10
Happy Mother's Day!

Proverbs Chapter 31, verses 26-28:
She openeth her mouth with wisdom; and in her tongue is the law of kindness. She looketh well to the ways of her household, and eateth not the bread of idleness. Her children arise up, and call her blessed; her husband also, and he praiseth her.

Prayer; Dear God, thank you for the gift of motherhood, given to all humankind as we ask for your special blessing on our mothers this and every day. Empower us to live for you, showing honor and kindness to our mothers. May their godly legacy continue in and through us. In Jesus' Name, Amen.

Thank God for mothers! Thank God especially for my blessed mother; the best mother in the world! We choose our friends but God chose our mothers. I am grateful to have a mother who taught us by example, who was kind to family, friends, neighbors and all children and encouraged each of her children to pursue our dreams. She still continues to encourage us to pursue God. My mother is beautiful inside and out and I have always considered her my dad's trophy wife because he made a great choice when he chose her to be his wife. And so her living legacy continues. Do mothers make mistakes? Of course! They are human, just as we are. However, mothers usually have their families' best interests at heart. Take time to thank God for and to honor your mother. And decide to make this day and every day a "Happy Mother's Day!"

© By Dr. Sheila Hayford.

May 11
Prayer - More than a Pastime!

1 Thessalonians Chapter 5, verse 17:

Pray without ceasing.

Luke Chapter 11, verse 1:

And it came to pass, that, as he was praying in a certain place, when he ceased, one of his disciples said unto him, Lord, teach us to pray, as John also taught his disciples.

Prayer: Dear Lord Jesus; Prayer is an important discipline for all your disciples. Thank you for teaching us how to pray and so we pray as you taught us in Luke Chapter 11, verses 2-4: Our Father which art in heaven, Hallowed be thy name. Thy kingdom come. Thy will be done, as in heaven, so in earth. Give us day by day our daily bread. And forgive us our sins; for we also forgive every one that is indebted to us. And lead us not into temptation; but deliver us from evil. Amen.

In the United States, the first Thursday in May is our National Day of Prayer, where people are encouraged to turn to God in prayer and reflection. That is very honorable for we all know the deep seated divisions and strife that we read about every day require God's intervention through prayer. However, Prayer is a Christian discipline and not a pastime and thus the discipline of prayer is to be exercised daily. The Scripture reading today says we should pray without ceasing. How is that possible? You see, some equate prayer with words spoken to God in a special position or in a special place. Actually, prayer can take place between you and God at any time; lying down, waking up, it may be a prayer thought, a prayer song, a prayer cry, there are spontaneous prayers, there are formal or written prayers, there are prayers you can listen to and pray along with, you can pray however you choose to have a conversation with God. And prayer can also be corporate; praying as a family, as a school, as a church, as a community, as a nation and globally. Things do change when we pray because we get God involved in the affairs of humankind. Let us pray without ceasing!

© By Dr. Sheila Hayford.

May 12
The Singing of the Birds

Song of Solomon Chapter 2, verse 12:

The flowers appear on the earth; the time of the singing of birds is come, and the voice of the turtle is heard in our land;

Prayer: Dear God; today is a good day because you are with us. Hallelujah! Amen.

It was the month of December and the weather was forecast to be warmer than normal; just like the day before, the high temperatures outside would be in the sixties. It would still be a cool night. As soon as I got up from bed, the birds started chirping. I walked downstairs to the kitchen and the cheery birds were chirping their lovely songs. I felt God had sent his birds to sing to me and I enjoyed it. Looking outside the kitchen window I saw heavy fog. I opened the kitchen door and it was still very cold outside. However, the birds had cheered me up, I knew the temperatures outside would warm up and I prepared for a blessed day. In life there may be circumstances that appear dreary at the beginning. Your mind may want to assume things would not work out well based on what you see. However, God's word to you is to never leave you or forsake you. So with God on your side, you're on God's winning side. Start your preparations for a good day!

© By Dr. Sheila Hayford.

May 13
True Repentance? Yes, It's A Discipline!

Psalm 51, verses 1-4:

Have mercy upon me, O God, according to thy lovingkindness: according unto the multitude of thy tender mercies blot out my transgressions. Wash me throughly from mine iniquity, and cleanse me from my sin. For I acknowledge my transgressions: and my sin is ever before me. Against thee, thee only, have I sinned, and done this evil in thy sight: that thou mightest be justified when thou speakest, and be clear when thou judgest.

Prayer: Dear God; help us to truly repent when we sin and to come to you in humility for you will forgive us. In Christ's Name. Amen.

Have you met someone who found it very hard to say they were sorry for something they did? After a while, you probably just let it go as there was no point in arguing with them. We know that for a person to be born again, that person first has to acknowledge their sin and their need for a Savior. Then, as a result of the finished work of the Lord Jesus on the cross to die for the sins of humanity, that person repents or is truly sorry for their sins and decides to walk in a different direction by inviting the Lord Jesus into their life as Lord and Savior. However, true repentance is not a one-time event. As a disciple of the Lord Jesus, true repentance towards God and our fellow humankind is an ongoing occurrence. A person must not hold onto arrogance and pride when repentance before God is needed and no disciple of our Lord Jesus should feel it is beneath them to show true repentance and do better towards their fellow man. King David's sin was great. However, in the Psalm above, King David did not run from God, King David ran to God. Indeed, true repentance should always lead a person to God's mercy. Do not despair when you sin, do not look for short cuts; acknowledge your sins to God and those you have wronged in God's power and wisdom and live free!

© By Dr. Sheila Hayford.

May 14
Gentleness: It's A Fruit!

2 Samuel Chapter 22, verse 36:
Thou hast also given me the shield of thy salvation: and thy gentleness hath made me great.

Prayer: Dear God; gentleness is very attractive to you. May we yield to the Holy Spirit in the cultivation of gentleness and in so doing attract others to our Lord Jesus Christ, in whose Name we pray. Amen.

Is gentleness as a human characteristic a fruit? It is. How so? It is because gentleness does not come naturally, it has to be cultivated. Children love playing together but have you noticed that children can sometimes be selfish? A child may not want to share her toys, a young boy may not want to play with the new kid on the block or the bully may try to intimidate another child. When we train our children, we teach them to show love and kindness towards others and also teach them to be gentle when playing with others, especially with their younger siblings or the new baby. As a disciple of the Lord Jesus the Holy Spirit indwells us and gentleness is a fruit of the Holy Spirit. As we grow in Christ in God, we should grow in gentleness. Can a person be gentle and yet stand up for what is right? Of course. A show of force or violence does not mean that a person is tough; it may sometimes indicate a person has not yet mastered their emotions. The world needs role models with Jesus Christ's discipline of gentleness on display. Do your part in displaying this fruit. It will attract many and cause some to desire to experience the source of your good fruit, the Lord Jesus Christ, for themselves. Hallelujah!

© By Dr. Sheila Hayford.

May 15
Longsuffering

Galatians Chapter 5, verse 22:
But the fruit of the Spirit is love, joy, peace, longsuffering, gentleness, goodness, faith,

Prayer: Dear Holy Spirit; longsuffering as a fruit of the Holy Spirit is one that only you can enable us to produce without bitterness, wrath, evil or the giving of any place to the devil. So help us, in Jesus' Name. Amen.

Longsuffering is a combination of two words, long and suffering which implies that a person is going through some discomfort over a long time. What longsuffering indicates, however, is that a person who is longsuffering has a good or even calm disposition while they are going through their particular challenge. As disciples of the Lord Jesus, we are called to bear our cross daily. Thus, there are some situations we may face as a result of our stance for the Lord Jesus that we must endure in the power of God the Holy Spirit, with God's wisdom and power. Sometimes the situation may change for the better; but when it comes to a person's freewill God always respects that. I recall one time a particular vote was coming up and many Christians prayed. When the vote passed it was not in accordance with God's principles. I was upset when I went to God in prayer. I was like, See, dear God! Can you believe what was voted? ... on and on and on! After I was done, GOD CALMLY responded, "It's my battle." I got the message and shut up! You see God is longsuffering towards us and the longsuffering fruit of the Holy Spirit will enable us to be longsuffering towards others.

© By Dr. Sheila Hayford.

May 16
Rejoice Always

Philippians Chapter 4, verse 4:
Rejoice in the Lord always: and again I say, Rejoice.
Prayer: Dear God: you have filled us with great joy! Thank you for bringing us into your family though our Lord and Savior Jesus Christ, and for the indwelling Holy Spirit who enables to always rejoice in you. May you be forever blessed! In Jesus' Name, Amen.

Rejoice! Whether you feel like it or not? Precisely! For you see, rejoicing is also a discipline of the disciples of our Lord Jesus that must be exercised in order to grow in our relationship with God. Rejoicing does not necessary mean singing songs, even though that may be a part. Rejoice gets its root from French and Latin; one implies enjoying the possession of something you own and the other implies a feeling of gladness. Either way, as born again believers we received ownership when we were made a part of the family of God. We are now sons and daughters of the Most High God Almighty and that should make our heart glad. No matter the challenge, when we reflect on whose we are, we should be filled with gratitude and gladness. So go ahead and rejoice!

© By Dr. Sheila Hayford.

May 17
Seasons

Ecclesiastes Chapter 3, verses 1,2:
To every thing there is a season, and a time to every purpose under the heaven: A time to be born, and a time to die; a time to plant, and a time to pluck up that which is planted;

Prayer: Dear God; every season you give us is a gift from you. Help us to use each season to its fullest potential and may our experience in each season bring you glory. In Jesus' Name. Amen.

We are getting to the midpoint of the month of May and soon the Memorial Day Holiday will be here, the unofficial start of the summer season. Thus, this is a good time for reflection. Seasons change; that is a given. Another given is that some things or opportunities we receive during specific seasons may never come back in exactly the same way. So it is a time of sober reflection. Yes, the upcoming vacation is important but we cannot spend more time planning for our vacation and neglect planning our year and our life with God. Take time to review the goals and plans you wrote down for this year. If there are areas where you have fallen short, how are you going to make up for them? Do you have to tweak those goals with God in prayer? How are we doing with our disciplines as disciples of our Lord Jesus? And are we yielding to the Holy Spirit daily as God cultivates his fruit in us? There are many spiritual and physical resources available to us so let us take action. Make a phone call, set up an appointment, implement the plan, ask for forgiveness from the one you said you would ask, set up a time schedule for specific disciplines and let God know we are committed in our relationship with and service to God. Since our life here on earth will determine how we live in eternity, let us persevere and not grow weary. God's rewards will be priceless!

© By Dr. Sheila Hayford.

May 18
Fasting

Mark Chapter 9, verses 28-29:
And when He had gone indoors, His disciples asked Him privately, Why could not we drive it out? And He replied to them, This kind cannot be driven out by anything but prayer and fasting. (AMPC)

Prayer: Dear God; you require we take good care of our bodies and we know fasting and prayer is an effective Christian discipline, necessary for breakthrough answers to prayer. So help us. In Jesus' Name, Amen.

Fasting is a Christian discipline. What did you just say? I thought a person can fast when they feel like it or not at all. What does the Bible say? The Bible says there are certain results in answer to prayer that will only occur when fasting accompanies the praying. Could that be why some have not had certain prayers answered? The disciples had been asked to pray for a person who was demon possessed and could not cast the demon out so they privately asked the Lord Jesus why the Lord Jesus was successful in that healing when they were not. It was in reply to that question that the Lord Jesus explained to them and to us, that person's healing and deliverance could only come about by prayer and fasting. Fasting is not the same as starvation. How so? With fasting, you go without food in order to devote your fasting time to prayer, Bible reading and hearing more clearly from God. You can chose how long to fast; some hours or some days and the type of fast. Of course, if you have any medical or other considerations you should seek expert counsel before embarking on a fast. God know what breakthroughs will be achieved by prayer and fasting. Allow God the honor of a fasting with prayer adventure with you as you exercise this Christian discipline!

© By Dr. Sheila Hayford.

May 19
Don't Faint!

Proverbs Chapter 24, verses 5, 10:
A wise man is strong; yea, a man of knowledge increaseth strength. If thou faint in the day of adversity, thy strength is small.

Romans Chapter 8, verse 28:
And we know that all things work together for good to them that love God, to them who are the called according to his purpose.

Prayer: Dear God: give us the wisdom, courage and strength we need in times of adversity for we know you will work all things together for our good. In Jesus' Name. Amen.

We all face adversity in some form in life. Sometimes it might be just an inconvenience. At times it may be overt; you are working towards a good cause but find some who are determined to oppose you. What do you do? First, be sure to be in right alignment with the Word of God. Then bring the situation before God in prayer and ask the Holy Spirit for wisdom on what to do. You see, the Bible says that a wise man is strong, and as your knowledge increases your strength increases. There may be others who have overcome the challenges a person is facing that could help with wise counsel and knowledge. As you work on the task at hand, do not allow your detractors to become a distraction. Don't faint and don't give up! The impact of your work may be life changing for someone. What looked like adversity might turn out easier than you thought. If your challenge turns out to be more difficult than you anticipated, remember that with God on your side, no experience is wasted because God will work things out for your good.

© By Dr. Sheila Hayford.

May 20
Graced To Give

2 Corinthians Chapter 8: 1-5:
Brothers and sisters, we want you to know about the grace that God has given to the churches in Macedonia. They have suffered a great deal. But in their suffering, their joy was more than full. Even though they were very poor, they gave very freely. I tell you that they gave as much as they could. In fact, they gave even more than they could. Completely on their own, they begged us for the chance to share in serving the Lord's people in that way. They did more than we expected. First they gave themselves to the Lord. Then they gave themselves to us because that was what God wanted. (NIV)

Prayer: Our heavenly Father; all we have comes from you. And what we receive from you is not always just for us, for you give us the privilege of blessing others as well. Help us not to be selfish. In Jesus' Name. Amen.

The grace of giving! What an example we see in the Christians in Macedonia. We note that they gave freely even though they did not have much and gave what they had joyfully. In other words, one does not need to have a lot of possessions in order to give. Moreover, their giving was not based on their challenging circumstances. We all have something to give or to share with another person. We may give of our time, our talent, our resources, we may give gifts of food to the hungry, financial or material resources to the needy, a place of safety to the homeless and so on. Giving is always an antidote to selfishness. The Macedonian Christians had found the secret to the grace of giving; first give yourself to God and then give to others as God leads. Through our Lord Jesus Christ, in the power of the Holy Spirit, we too have been graced to give.

© By Dr. Sheila Hayford.

May 21
Hope: A Christian Discipline

Romans Chapter 8, verse 25:
But if we hope for that we see not, then do we with patience wait for it.

Romans Chapter 15, verse 13:
Now the God of hope fill you with all joy and peace in believing, that ye may abound in hope, through the power of the Holy Ghost.

Prayer: Dear God; we thank you that our hope and trust is in you and in your Word and you will never fail us. In Jesus' Name. Amen.

As a Christian believer you have got to have hope. That is, hope is a required discipline. How so? The Word of God tells us the Lord Jesus will come back to earth again, so we must rejoice in hope as we anticipate that joyous union and wait patiently for that day. God, our heavenly Father is the God of hope, and expects us to display his characteristic of hope. As long as a person is alive on this earth, there is hope for the person for the better. So no matter how it hopeless the scenario when you pray, exercise your hope discipline. The Holy Spirit will keep you in joy and at peace as you trust and wait on God.

© By Dr. Sheila Hayford.

May 22
No Offense

Luke Chapter 17, verses 1-3:

Then said he unto the disciples, It is impossible but that offences will come: but woe unto him, through whom they come! It were better for him that a millstone were hanged about his neck, and he cast into the sea, than that he should offend one of these little ones. Take heed to yourselves: If thy brother trespass against thee, rebuke him; and if he repent, forgive him.

Prayer: Dear God; we receive forgiveness from you so help us extend forgiveness to our fellow man. And grant that we may live in such a way that we do not cause another person to stumble. In Jesus' Name, Amen.

The offended or the one doing the offense, we all need the Lord Jesus Christ. In the world we live in, the Lord Jesus tells us we can all expect someone to offend us. It is a part of the sin problem of the human race. How do we handle offense? God does not want us to hold grudges and God does not want us to walk in unforgiveness. So if someone offends you, it is usually better to let them know of your displeasure at that time, so if the person repents and genuinely apologizes, you can forgive them right away. If a person offends you but is unrepentant concerning their offence, forgive them anyway and allow God to exert vengeance on your behalf. What if you offend someone? Your offence may have been unintended but was perceived as intentional. If you are made aware of the offence, real or perceived, be humble enough to acknowledge your error and apologize. God has given us the Holy Spirit who is a wise counselor. Pray and ask God for wisdom to relate to others in your relationships. It might not be wise to continue in some relationships, depending on the offense. If a person is abused by another, accepting their apology and forgiving them is a commendable Christian attribute, but that does not mean that person has to place themselves in harm's way for further abuse. If a person is offended with God and God's principles, in the long run their issue is with God and not with you; forgive them for any real or perceived offense they may feel you did as you depend on the Holy Spirit to help you explain that their issue is with your godly stance for our Lord Jesus Christ. Forgiveness is a Christian discipline. Let us exercise the forgiveness discipline daily!

© By Dr. Sheila Hayford.

May 23
Remind God

Psalm 119, verse 49:

Remember the word unto thy servant, upon which thou hast caused me to hope.

Prayer: Dear God; I love when you speak to me. It gives me the faith to believe you for what looks impossible to man. I rejoice exceedingly as I see your hand at work and your words fulfilled. Thank you. In Jesus' Name, Amen.

We know children will remind their parents of what it is they want or desire for Christmas. However, God is God and God is all-knowing so why should we remind God? Does God want to be reminded? Yes, God loves to be put in remembrance of His Word. You see, reminding God says you are paying attention to what God has said and you are expecting God to be faithful to what God has said and that kind of faith pleases God. We all have needs, wants and desires. And God, who knows what is best for us, reveals His will and plans for us as we spend time with God. What promises from God are you waiting to be manifested? Remind God of them, get an update from God and allow God to do what God said in God's time.

© By Dr. Sheila Hayford.

May 24
Is It Possible?

Luke Chapter 1, verse 37:

For with God nothing shall be impossible.

Prayer: Dear Holy Spirit, I appreciate the reminder for with God all things are possible. Help me to live to my fullest potential in Christ in God. In Jesus' Name I pray. Amen.

Rain was forecast for the afternoon for what was an unusually warm day for the time of year and I started to pray to God, "Is it possible ... and was going to finish the sentence by saying "... to hold off the rain till much later in the day" when the Holy Spirit reminded me that with God all things are possible. Speaking to the weather in Jesus' Name to effect change now comes easy to me after years of practice and experienced results so I could have exercised that speaking discipline right then instead of starting to ask a lazy attitude question. In what may look like an impossible situation, when you are tempted to ask the question "Is it possible?" remind yourself that **With God All things are possible**. The key is to make sure you are in the will of God and you are about to embark on the endeavor with God. It is possible!

© By Dr. Sheila Hayford.

May 25
Kindness - It's A Fruit And A Seed

Psalm 117, verses 1-2:

O praise the Lord, all ye nations: praise him, all ye people. For his merciful kindness is great toward us: and the truth of the Lord endureth for ever. Praise ye the Lord.

Prayer: Dear God, help me to be good soil when I receive kindness from you and enable me to display your kindness fruit, by the power of the Holy Spirit. In Jesus' Name, Amen.

Kindness is a fruit of the Holy Spirit but it is also a seed. As we grow in our relationship with the Holy Spirit, we become more like our Lord Jesus Christ and display the fruit of Kindness. God is kind to the just and the unjust. In these days of grace, God allows rain to water the earth on the lands of both the just and the unjust and free fresh air is available to both the righteous and the wicked. Why do I say that kindness is also a seed? When you sow kindness you usually reap kindness in return. So do we show kindness in order to reap kindness back? No! We show kindness because we are God's children and our character should reflect our God. When the seed of kindness is sown, only the recipient can decide what soil they will be in order for that seed of kindness to survive or to thrive. Just like the Word of God, if the seed of kindness falls on hard soil or among weeds it may not have the conditions necessary to survive. If the seed of kindness falls on good ground, it grows and multiplies and kindness is then extended to others, many times beyond the initial seed. What soil are you when you receive a seed of kindness? Are you bearing the kindness fruit of the Holy Spirit? With the help of the Holy Spirit, be good ground for the seed and the fruit of kindness.

© By Dr. Sheila Hayford.

May 26
It's A "Go"!

John Chapter 14, verse 12:
Verily, verily, I say unto you, He that believeth on me, the works that I do shall he do also; and greater works than these shall he do; because I go unto my Father.

Prayer: My Lord Jesus; you always speak truth to me and to all. Thank you for the miracles I have seen in answer to prayer, the miracles I still experience and for your promise to expect greater with you. I believe you. Let's go. Amen.

There are answers to questions you may have that God has already provided the answer in Scripture. The Lord Jesus tells us in the above verses that we will do greater works than the Lord Jesus did on this earth because he returned to his place in divinity at the right hand of God our heavenly Father. So you do not need to wonder if you can do anything the Lord Jesus did on this earth. The Lord Jesus taught us by example to pray, to fast, to teach, to lead, to care for, to provide, to heal and more. The Lord Jesus has also given us delegated authority in His Name to do those works that he did and greater in the power of God the Holy Spirit. So doing the works of our Lord Jesus Christ is a "Go" with God. Get with God and Go with God!

© By Dr. Sheila Hayford.

May 27
Remember The Cost!

John Chapter 19, verses 16-18:

Then delivered he him therefore unto them to be crucified. And they took Jesus, and led him away. And he bearing his cross went forth into a place called the place of a skull, which is called in the Hebrew Golgotha: Where they crucified him, and two other with him, on either side one, and Jesus in the midst.

Prayer: Dear Lord Jesus: we love you and are eternally grateful to you for coming to our aid and saving us from sin, satan and the punishment of hell. You more than proved to us the value you place on us. May we remember what our salvation cost you and not take a life worthy of your sacrifice lightly. Amen.

The holiday this week stated Memorial Day but how many reflect on the cost or the toll it took, including the lives lost, to ensure the celebrations many today take for granted? When a person buys an expensive luxury car, maybe a BMW, they usually take good care of it. Not only that, they will remind their children and others to take good care of it as well. They might even enforce special rules for their cars; no eating inside the car, no speeding, etc. Why? They know how much the car cost them and they consider their purchase of great value. When it comes to our salvation through our Lord and Savior Jesus Christ, let us remember the cost. It cost the Lord Jesus an unfair trial, torture, mistreatment and death by hanging on a cross in public death meant for criminals in order to shed his blood for the sins of a lost humanity. Without the Lord Jesus' death, burial and resurrection, there would not be hope for mankind. But thank God, we now have salvation, the indwelling of the Holy Spirit and eternal life with our Lord and Savior, Jesus Christ. How do we value our salvation? Do we allow others to talk bad about our God in our presence? Do we reverence God in our hearts, our speech and our lives? Remember, The Lord Jesus paid the ultimate price for us. Yes, the Lord Jesus **purchased** our salvation when he redeemed us from satan and hell. We are valuable to our Lord Jesus Christ and our Lord and Savior is more than priceless to us.

© By Dr. Sheila Hayford.

May 28
Early In The Morning

Psalm 5, verse 1-3:

Give ear to my words, O Lord, consider my meditation. Hearken unto the voice of my cry, my King, and my God: for unto thee will I pray. My voice shalt thou hear in the morning, O Lord; in the morning will I direct my prayer unto thee, and will look up.

Prayer: Dear God; thank you for the gift of today. Strengthen me by your power, forgive me of all sin in what I should not have done and in what I should have done but did not do and grant me the grace to represent you well. In Jesus' Name, Amen.

What is the first thing you do in the morning when God wakes you up? In life's busy moments, it can be easy to take for granted God's mercy in waking you up. Yes, the day's schedule may be filled with a lot of work, the children have to be get ready for school, you have to prepare breakfast and so on, and if you are not intentional about it, you might not pray or thank God for the gift of another day. Let us take the time to thank God and acknowledge God early in the morning. Don't give God your second best time. Give God your first fruits time, that is, the first fruits of the time you are going to spend the rest of the day. And see the difference it makes!

© By Dr. Sheila Hayford.

May 29
Enjoy The Fruit of Your Work

Psalm 128, verse 2:
For thou shalt eat the labour of thine hands: happy shalt thou be, and it shall be well with thee.

Prayer: Dear God, thank you for the gift of work and the rewards that come from working. May we be faithful to you and others as we do our work. In Jesus' Name, Amen.

It is okay to take that vacation! Really? Yes, after all that hard work you put in at work and all the time you may have had to spend away from your family. Work, or labor, is God instituted; given to Adam when God created the first human being and placed Adam in the Garden of Eden. Work should be enjoyable. However, working at something you enjoy is still work. And work is not always easy; sacrifices are sometimes made and some may have temporarily put off their personal life schedule in order to achieve the company's goals. When you are rewarded with your vacation, your pay raise bonus or that company reward, enjoy it since you must have worked hard to earn it. Always remember to praise and thank God for giving you the strength to work and the favor to earn the rewards. Bless and serve God with your tithes and offerings as you advance God's work and continue to seek and fellowship with God while you are enjoying your vacation and as you are favored by God and man. When a person is in right alignment with God through our Lord Jesus Christ, their work is an extension of their relationship with and service to God. Thus, an excellent work ethic is pleasing to God. As the psalmist reminds us; Happy shall we be and it shall be well with us.

© By Dr. Sheila Hayford.

May 30
The Promise

Judges Chapter 13, verses 2-6:

A certain man of Zorah, named Manoah, from the clan of the Danites, had a wife who was childless, unable to give birth. The angel of the Lord appeared to her and said, "You are barren and childless, but you are going to become pregnant and give birth to a son. Now see to it that you drink no wine or other fermented drink and that you do not eat anything unclean. You will become pregnant and have a son whose head is never to be touched by a razor because the boy is to be a Nazirite, dedicated to God from the womb. He will take the lead in delivering Israel from the hands of the Philistines." Then the woman went to her husband and told him, "A man of God came to me. He looked like an angel of God, very awesome. I didn't ask him where he came from, and he didn't tell me his name. (NIV)

Prayer: Dear God, I thank you for The Promise. You are a great God and you do great things. We believe you and we expect good and great from you. In Jesus' Name, Amen.

I love God and you do too! Even though Manoah's wife did not have any biological children, we do not read of her complaining. However, God had great plans for her and through her, Israel would begin to be delivered from their oppressors, the Philistines. And so, while she was minding her business God's angel came to her and gave her **The Promise** from God. It was an astounding declaration with conditions attached. With faith and excitement she shared the good news with her husband. Later, they had a child, Samson. Samson fought the Philistines and indeed began the deliverance of Israel from the hand of their enemies. What is "The Promise" God has made to you? You know, that astounding promise! Have faith, share it with those God leads you to and make sure to fulfill God's conditions necessary for its manifestation. Then be ready to experience The Promise.

© By Dr. Sheila Hayford.

May 31
It Matters How You Live

Romans Chapter 12, verse 1:
I beseech you therefore, brethren, by the mercies of God, that ye present your bodies a living sacrifice, holy, acceptable unto God, which is your reasonable service.

Prayer: Dear God; it matters to you how we live and that is the most important reason of all, so help us live lives that please you. In Jesus' Name, Amen.

We are living in the 21st century and some would like you to believe that a person can live anyhow and get away with it. Of course, satan will not tell a person the consequences of living outside of the will of God and satan would have some feel like holy living for God is too restrictive. God's truth is that living in sin is bondage and living a holy live for God through the Lord Jesus and in the power of the Holy Spirit is true freedom. It not only matters how we live; how we live on this earth will determine how we live in eternity. Let us resolve to live right, to live holy and to please God, in the power of God the Holy Spirit. Amen.

© By Dr. Sheila Hayford.

June 1
The Purpose

Isaiah Chapter 61, verses 1-3:

The Spirit of the Lord God is upon me; because the Lord hath anointed me to preach good tidings unto the meek; he hath sent me to bind up the brokenhearted, to proclaim liberty to the captives, and the opening of the prison to them that are bound; To proclaim the acceptable year of the Lord, and the day of vengeance of our God; to comfort all that mourn; To appoint unto them that mourn in Zion, to give unto them beauty for ashes, the oil of joy for mourning, the garment of praise for the spirit of heaviness; that they might be called trees of righteousness, the planting of the Lord, that he might be glorified.

Prayer: Dear God, thank you for bringing each person to earth with purpose. When we each fulfil our part, society is changed for the better and we bring you glory. So help us yield to the work of the Holy Spirit in and through us. In Jesus' Name, Amen.

As a child of God, have you ever wondered what your purpose for living on this earth is? True, the Holy Spirit indwells you and is your seal that you are a child of God. However, God has purpose for your life and it is found in the above verses. God has given you natural talents, gifts and abilities, the indwelling of the Holy Spirit and various vocations to fulfil God's plan and purpose on this earth and for eternity. We are called to share the good news of salvation through our Lord Jesus Christ, to care, to teach, to empower, to encourage, to help others grow in their relationship with God, to allow place for God's vengeance and to give hope, all to the glory of God. And how do we do this? In the power of God the Holy Spirit who is at work in and through us. Go forth and be who God called you to be!

© By Dr. Sheila Hayford.

June 2
The Power of Togetherness

Acts Chapter 2, verses 1-4:

When the day of Pentecost came, they were all together in one place. Suddenly a sound like the blowing of a violent wind came from heaven and filled the whole house where they were sitting. They saw what seemed to be tongues of fire that separated and came to rest on each of them. All of them were filled with the Holy Spirit and began to speak in other tongues as the Spirit enabled them. (NIV)

Prayer: Dear Lord Jesus, may your disciples be united and in one accord to see God's kingdom advanced, with our focus on the case for God and not on frivolous rivalries. In Jesus' Name, Amen.

Good is multiplied when Christians are united for good. When Christians pray together, the effects of their prayers are multiplied. When Christians embark on a period of fasting together, the change that is effected is multiplied and when Christians embark on evangelistic missions together, nations are saved. So whose fault is it when we see a society in disarray? I say it is a reflection of the collective state of the Christians in that society to effect change. God will still hold a person fully accountable for their action. However, is it also possible that God might hold Christians accountable for what they did not do to effect change in society? Sobering! When Christians want God's intervention, the power of togetherness must not be underestimated. Discord and strife are tools satan tries to use to prevent God's work from going forward. So pray and make sure those you align with are in alignment with God's will and with the endeavors you desire. Then work together in the power of God.

© By Dr. Sheila Hayford.

June 3
Favor

Acts Chapter 27, verses 41-44:
But the ship struck a sandbar and ran aground. The bow stuck fast and would not move, and the stern was broken to pieces by the pounding

of the surf. The soldiers planned to kill the prisoners to prevent any of them from swimming away and escaping. But the centurion wanted to spare Paul's life and kept them from carrying out their plan. He ordered those who could swim to jump overboard first and get to land. The rest were to get there on planks or on other pieces of the ship. In this way everyone reached land safely. (NIV)

Prayer: Dear God; help us to be mindful of the fact that favor with you can show up in many different ways. Paul was in a difficult place but he was favored by you and so his life was spared and the lives of those who were with him were spared. Help us to always share the Lord Jesus as you give us opportunities to do so. In Jesus' Name, Amen.

The Apostle Paul was on board a ship with many others and while there, the ship was involved in a shipwreck. God had promised the Apostle Paul that despite the shipwreck, no one on board with the Apostle Paul would lose their life. Think about this; all who were on board with the Apostle Paul were favored by God to be protected from losing their life during the shipwreck. When the ship ran aground, the soldiers panicked. They wanted to kill the prisoners to prevent them from escaping. However, God had told the Apostle Paul he would stand before Caesar and God's word will always come to pass. So Paul found favor in the eyes of the centurion, Paul's life was spared and those with him benefitted as well. A person who is a born again believer has favor with God through our Lord Jesus Christ. So if a person says they are born again into God's family, there has to be some demonstration of God's favor. That person can pray and see God's intervention in answer to prayer. People who need encouragement, peace and godly counsel should be able to observe these in the life of a Christian. And those in good relationship with a born again believer should experience God's favor in some fashion. Some are 'ship-wrecked' in life, battling challenges left and right, without a clue as to what to do to survive. They have friends, co-workers and acquaintances who are born again believers. What are you going to do or say to those 'ship-wrecked' in life and without hope? Are you going to introduce them to the Lord Jesus, the life guard that can save them? Are you going to encourage them, help them or lead them to resources that may benefit them? Jesus' favor with God brings us into right standing with God. God's favor on a person will cause that person to be favored by man. Your favor with God has to impact someone for good.

© By Dr. Sheila Hayford.

June 4
Favored? Get ready!

1 Samuel Chapter 18, verses 28-30:
When Saul realized that the Lord was with David and that his daughter Michal loved David, Saul became still more afraid of him, and he remained his enemy the rest of his days. The Philistine commanders continued to go out to battle, and as often as they did, David met with more success than the rest of Saul's officers, and his name became well known.

Prayer: Dear God, Thank you for unmerited favor; favor with you that is ours through our Lord Jesus Christ. Help us to focus on pleasing you and not to be distracted by those who wish to detract us. In Jesus' Name, Amen.

So you are favored of God! It is a wonderful feeling! Your soul is at peace and you are enjoying life in unhindered fellowship with God. You would think everyone would be happy for you and with you. Some assume that because a person favored by God has favor with God and man, it means that person has favor with **all** men. That is the way it should be. However, the reality is that some become angry, upset, jealous and hateful when a person is favored by God. When King Saul realized that God was with David and that King's Saul's daughter loved David, you would expect King Saul to be happy. Instead, King Saul hated David, was increasingly fearful of David and became David's enemy until the day King Saul died. David's favor with God could have rubbed off on King Saul, but King Saul was so hateful that all he could think towards David was evil. So get ready, you favored one, if some who should be rejoicing with you chooses to make you their enemy. You know you cannot force anyone to like you; however, you must not be distracted by their actions. David continued his walk and work with God and had more success than the rest of those working under King Saul. So let God's works in you speak for themselves. Continue to walk in success. Get ready!

© By Dr. Sheila Hayford

June 5
Your Legacy

Deuteronomy Chapter 34, verses 7-12:
Moses was a hundred and twenty years old when he died, yet his eyes were not weak nor his strength gone. The Israelites grieved for Moses in the plains of Moab thirty days, until the time of weeping and mourning was over. Now Joshua son of Nun was filled with the spirit of wisdom because Moses had laid his hands on him. So the Israelites listened to him and did what the Lord had commanded Moses. Since then, no prophet has risen in Israel like Moses, whom the Lord knew face to face, who did all those signs and wonders the Lord sent him to do in Egypt - to Pharaoh and to all his officials and to his whole land. For no one has ever shown the mighty power or performed the awesome deeds that Moses did in the sight of all Israel. (NIV)

Prayer: Dear God; thank you for working in the lives of each of your children as we submit to your authority and yield to the Holy Spirit. It is a privilege to be part of the legacy of our Lord and Savior, Jesus Christ. In Jesus' Name, Amen.

What a Legacy! There will never be another prophet like the Prophet Moses! God's prophet, Moses, had an extraordinary life. As a Hebrew male baby, he was slated to be killed after birth by order of Pharaoh, the King, but God miraculously spared him and had him raised in the home of the ones who sought the lives of his people. God then employed his natural mother to take care of him! However, Moses was touched by the suffering of his people even though he was raised in a comfortable palace and set about to right a wrong, committing murder in the process. Many would have written Moses off, but not God. In God's perfect timing, after Moses had lived in the wilderness for a while, God called Moses to deliver the people of Israel. And so it was that Moses became a friend of God, performing amazing signs and wonders in the power of God. When Moses died at 120 years of age, Moses had already prepared Joshua as his successor and the people listened to Joshua. Your legacy began the day you were born and it is still in progress. Like the prophet Moses, there will only be one 'you' for you are an original. Do you know the Lord Jesus as your Lord and Savior? Do you know God's call, plan and purpose for your life? Are you friends with God? Who are you teaching and training? God wants you healthy and strong when your life on this earth is completed so take good care of yourself. Finish your fulfilled life strong!

© By Dr. Sheila Hayford.

June 6
The Power Of Encouragement

Proverbs Chapter 12, verse 25:
Heaviness in the heart of man maketh it stoop: but a good word maketh it glad.

Prayer: Dear God; you are always encouraging us. Help us to be a source of encouragement to many. In Jesus' Name, Amen.

Encouragement is a very powerful tool. There are many, especially children, who find themselves faced with challenges that are not of their direct choosing. How they respond to those challenges will either make them stronger or have the potential to destroy them. Encouragement can thus effect life and the lack thereof may lead to despair. Encouragement does not have to be wordy. Putting in a good word for your co-worker is a powerful form of encouragement. It lets the person know that their work is appreciated and they are more inclined to do good work on the job. No one is too young or too old to be encouraged. A child who has completed their chores satisfactorily stands taller when they are encouraged whereas a child that is constantly berated becomes discouraged and tends to look at the negatives in life because that is what they have been taught. A young Christian who is constantly criticized for their decisions instead of being encouraged and taught to make better decisions with God's help may become frustrated. Encouraging the young Christian may cause them to become 'all things are possible with God' oriented. We all need encouragement in life; give encouragement to others and allow others to encourage you.

© By Dr. Sheila Hayford.

June 7
What Are You Saying?

Proverbs Chapter 12, verse 14:
A man shall be satisfied with good by the fruit of his mouth: and the recompence of a man's hands shall be rendered unto him.

Prayer: Dear God; may the fruit of our thoughts, our words and our actions be a blessing to you and to humanity. In Jesus' Name, Amen.

What are you saying to others? More importantly, what are you saying to yourself? In these verses, we are told that a person will be satisfied with the fruit of his mouth. In other words, your words are seed and in due time, your words grow, multiply and bear fruit. That is, you reap the result of what you say to yourself. Every person is, in a sense, the sum total of their thoughts, words and actions. The situations a person faces may have been the result of the actions of someone else, but each adult is responsible for how he or she will respond to the situation, challenges and opportunities in life. If a person decides to surrender their lives to God, agree with God in their words and live for God, it will show in that person's life. If a person decides they are going to live for themselves and themselves only, that will also show up in their life. So, in the middle of this New Year, if you would like to change some things for the better, one of the ways to do so would be to change the way you think and to be careful about the words that you speak. Since what we think and what we say affects our actions, it stands to reason we will also be rewarded by the fruit of what we do. If our work is good, the fruit of our work should be good. What are you thinking? What are you saying? How are you living?

© By Dr. Sheila Hayford.

June 8
A Fair Deal

Colossians Chapter 4, verse 1:

Masters, give unto your servants that which is just and equal; knowing that ye also have a Master in heaven.

Proverbs Chapter 21, verses 2, 3:

A person may think their own ways are right, but the Lord weighs the heart. To do what is right and just is more acceptable to the Lord than sacrifice.

Prayer: Dear God; you know every heart. May our faith produce the fruit of godly living at home, at work and in our society. In Jesus' Name, Amen.

Is God really that concerned about how a company pays their workers, or whether the employees are treated right? Of course, He is! In fact, God is reminding us in these verses that God is our heavenly Master and we want God to treat us well. A Fair Deal is not a one way deal; it involves the commitment of both parties. If an employee expects to be treated well, there is the expectation that the employee will do his or her job satisfactorily and that the employer will give the employee fair wages and benefits commensurate with the ability of the employer. On a larger scale, fairness and justice must be at the core of any society. When inequality and injustice prevail and many feel they are getting a raw deal instead of a fair deal, there is strife, there are protests and the fabric of the society unravels. Thus, it is in the best interests of humankind for God's principles of justice and fairness to prevail. Will God force His will of us? No, because God chooses to accept man's freewill. However, some day each of us will be personally accountable to God for our actions and on that day God is the one who will mete justice. May God's will be done on this earth as it is in God's heaven.

© By Dr. Sheila Hayford.

June 9
Abigail - Wisdom On Display

1 Samuel Chapter 25, verses 26-27:
And now, my lord, as surely as the Lord your God lives and as you live, since the Lord has kept you from bloodshed and from avenging yourself with your own hands, may your enemies and all who are intent on harming my lord be like Nabal. And let this gift, which your servant has brought to my lord, be given to the men who follow you. (NIV)

Prayer: Dear God; your wisdom astounds me. And you given us this wisdom freely, when we ask and when we obey your instructions. Help us to be found faithful in this grace of wisdom. In Jesus' Name, Amen.

Nabal was a wealthy man and he had a lot of flocks. He also had a wife who was filled with God's wisdom. It so happened that David and his men were out when Nabal's servants were tending their flocks.

David's men protected Nabal's men and their flocks from harm and none of their flocks were lost or missing. So when David sent greetings to Nabal asking for some provisions for his men in gratitude for their protection, David was obviously upset with Nabal's rudeness and stinginess. David was inclined to take matters into his own hands and go and destroy Nabal's household in what David felt would be revenge for him and his men. Enter Abigail. When one of the servants told her what had happened to David and David's men she loaded her servants with food and provisions and rode behind them to David and David's men to appease them and to provide for them. David was very impressed with and grateful to Abigail and accepted her food and provisions. He was even more grateful that she had prevented him from shedding innocent blood in his desire to destroy all Nabal and Nabal's household. When the Lord God struck Nabal and Nabal died about ten days later, David asked Abigail to become his wife and she did. Abigail's wisdom not only saved her and her entire household, it prevented David from exacting revenge against Nabal and allowed the vengeance of God on David's behalf to take effect. Furthermore, it caused Abigail to be favored and noticed by David and in the end Abigail was promoted to become David's wife. All of this from the display of a single act of wisdom. Make no mistake, Abigail private acts of wisdom and her life of wisdom had prepared her for that grand display of wisdom and her story continues to be read today. What gifts and abilities has God given you? As you exercise those gifts and abilities in God's wisdom and are faithful in the little things, you will get God's attention and God's promotion. And when your time to shine comes, on this earth or as the stars in eternity, you will have been well prepared.

© By Dr. Sheila Hayford.

June 10
Be Nice to The Messenger!

Hebrews Chapter 13, verse 2:

Be not forgetful to entertain strangers: for thereby some have entertained angels unawares.

Prayer: My heavenly Father; you know I love you. I am especially grateful I am your child and love that you send your holy angels to minister and to war on my behalf, through my Lord and Savior, Jesus Christ in whose Name I pray, Amen.

I could tell you story after story of strangers who have showed up at various times in my life who I am forever convinced were God's angels appearing in human form. They showed up and spoke and some engaged in conversation with others present and I never saw them again. God sends angels, appearing to be strangers in human form but sent to humanity on assignment; be nice to them! I wanted to buy a living room music system; a set to play all the different modes of music at the time, speakers, added cabinets to place the music with closing doors, etc. I saw one music system set advertised on sale so I went to the store to buy it. When I got to the store they had run out of the set advertised but said that they would honor that price for an upgraded system. I looked at the upgraded system, all nicely decked out and I liked it. I bought it, paid for it and was told the set would be brought to my car. Nice! Well, when I saw the guy bringing my set to my car I was like, "What in the world…?" There was this L…O…N...G… tall cardboard box with all the different parts of the music system set placed on top of each other! I thought they would be packed into smaller separate boxes and as I looked at that long box I knew there was no way it would fit inside my car, even with the windows down. What was I to do? Suddenly out of nowhere a white pickup truck appeared. The guy who got out of the truck seemed to know my challenge; he offered to place the long box in his truck and said he would follow me and bring my music system to my house. I am a trusting person and have said many times I start off giving everyone the benefit of being trustworthy so I happily agreed. The store person put the box in the truck and we were ready to pull off! Right then, the store person comes to me, I pull down the car window and he quietly asks if I wrote down the guy's license plate. I said "No" and wondered why he waited till then to ask me but I was at peace. The guy in his truck brought my system to my house. Then he said the system was too heavy and needed men to do the job so I called my immediate neighbor and the neighbor next to him. All three men put the system in my living room, set it up, some extra wire was needed that my immediate neighbor had and we had good conversation. It was a very nice meeting. Afterwards the guy said he lived … and gave me the place, I thanked him and that was it. Well, after some months I thought to myself that it was not right that I never went back to say thank you, especially since I enjoyed playing music using that set, so I drove in what I thought was the area he said he lived. No one I asked knew who I was talking about! I am convinced he was my God sent angel and I am grateful I was nice to him, didn't brush him off nor was I rude or unkind to him. I enjoyed that music system for many years. God tells us to be careful to entertain strangers because some may be angels sent from God. God especially warns us to be careful how we talk to those angels who appear to be strangers because God has given them authority to make certain proclamations and have God back up their words. Don't try to shoot God's messenger; that would be a disaster and not for the angel. Be nice to God's messenger!

© By Dr. Sheila Hayford.

June 11
Health

1 Samuel 16:11-13: So he asked Jesse, "Are these all the sons you have?" "There is still the youngest," Jesse answered. "He is tending the sheep." Samuel said, "Send for him; we will not sit down until he

arrives." So he sent for him and had him brought in. He was glowing with health and had a fine appearance and handsome features. Then the Lord said, "Rise and anoint him; this is the one." So Samuel took the horn of oil and anointed him in the presence of his brothers, and from that day on the Spirit of the Lord came powerfully upon David. Samuel then went to Ramah. (NIV)

Prayer: Dear God; Thank you for the gift of good health and for the healing that is available in Jesus Christ. Help me exercise my freewill to make healthy decisions and to follow through on them. In Jesus' Name, Amen.

I have a question. What if David came in from tending the sheep and was not glowing with health, with a fine appearance and handsome features? Would God have chosen him for the job? You must understand that I am not talking about age, gender, race or other discrimination for a job where two or more people are equally qualified for the position. We know you have to be at least thirty-five years of age in addition to other requirements to be President of the United States of America and yet voters want to know if a person will be physically able to stand the rigorous work of the U.S. Presidency. God wants us healthy. God has a lot of work that needs to be done on this earth and God has chosen humankind, working in the power of God, and within the will of God to accomplish God's work on earth. Not only does God want you healthy, God wants everyone on your team healthy as well. I know I have sometimes skipped breakfast when I got busy. That is not healthy. God has given us so many foods, including meats, vegetables, fruits and healthy drinks. We have so many ways to exercise and so much outdoor beauty to relax in and enjoy. We also have the freewill to make and practice good health choices. Moreover, we must not take the amazing body with all the amazing organs God gives humanity for granted. Money cannot buy health, even though it can buy good medical care and treatments. So do not take good health for granted and do not abuse your body. As you invest in your wellbeing, it would be good to write down your wellbeing goals for the remainder of this year and then start working on them, even if it means baby steps at first. Exercise your freewill and self-discipline as you ask and trust God to help you achieve your goals.

© By Dr. Sheila Hayford.

June 12
Earth's Custodians

Genesis Chapter 1, verse 26-27:
And God said, Let us make man in our image, after our likeness: and let them have dominion over the fish of the sea, and over the fowl of the air, and over the cattle, and over all the earth, and over every creeping thing that creepeth upon the earth. So God created man in his own image, in the image of God created he him; male and female created he them.

Genesis Chapter 2, verse 15:
And the Lord God took the man, and put him into the garden of Eden to dress it and to keep it.

Mark Chapter 13, verses 34-35:
For the Son of Man is as a man taking a far journey, who left his house, and gave authority to his servants, and to every man his work, and commanded the porter to watch. Watch ye therefore: for ye know not when the master of the house cometh, at even, or at midnight, or at the cockcrowing, or in the morning:

Prayer: Dear God, help me to be a good steward of all you have entrusted me with. In Jesus' Name I pray, Amen.

I find it disconcerting that some will walk their dog in the free park but not pick up their dog litter after their dog. Some chew gum and after they are done just spit out the gum wherever they may be. Others may throw their food wrapper out of their car while they are driving. On a larger scale it is appalling that some will pollute drinking water with toxic chemicals in order to make a profit for the company and not care about the individuals being harmed in the process. Does God care? In the first chapter of the Holy Bible God gives us the mandate he gave to humanity. Earth was man's territory and man had authority over the earth. In the second chapter of the book of Genesis, God gave Adam stewardship of the Garden of Eden, to tend to the beautiful garden and to maintain it. And the Lord Jesus Christ, to whom God has made the Righteous Judge, warns us to be careful to be good stewards over whom and what God has given us authority over and to do the work we each need to do for the benefit of the society at large. Will we be found faithful?

© By Dr. Sheila Hayford.

June 13
Travel and Sea

Jonah Chapter 1, verses 1-3:

Now the word of the Lord came unto Jonah the son of Amittai, saying, Arise, go to Nineveh, that great city, and cry against it; for their wickedness is come up before me. But Jonah rose up to flee unto Tarshish from the presence of the Lord, and went down to Joppa; and he found a ship going to Tarshish: so he paid the fare thereof, and went down into it, to go with them unto Tarshish from the presence of the Lord.

Ezekiel Chapter 3, verses 18-19:

When I say unto the wicked, Thou shalt surely die; and thou givest him not warning, nor speakest to warn the wicked from his wicked way, to save his life; the same wicked man shall die in his iniquity; but his blood will I require at thine hand. Yet if thou warn the wicked, and he turn not from his wickedness, nor from his wicked way, he shall die in his iniquity; but thou hast delivered thy soul.

Prayer: Dear God, it is our heart's desire to obey you even when it may not always be easy or convenient. So help us by the power of the Holy Spirit. In Jesus' Name, Amen.

God is a God of mercy and even though the people in the city of Nineveh were very wicked, God asked Jonah to travel to Nineveh and warn them of God's impending judgment against them if they did not repent and turn away from their evil doing. You might think Jonah would be happy to oblige. Not so! Jonah made up his mind he would rather disobey God than warn the wicked to turn from their evil ways and so he decided to travel by sea away from the presence of God. Isn't it the same way today? Many are hurting, many are hell bound knowingly and unknowingly. The Lord Jesus has given every believer the command to share the good news of salvation through our Lord Jesus with the billions of souls in humanity. God is also very clear. If a person warns the wicked of God's impending judgment and offers the Lord Jesus' salvation and the wicked person refuses to repent and accept the Lord Jesus as their Lord and Savior, then if the wicked dies they will be judged by God for their sins but the person who obeyed the Lord Jesus and warned them will have saved their own soul. However, if a person fails to warn the wicked and offer the Lord Jesus' salvation and the wicked person dies in their sin, God will require the blood of the wicked at their hand of the person who disobeyed the Lord Jesus' command to preach the good news of salvation. Jonah eventually repented, but not before he had involved a lot of others in his mess, and God allowed him the grace to go back to Nineveh and warn that city's inhabitants. The good news is the people in that city repented, and God's judgement at that time was averted. One man's obedience saved a whole city from destruction. What will your obedience to God do?

© By Dr. Sheila Hayford.

June 14
The Forest

Psalm 50, verses 10-15:

For every beast of the forest is mine, and the cattle upon a thousand hills. I know all the fowls of the mountains: and the wild beasts of the field are mine. If I were hungry, I would not tell thee: for the world is mine, and the fulness thereof. Will I eat the flesh of bulls, or drink the blood of goats? Offer unto God thanksgiving; and pay thy vows unto the most High: And call upon me in the day of trouble: I will deliver thee, and thou shalt glorify me.

Prayer: Dear God, we expect you to keep your vows and promises, so we should expect you to expect us to keep our promises and vows to God. Help us not to be rash in making empty promises, but to be careful and to be found faithful in our promises to you. In Jesus' Name, Amen.

Everything belongs to God; the forests, the wild beasts, the land, the seas. All God gives us is entrusted to us, we are stewards. So what does God desire of us, since God owns everything he placed on this earth under the dominion of humankind? We know, through our Lord Jesus Christ, that God desires for everyone to be a part of God's family and that God respects the freewill of every individual's choice. And how about what God has given to us? God wants us to be appreciative and respond to God's goodness with thanksgiving. We know it takes money, time and commitment to do the work of God's kingdom in sharing the good news of salvation through the Lord Jesus and to perform works that will benefit society and bring glory to God. When we make promises or vows to God to contribute money, resources, time or talent that we receive from God for God, God expects us to honor and fulfil our vows and promises to God. As we are faithful in keeping our vows and promises to God, let us expect God to be faithful in keeping His vows and promises to us.

© By Dr. Sheila Hayford.

June 15
Hobbies

Genesis Chapter 4, verses 20-22:

Adah gave birth to Jabal; he was the father of those who live in tents and raise livestock. His brother's name was Jubal; he was the father of all who play stringed instruments and pipes. Zillah also had a son, Tubal-Cain, who forged all kinds of tools out of bronze and iron. Tubal-Cain's sister was Naamah. (NIV)

Prayer: Dear God; thank you for the gifts, talents and beauty you have so blessed humanity with and for the creative ability to develop even more innovative crafts, sculptures, hobbies, instruments and more. We appreciate your gifts and even more, we appreciate You. In Jesus' name, Amen.

I love the fact that everyone has unique talents, abilities and hobbies. I love buying and gifting handmade crafts because they are one of a kind. I also enjoy listening to those with musical abilities or play musical instruments. A friend of mine enjoys knitting. She knits sweaters, scarfs, and mittens for herself and some accessories and sweaters to give as gifts. When I received a sweater she had knitted as a gift I was impressed with the design, honored that she had chosen to honor me with her handcrafted labor of love and, of course, I enjoyed wearing it. It is spring time, time to enjoy the outdoors! What hobbies do you enjoy? What hobbies would you love to share with your family? Jabal was the father of those who loved farming. In other words, Jabal passed on his love for farming to his children and his descendants. Jabal's bother, Jubal, raised those who played stringed instruments [such as the harp I would imagine] and pipes, [probably what we would refer to today as the organ]. How beautiful! Your talent, your hobby, your abilities are gifts you give to you, to your family, to your descendants, to the world at large through your influence and work and to your God. Share them!

© By Dr. Sheila Hayford.

SIMPSON'S HOBBIES AND GIFTS
Serving Generations of Satisfied Families!

TOYS. COLLECTIBLES. ANTIQUES. GIFTS. REPAIRS.

709 Foulk Rd, Wilmington, DE 19803
Telephone: (302) 654-5022

Hours of Operation:
Monday to Friday: 12 noon to 5pm
Saturdays: 12 noon to 5pm
Sundays: 12 noon to 2pm

WE HAVE WHAT YOU ARE LOOKING FOR!

- ✓ Model Cars, radio controlled toys
- ✓ Trains
- ✓ Supplies and Parts
- ✓ Repairs, Custom Orders to your specifications may also be available

Call (302) 654-5022 Today!

June 16
God - The Patriot

2 Kings Chapter 19, verses 32-35:

Therefore thus saith the Lord concerning the king of Assyria, He shall not come into this city, nor shoot an arrow there, nor come before it with shield, nor cast a bank against it. By the way that he came, by the same shall he return, and shall not come into this city, saith the Lord. For I will defend this city, to save it, for mine own sake, and for my servant David's sake. And it came to pass that night, that the angel of the Lord went out, and smote in the camp of the Assyrians an hundred fourscore and five thousand: and when they arose early in the morning, behold, they were all dead corpses.

Prayer: Dear God, we entrust our being and our lives to you for you are the Ultimate Authority and the Ultimate Defender of Truth and Righteousness. Help us to stand for your truth. In Jesus' Name, Amen.

We often hear the word Patriot used in many forms, usually to denote someone who is willing to defend his or her country. Do you know that God is a Patriot, willing to defend his chosen city and his people? The King of Assyria was issuing threats to King Hezekiah, the righteous king of Judah, and not only that, the King of Assyria put God in the mix by saying that King Hezekiah should not think that God in whom King Hezekiah trusted would be able to defend King Hezekiah from the hands of the King of Assyria. What was God to do when the King of Assyria put God on the spot like that? It depended on what King Hezekiah did! Really! God was waiting on what a man would do to determine how God would act? Aha! Well, King Hezekiah prayed. King Hezekiah worshipped God, laid out the reality of the threats of the King of Assyria before God and asked for God's deliverance and intervention. Of course, God the Ultimate Patriot, was ready to defend his city and King Hezekiah who had placed his trust in God. God sent his angel into the camp of the Assyrians and that angel killed 185,000 of the Assyrian troops. With that news, the King of Assyria turned back. Thus, God defended King Hezekiah and the city and saved it. Isn't it interesting that Judah means praise and that when King Hezekiah brought praise and worship to God first, then presented his adversary's threat and ridicule of his God in prayer, God saved and delivered King Hezekiah and his city. Offer praise and worship to God first, then present your adversary and detractors threats and ridicule of God to God in prayer and allow God to save and deliver in accordance with God's will.

© By Dr. Sheila Hayford.

June 17
Graduation Times

Hebrews Chapter 12, verse 1:
Wherefore seeing we also are compassed about with so great a cloud of witnesses, let us lay aside every weight, and the sin which doth so easily beset us, and let us run with patience the race that is set before us,

Prayer: Dear God; I am looking forward to completing every area of my life's race strong, by the power of God the Holy Spirit. So help me, in Jesus' Name, Amen.

It is that time of the year; students are graduating from school and graduation celebrations seem to be everywhere. Rejoicing with the new graduates on their hard won achievements, considering the disciplines and sacrifices many of them had to make is commendable. We all love to have others celebrate our joys with us. Have you considered your earthly graduation? And the celebration that will be yours if you graduate with at least a passing grade in God's school of life. In this verse, life is likened to a race. There are many who start the race but in order to cross the finish line you have to put aside distractions, hindrances and things that are not beneficial to your race. The race of life is not a sprint, it requires patience and perseverance. As Christians, the first qualification to start this race in God and with God is to accept the Lord Jesus Christ into our life as Lord and Savior. God has a specific race for each person, so although our destination with the Lord Jesus is the same, our specific life experiences may vary. God wants us to get to know him, spend time with him and receive his instructions on the details of and the rules for our race in life. With the gift of the Holy Spirit to enable and empower us, we can ran our race and finish strong. We work with God to run our race and God gives us the prize. How easy is that? Or, how hard is that? It depends; the start may be relatively easy, the middle may be challenging, towards the end may be easy or hard. Only God knows the details of your race in its fullest, before you started to when you will finish. Many are ready to rejoice in our life's graduation celebration. There is no letting them down!

© By Dr. Sheila Hayford.

June 18
The Bride Caregiver

Ruth Chapter 1, verses 16, 17:

And Ruth said, Intreat me not to leave thee, or to return from following after thee: for whither thou goest, I will go; and where thou lodgest, I will lodge: thy people shall be my people, and thy God my God: Where thou diest, will I die, and there will I be buried: the LORD do so to me, and more also, if ought but death part thee and me.

Prayer: Dear God, thank you for sharing Ruth's story with humanity. She is an inspiration and an example of your mighty hand at work in the lives of caregivers at home, caregivers at work and caregivers in society. We all have something to give and to share so help us to be found faithful. In Jesus' name, Amen.

What an amazing woman Ruth is! Ruth was a Moabite, and she was the Bride of one of Naomi's sons after Naomi, Naomi's husband and Naomi's two sons came to Moab to escape the famine in Naomi's hometown. While in Moab, Naomi's husband and both of her sons died.

Naomi was now left with her two daughters-in-law. Her daughters-in-law lovingly and dutifully cared for Naomi. But this time, Naomi heard that there was food in her hometown and yearned to return to her homeland. She had much love and gratitude for her daughters-in-law as Naomi told them of her decision to return to her homeland. She encouraged them to stay in their country and move on with their lives. Orpah agreed with Naomi and tearfully kissed Naomi goodbye. Ruth was determined to continue to be Naomi's caregiver. Nothing Naomi said would convince Ruth to leave her. And in the verses above, Ruth made her stand for God known. Naomi's God would be Ruth's God and Naomi's people would be Ruth's people. So Ruth went with Naomi to Bethlehem. Whilst there, Ruth continued to be faithful to Naomi, doing whatever menial jobs she could get to take care of Naomi and herself; but, oh, did God have a wonderful surprise for Ruth! Ruth became the bride of Boaz and they had a son named Obed. Obed was the grandfather of King David through whom the genealogy of the Lord Jesus Christ came. Wow! Ruth, the Bride Caregiver became a part of the lineage of the Great Caregiver. Don't worry when it seems your faithfulness and small acts of sacrifice and kindness go unnoticed by men. Faithfulness and service is always noticed by God, and God, the Ultimate rewarder, will give the rewards.

© By Dr. Sheila Hayford.

June 19
Wedding Invitations

Luke Chapter 14, verses 16-18, 23:

Jesus replied: "A certain man was preparing a great banquet and invited many guests. At the time of the banquet he sent his servant to tell those who had been invited, 'Come, for everything is now ready.' "But they all alike began to make excuses. The first said, 'I have just bought a field, and I must go and see it. Please excuse me.' "Then the master told his servant, 'Go out to the roads and country lanes and compel them to come in, so that my house will be full.

Prayer: Dear Lord Jesus; help me to do my part in inviting many to our wedding banquet, in the power and leading of the Holy Spirit. Amen.

June is one of the favorite months many chose to have their wedding. We too, have a wedding celebration coming up; our wedding feast celebrating the marriage of our bridegroom, the Lord Jesus Christ, to his bride, his church of born again believers. And we have the wedding invitations. As we know, a wedding is a joyous occasion. And the wedding feast is cause for much celebration. However, in this parable, some of the invited guests began to give excuses. Nevertheless, the Master of the house wanted as many people as possible to take part in the celebrations so he told his servants to go to the highways and byways and compel people to come in. The Lord Jesus is talking to us in this parable. Hell is a real place and without the Lord Jesus in their lives many people are headed there. When we share the good news of salvation with others, some will give excuses. However, God does not want to see anyone go to hell, especially since the Lord Jesus Christ has paid the price for sin. Salvation through the Lord Jesus is a freewill decision; we do the sharing and each individual does the responding, either positively or negatively to the Lord Jesus. Let us be diligent in handing out those invitations. Wouldn't you like to see some of those you invited at the wedding banquet?

© By Dr. Sheila Hayford.

June 20
Honeymoon – "Us" Time

Deuteronomy Chapter 24, verse 5:
When a man hath taken a new wife, he shall not go out to war, neither shall he be charged with any business: but he shall be free at home one year, and shall cheer up his wife which he hath taken.

Prayer: Dear God, marriage is your idea and the honeymoon between husband and wife is your wise counsel. Let us not allow satan to deceive many into thinking that you want to deprive them of joy because you are the originator of all things good. We thank you and we bless you. In Jesus' Name, Amen.

Did you know that the honeymoon after marriage is God's idea? And God's verses above sound even better! Have your husband take a year off to cheer his wife! We get the principle, dear God. When a person enters into marriage, they are bound to face new challenges. Each person has their own preferences and idiosyncrasies and the husband and wife have to adjust to living in a committed marriage relationship together. It is usually not as easy as it seems. Thus, the honeymoon is your "Us Time" when you get to enjoy each other and start your new life with God on a strong foundation, relatively free of distractions. Your honeymoon is not a luxury that should be skipped because you have "more important" things like work to do. You may not be able to take a whole year off and still have a job to take care of your spouse but most can take some time off; it is that important. Set up the spiritual foundations for your marriage now. Resolve to have personal quiet time with God, family time as husband and wife with God, family time with parents and children with God and time for teaching and instructing children on how to have a personal relationship with our Lord and Savior, Jesus Christ. Set goals and plans for your marriage, depending on the Holy Spirit for guidance, direction and the power to accomplish. Enjoy your "us time" together!

© By Dr. Sheila Hayford.

June 21
Father's and Step Up Father's Day

Ruth Chapter 4, verses 20-22:

Amminadab the father of Nahshon, Nahshon the father of Salmon, Salmon the father of Boaz, Boaz the father of Obed, Obed the father of Jesse, and Jesse the father of David.

Prayer: Dear Heavenly Father, you are the best father there is. Thank you. Thank you for giving us earthly fathers and step up fathers, without whom your work on this earth would not be possible. May their lives reflect your glory. In Jesus' Name, Amen.

What an honor to celebrate Father's, especially our Heavenly Father. None of us would be alive without our biological fathers and for that we all ought to be grateful. It comes easy to many to acknowledge and thank their fathers who continue to be role models for their family and for society. However, we must not forget those families who have absent fathers, fathers who abuse them or fathers who constantly belittle or demean them. Is there hope in those situations? Of course? Even though you may not be a biological father to a person, if helping to encourage, mentor and provide spiritual teaching and training to another is within your ability, your means and is appropriate, deliberate with God in prayer and if it is a "go" with God, step up and do so.

So to all biological fathers, Step up fathers, godfathers, grandfathers, great grandfathers, great great …, Happy Father's Day!

© By Dr. Sheila Hayford.

June 22
The Blessed Home

Proverbs Chapter 3, verse 33:

The Lord's curse is on the house of the wicked, but he blesses the home of the righteous. (NIV)

What agreement is there between the temple of God and idols? For we are the temple of the living God. As God has said: "I will live with them and walk among them, and I will be their God, and they will be my people." (NIV)

Prayer: Our Heavenly Father, thank you for blessing us through my Lord and Savior Jesus Christ. Dear Lord Jesus, we love you and are eternally grateful to you. Dear Holy Spirit, thank you for abiding in us. Thank you for the blessed home. In Jesus' Name, Amen.

Is your home blessed? God promises to bless the home of the righteous. We know that in and of ourselves, we have no righteousness of our own. However, when we believe, accept and receive the Lord Jesus and his death on the cross for our sins, we receive the righteousness of our Lord Jesus Christ. Thus, when we come to our heavenly Father through His Son, our Lord Jesus, God sees us clothed in the righteousness of the Lord Jesus. So, it is through our Lord Jesus Christ that God blesses the home of the righteous. We must note that God's desire is for us to live lives that are pleasing to God and give glory to God so we must be mindful how we live. God the Holy Spirit who abides in us will empower us to live for God and when we sin in our humanity, we must be quick to repent of sin, confess our sins to God and receive God's forgiveness. As living temples or houses of the indwelling Holy Spirit, God abides in our home. Enjoy God's blessed home, on this earth and in eternity.

© By Dr. Sheila Hayford.

June 23
Gardens

Luke Chapter 13, verses 18-19:

Then said he, Unto what is the kingdom of God like? and whereunto shall I resemble it? It is like a grain of mustard seed, which a man took, and cast into his garden; and it grew, and waxed a great tree; and the fowls of the air lodged in the branches of it.

Prayer: Dear God; may our hearts be fertile ground for the Word of God to grow, thrive and produce good fruit, great trees and a haven that will direct many to you. In Jesus' Name, Amen.

I am in awe of God's creative genius in nature and I enjoy gardens. Gardens are so reflective of the creativity of God. Gardens can be designed and created in so many different ways. There are small gardens for the pleasure of the owner and those associated with them and then there are large gardens, created for the enjoyment of larger communities, and in some cases, for worldwide enjoyment. The thing about gardens is that they take a lot of work to maintain. The plants have to be watered, weeds removed, the ground fertilized, trees and shrubs pruned, leaves raked, in some cases bird habitats kept clean, it is no easy feat. Of course, the end result of the beautiful gardens are worth the work and the work involved to keep the garden is in itself rewarding. The mustard seed used in the illustration above is a small seed but in the right soil it grew to become a great tree. When you start your spiritual journey with God, your faith may be small. But as you feed your faith with the Word of God and exercise the disciplines of your Christian faith, the Word of God produces good fruit and becomes a gorgeous garden. Many will come to you to be shown the way of your Savior and you will not only provide knowledge sharing the good news of salvation, you will also provide nourishment and refreshing to many. God will be your Master Gardener and he will take delight in you. God's kingdom is growing in and through you!

© By Dr. Sheila Hayford.

June 24
In Whom Do You Trust?

Isaiah Chapter 31, verse 1-3:

Woe to them that go down to Egypt for help; and stay on horses, and trust in chariots, because they are many; and in horsemen, because they are very strong; but they look not unto the Holy One of Israel, neither seek the Lord! Yet he also is wise, and will bring evil, and will not call back his words: but will arise against the house of the evildoers, and against the help of them that work iniquity. Now the Egyptians are men, and not God; and their horses flesh, and not spirit. When the Lord shall stretch out his hand, both he that helpeth shall fall, and he that is holpen shall fall down, and they all shall fail together.

Prayer: Dear God; my trust is first and foremost in you. I know you cannot and will not fail for you are the ultimate in truth and the ultimate in faithfulness. In Jesus' Name, Amen.

Even though our money notes say in God we trust, God is asking each of us a very personal direct question, "In whom do you trust?" When you face a challenge who do you go to **first**? The warning here is of a people who in a time of war or other challenge put their trust in what they can see; strong horses, solid chariots, large numbers of horsemen and depend on those for victory instead of first consulting with God to find out what their response to the challenge should be. Why does God use the word "woe" in describing them? It is because when God brings about God's judgment, the evildoer and the one who helps the evildoer will both fall. So look to God when you are facing your challenge. Pray, seek God for guidance and direction, find out what God's word says, seek counsel from those who have knowledge in that area and then make your decisions with the blessing of God.

© By Dr. Sheila Hayford.

June 25
The Vow

1 Samuel Chapter 1, verse 11, 20, 26-28:

And she vowed a vow, and said, O Lord of hosts, if thou wilt indeed look on the affliction of thine handmaid, and remember me, and not forget thine handmaid, but wilt give unto thine handmaid a man child, then I will give him unto the Lord all the days of his life, and there shall no razor come upon his head. Wherefore it came to pass, when the time was come about after Hannah had conceived, that she bare a son, and called his name Samuel, saying, Because I have asked him of the Lord. And she said, Oh my lord, as thy soul liveth, my lord, I am the woman that stood by thee here, praying unto the Lord. For this child I prayed; and the Lord hath given me my petition which I asked of him: Therefore also I have lent him to the Lord; as long as he liveth he shall be lent to the Lord. And he worshipped the Lord there.

1 Samuel Chapter 2, verse 21:

And the Lord visited Hannah, so that she conceived, and bare three sons and two daughters. And the child Samuel grew before the Lord.

Prayer: Dear God, thank you that you allow our sincere vows to you to influence your actions towards us. In Jesus' Name, Amen.

Can your vow have influence with God? Let's find out from the life of Hannah. Hannah's husband loved her and was kind to her. However, they had no children and Hannah was distraught so she went to God in prayer. Hannah had obviously been praying to God for a while because every year they went to worship the Lord in Shiloh but that year her prayers would be different; different because Hannah made a vow to God. If God gave Hannah a son, Hannah vowed to give him back to the Lord God. So what happened? Hannah's vow influenced God and she gave birth to a son named Samuel. Hannah kept her promise and brought her child to the priest Eli, offered her child back to God and left Samel under Eli the priest. Samuel grew to become one of the great judges of

Israel, used mightily by God. And when Hannah gave God her son, Samuel, God gave Hannah sons and daughters. Wow! What vow do you need to make to God? God is not interested in rash vows made with no intention of keeping. However, your genuine vows do get God's attention. What is it that you want?

© By Dr. Sheila Hayford.

June 26
The Caregiver's Reward - Motherhood

2 Kings Chapter 4, verses 9-10, 13-17:

She said to her husband, "I know that this man who often comes our way is a holy man of God. Let's make a small room on the roof and put in it a bed and a table, a chair and a lamp for him. Then he can stay there whenever he comes to us." Elisha said to him, "Tell her, 'You have gone to all this trouble for us. Now what can be done for you? Can we speak on your behalf to the king or the commander of the army?'" She replied, "I have a home among my own people." "What can be done for her?" Elisha asked. Gehazi said, "She has no son, and her husband is old." Then Elisha said, "Call her." So he called her, and she stood in the doorway. "About this time next year," Elisha said, "you will hold a son in your arms." "No, my lord!" she objected. "Please, man of God, don't mislead your servant!" But the woman became pregnant, and the next year about that same time she gave birth to a son, just as Elisha had told her. (NIV)

Prayer: Dear God, I am so touched by the acts of kindness of this beautiful woman, a woman who was not only wealthy, she was beautiful inside and out. She did not have to, but she chose to be a blessing and you rewarded her beyond her imagination. Thank you for the lessons she teaches. In Jesus' Name, Amen.

We do not know her name but we know she was a wealthy Shunammite woman. She discerned the prophet Elisha to be a man of

God and she urged him to stay for a meal so he would do so when he was in her area. The Shunammite woman also decided to make available for the use of the prophet Elisha a furnished room where the prophet Elisha could stay whenever he stopped by on his travels. No one asked her to do this; it was of her own initiative. However, the prophet of God took notice and asked his servant what could be done for her to show his appreciation and gratitude. The Shunammite woman was not looking for a reward from Elisha and did not request anything in return. But the prophet Elisha went further. When his servant told him that she did not have any children, the prophet Elisha knew what to do. "Call her" he told the servant and when she came, the prophet Elisha prophesied she would have a son the following year at about the same time. And it happened just like that! Wow, Motherhood became the reward of the wealthy Shunammite woman. She who had what her money could buy received from the man of God what her money could not buy. So do not look down on God's chosen servant, sent by God to be a potential blessing to you, or you may lose out on more than you will ever know, in this earth realm and in eternity. Bless God and bless God's chosen!

© By Dr. Sheila Hayford.

June 27
Finish It

Zechariah Chapter 4, verse 9:
The hands of Zerubbabel have laid the foundation of this house; his hands shall also finish it; and thou shalt know that the LORD of hosts hath sent me unto you.

Prayer: Dear God, we trust you to bring to a successful completion all the good works you have ordained and purposed for us. In Jesus' Name, Amen.

The Lord Jesus encourages us to count the cost before we start a project or commit to a cause. If you want to commit your life to living for God and receiving the Lord Jesus Christ as Lord and Savior you have to understand that your decision will not be popular with everyone and you might even lose a few friends. If you want to build a house, the Lord Jesus says to consider the cost so you do not start it and stop before it is completed. One of the secrets to a successful project is to have the backing of God. If God asks you to do something and you respond in obedience and trust, God is obligated to help you bring the project to completion according to his specifications. So discuss your project with God first and find out if that is what God will have you do. If God says "yes!" you must seek God's counsel as to when and how to proceed. Then work at the project and bring it to a successful completion. God in you and God working through you brings God glory!

© By Dr. Sheila Hayford.

June 28
Fits of Jealousy

2 Corinthians Chapter 12, verse 20:
For I am afraid that when I come I may not find you as I want you to be, and you may not find me as you want me to be. I fear that there may be discord, jealousy, fits of rage, selfish, ambition, slander, gossip, arrogance and disorder.

Prayer: Dear God; may the character of my Lord and Savior Jesus Christ be expressed in and through me. In Jesus' Name, with much thanksgiving. Amen.

Just look at all the horrible things that accompany jealousy; discord, fits of rage, selfish ambition, slander, arrogance and gossip. That is a sorry state of affairs the Apostle Paul was describing! By the grace of God, I have not been raised by God to be jealous because God saved me in my teen years. I was, therefore, disappointed to find out that jealousy and its associated carnal sin of covetousness was so prevalent in some older Christians and, in some cases, Christian congregations. If a person cannot celebrate another person's successes, why should God grant that person success? A person sowing to their fleshly desires will reap carnal results. God is looking for mature Christians and not carnal Christians. Let us grow in faith and in the disciplines of Christ like character and give God many good things to say about us.

© By Dr. Sheila Hayford.

June 29
Compromising Situations

Matthew Chapter 5, verses 29-30:

If your right eye causes you to stumble, gouge it out and throw it away. It is better for you to lose one part of your body than for your whole body to be thrown into hell. And if your right hand causes you to stumble, cut it off and throw it away. It is better for you to lose one part of your body than for your whole body to go into hell.

Matthew Chapter 16, verse 25:

For whosoever will save his life shall lose it: and whosoever will lose his life for my sake shall find it.

Prayer: Dear God, we chose life when we chose you. Enable us to always stand for you, in your grace, power and mercy. In Jesus' Name, Amen.

Don't put yourself in compromising situations. God's command is simple and to the point. If you have a problem with alcoholism do not go and sit at the bar and place yourself in position to be tempted. If you are engaging in acts of fornication with the man or woman you are in love with, get married; or if you are not serious about getting married, cut off that relationship. If you have a problem with gambling and put your rent money, your bills due money and money needed by your family into the slot machine instead of taking care of your responsibilities stay away from the casino. The issue becomes who you want to save face with. Do you want to save face with a person or situation that will lead you to sin or are you willing to give up that part of your life to gain the kingdom of God. The Lord Jesus Christ, the Righteous Judge, says whoever will lose his life, in whatever sacrifice, for the sake of the Lord Jesus will find it. Take the Lord Jesus at his Word.

© By Dr. Sheila Hayford.

June 30
God Has Always Been There

Deuteronomy Chapter 31, verse 6:
Be strong and of a good courage, fear not, nor be afraid of them: for the Lord thy God, he it is that doth go with thee; he will not fail thee, nor forsake thee.

Prayer: Dear God; you are always with me. Thank you for your keeping power. Enable me, in the power of the Holy Spirit to be strong, courageous and joyful for victory is mine; through my Lord and Savior, Jesus Christ. Amen.

Sometimes when you are facing a challenge you may wonder when God will show up. The truth is that God has always been there. And your God encourages you to be strong, courageous and fearless as you go through your test or trial. Remember God promised He will never leave you or forsake you. So walk in obedience to God and trust God with the outcome. Disobedience and sin separate a person from fellowship with God; God did not move, that person moved. However, God is always in a posture to receive everyone who comes to God in sincerity and in true repentance for sin. Exercise your faith in God at all times. Do not be fainthearted or weary; for God goes before you, God goes behind you and God goes with you!

© By Dr. Sheila Hayford.

July 1
Do Unto ...

Luke Chapter 6, verse 31:

And as ye would that men should do to you, do ye also to them likewise.

Prayer: Dear God, the do unto others command given to humanity by our Lord Jesus is poignant. Help us to put this command into practice, especially since we receive so much grace, love, kindness and mercy from you. In Jesus' Name, Amen.

If you have ever wondered whether you should do or say something to another person, the Lord Jesus gives a litmus test. Would you like someone to say or do to you what you are about to say or do to someone else if you were in their situation? In other words, God is challenging us to show some love, kindness and mercy in the same way we want God to show us love, kindness and mercy.

Now comes the 'it's time to practice that' part!

© By Dr. Sheila Hayford.

July 2
Direct My Steps

Luke Chapter 1, verses 39-44:

At that time Mary got ready and hurried to a town in the hill country of Judea, where she entered Zechariah's home and greeted Elizabeth. When Elizabeth heard Mary's greeting, the baby leaped in her womb, and Elizabeth was filled with the Holy Spirit. In a loud voice she exclaimed: "Blessed are you among women, and blessed is the child you will bear! But why am I so favored, that the mother of my Lord should come to me? As soon as the sound of your greeting reached my ears, the baby in my womb leaped for joy. (NIV)

Prayer: Dear Holy Spirit; I love it when I look back and see that what I thought would be 'ordinary' was actually a display of you directing my steps to bring about God's ordained outcome. Thank you. Help me to always yield to your promptings and follow your leading with joy and gratitude. In Jesus' Name, Amen.

Mary had just received the good news from the angel that she was going to give birth to the Lord Jesus Christ. What happened next? She hurried up and went to visit her relative, Elizabeth, who had experienced a miraculous pregnancy in her old age and who was in the sixth month of her pregnancy. Wow! God the Holy Spirit directed Mary who had received such a powerful revelation from God to her relative who was further ahead in the manifestation of a miraculous pregnancy. That was just what they both needed. Elizabeth was filled with joy as she began to prophecy over Mary, confirming what the angel had told Mary. And since Elizabeth's baby, John the Baptist, was born with a mandate from God to prepare for the coming of God's kingdom through the Lord Jesus Christ, the baby was so excited he leaped for joy in his mother's womb! Mary responded with her song of praise to God and stayed with Elizabeth for about three months before returning home. Direct our steps, dear Holy Spirit, according to God's will,

© By Dr. Sheila Hayford.

July 3
Live To Eat Or Eat To Live?

Luke Chapter 12, verses 19-21:
And I'll say to myself, "You have plenty of grain laid up for many years. Take life easy; eat, drink and be merry."' "But God said to him, 'You fool! This very night your life will be demanded from you. Then who will get what you have prepared for yourself?' "This is how it will be with whoever stores up things for themselves but is not rich toward God." (NIV)

Prayer: Dear God; you teach us that life involves more than what we can see physically because you created us as spirit, soul and body beings. Help us to get our priorities right and first be in right standing with you through your Son and our Lord and Savior, Jesus Christ. May we renew our mind with the word of God and live on this temporal earth with our eternal destiny in mind. In Jesus' Name. Amen.

The man in this parable the Lord Jesus told was a successful farmer. He had plenty of grain stored up and his philosophy on life was to take life easy, eating, drinking and being merry. No mention of God by this man. But then the God he had neglected spoke to him. God, his Creator, told him his life was going to end that very night! All the temporal things he had stored on this earth would be of no value for him in eternity and the God he had neglected would be the God to whom he would account for the way he lived life on this earth. Sobering, considering that once he departed this earth his opportunity to receive the Lord Jesus as his Lord and Savior would be gone forever. A parable is intended to teach a lesson in an easy to understand story. The message here is that while we have to eat to live, life is more than the physical or material things in life. As we accumulate wealth and achieve great successes in life, let us remember our Creator, the source of all the good things we enjoy and make sure we are in right standing with God, through our Lord and Savior, Jesus Christ.

© By Dr. Sheila Hayford.

July 4
A Solid Foundation

Matthew Chapter 7, verse 25:
And the rain descended, and the floods came, and the winds blew, and beat upon that house; and it fell not: for it was founded upon a rock.

Matthew Chapter 16, verses 16-18:

And Simon Peter answered and said, Thou art the Christ, the Son of the living God. And Jesus answered and said unto him, Blessed art thou, Simon Barjona: for flesh and blood hath not revealed it unto thee, but my Father which is in heaven. And I say also unto thee, That thou art Peter, and upon this rock I will build my church; and the gates of hell shall not prevail against it.

Prayer: Dear Lord Jesus; we thank you for being our sure and solid foundation. In you we have right standing with God our heavenly Father, we have the indwelling of God the Holy Spirit and we have the gift of eternal life with you. What a blessing! Hallelujah! Amen.

On what is your house built upon? Most people have either built a home or lived in one. We know how important the foundation of a physical home is. If the foundation is shaky, no matter how pretty the house may look, or how well built the actual house is, when the foundation is cracked or moves, that house will fall. It is the same principle in spiritual matters. There are many who tout opinions that contradict what God says in the Bible. They live their lives believing these false opinions and their opinions become their foundation in life. The Lord Jesus categorically says that He is The Way, The Truth and The Life and that no one gets to God the Father except through him. This truth is the solid foundation upon which the Lord Jesus says he will build his church, the body of born-again believers, and hell will never prevail against this strong and true foundation. What is the spiritual foundation of your life?

© By Dr. Sheila Hayford.

July 5
Star Wise

Daniel Chapter 12, verses 2-3:

And many of them that sleep in the dust of the earth shall awake, some to everlasting life, and some to shame and everlasting contempt. And they that be wise shall shine as the brightness of the firmament; and they that turn many to righteousness as the stars for ever and ever.

Prayer: Dear God: May I do my part to lead many to the true life that is only found in my Lord and Savior, Jesus Christ. In the power of the Holy Spirit and in Jesus' Name I pray, Amen.

Many have heard of Star Wars. I would like to introduce Star Wise. So you might ask what that is about. You see, sometimes wisdom can be very subjective depending on who you ask. So let us look at the gold standard for wisdom, God's standard. In God's eyes, a person who is wise is one that is in right standing with God and one who, in God's power, causes many to turn to our Lord and Savior Jesus Christ. At the resurrection, there will be those who are raised to everlasting life with God and those who are raised to eternal separation from God. The wise who have led many to righteousness will shine as the stars forever. Hence I say, star wise. Everyone has the opportunity while they are still alive on this earth to choose which side they will be at that great Resurrection Judgment; with the Lord Jesus or with the devil. Jesus Christ has paid the price for the sins of humanity so no one needs to join the devil in hell. However, God gives everyone the freewill to make that right choice. Choose eternal life with the Lord Jesus. And then lead others to eternal life with the Lord Jesus Christ.

© By Dr. Sheila Hayford.

July 6
Freedom

1 Corinthians Chapter 10, verse 23:
"I have the right to do anything," you say - but not everything is beneficial. "I have the right to do anything" - but not everything is constructive. (NIV)

Prayer: Dear God, help me to use my freedom in Christ for good and not as an excuse to cause a fellow believer to stumble. In Jesus' name, Amen.

As born again believers and disciples of our Lord Jesus Christ, we have been set free in Christ from bondage to sin. We are not bound by rules that tell us how long or how short our dress should be, whether or not to wear make-up, what we should eat, etc. However, as we celebrate Independence Day in the United States, we recognize that with freedom comes responsibility. The Apostle Paul says we must be considerate of others when we exercise our freedom. If you have been invited to sing or preach in a congregation where the women cover their heads during church service, take your scarf or handkerchief with you and cover your head when you go there. You are there to share the love of Christ and to lead others to God in the power of God the Holy Spirit and not to cause offense that will cause someone there to stumble or be distracted from the message of Christ. I know in my early born again Christian days, I would say to myself and to others, "Oh, these baby Christians!" I didn't understand then why I had to choose to limit my freedoms for the benefit of another Christian. I realized that was immature thinking and am thankful God gives all of us the grace to grow in our Christian journey. Use your freedom in Christ for good!

© By Dr. Sheila Hayford.

July 7
At What Price?

Numbers Chapter 23, verses 8, 19-21:
How shall I curse, whom God hath not cursed? or how shall I defy, whom the Lord hath not defied? God is not a man, that he should lie; neither the son of man, that he should repent: hath he said, and shall he not do it? or hath he spoken, and shall he not make it good? Behold, I have received commandment to bless: and he hath blessed; and I cannot

reverse it. He hath not beheld iniquity in Jacob, neither hath he seen perverseness in Israel: the Lord his God is with him, and the shout of a king is among them.

Prayer: Dear God; we stand with you and for you, in the power of the Holy Spirit and through our Lord and Savior, Jesus Christ, Amen.

The King of Moab, Balak, wanted Balaam to curse the people of Israel and offered Balaam material goods and promotion if he would curse God's people. Balaam who had disobeyed God earlier and for which it almost cost him his life was not about to displease God for a pot of gold or any other offer. Balaam would rather please God if it meant he would lose material wealth than disobey God. In other words, Balaam could not be bought. Some will stand for good but when tempted with evil, will succumb if the price is right. It is never worth sacrificing something that is of eternal value for temporal gain. Times may be challenging, but God is faithful. If God has blessed a person, no man can curse them and if a person brings about God's curse on them, they are cursed no matter how much temporal gains they acquire. Stand with God and stand for God!

© By Dr. Sheila Hayford.

July 8
Stubborn Mule

Genesis Chapter 36, verse 24:
And these are the children of Zibeon; both Ajah, and Anah: this was that Anah that found the mules in the wilderness, as he fed the asses of Zibeon his father.

James Chapter 1, verse 5:
If any of you lack wisdom, let him ask of God, that giveth to all men liberally, and upbraideth not; and it shall be given him.

Prayer: Dear God, I still laugh when I recall the first time I saw the actions of that stubborn mule. What an indelible lesson! I ask for your wisdom in my daily living for I do not want to be without understanding. In Jesus' Name, Amen.

The first time I saw a mule in action I didn't know whether to laugh or to cry! I immediately understood why Scripture encourages us not to be like the mule, without understanding. The mule I observed was stubborn. It was jumping haphazardly every way except in the direction the owner wanted. The mule seemed frustrated but it just kept doing the wrong things. The result looked hilarious but was for the mule, sad. Why? It was because the actions of the mule were against the best interests of the mule; they were self-destructive. Yet, the mule shows us a picture of what stubbornness looks like. In the Holy Bible, God, our Maker, teaches us the best way for humankind to live. When we submit to God and to God's words, our lives are in alignment with God's truth and we live at peace with God. If a person is stubborn and rejects God's truth, although they are very much alive, like the mule their life goes about in every direction except for the one God desires for them and as far as their eternal destiny is concerned, their lives on earth are self-destructive. Let us ask God for wisdom in our daily living for God has promised to give wisdom in abundance when we ask. In so doing, we will not be without understanding.

© By Dr. Sheila Hayford.

July 9
Tiger's Comeback

Mark Chapter 9, verse 23:
Jesus said unto him, If thou canst believe, all things are possible to him that believeth.
Prayer: Dear Lord Jesus, I am so amazed and happy to see Tiger Wood's golf comeback. Your grace, mercy, strength and hope are available to all. I believe I will accomplish my destiny in its fullest in you and I believe you. Amen.

Those who have read the Morning Glory - 365 devotionals like no other! to which this book is the sequel know I have a lot of respect for Tiger Woods golf talents and accomplishments. When he was dealing with his personal issues I said about three years ago that he had not been given the space or time to deal with those issues. Then came the year 2019, Tiger's Comeback year! In 2019, Tiger won his 5th Masters, his 15th Major Championship win and his 82nd PGA Tour. I was especially thrilled to see his 5th Masters win in the presence of his children. In May of 2019, Tiger Woods also received the Presidential Medal of Honor, a very fitting and deserving honor. Only a remarkable person with such focus, drive, determination, perseverance and work ethic could orchestrate such a comeback, thanks be to God. When God says that, all things are possible to him who believes, God is serious. Let Tiger inspire us to reach for our 'history in the making' wins.

© By Dr. Sheila Hayford.

July 10
Adorned

1 Peter Chapter 3, verses 3, 4:
Whose adorning let it not be that outward adorning of plaiting the hair, and of wearing of gold, or of putting on of apparel; But let it be the hidden man of the heart, in that which is not corruptible, even the ornament of a meek and quiet spirit, which is in the sight of God of great price.

Prayer: Dear God, we want to look beautiful to and for you. In Jesus' Name, we pray. Amen.

Summer is here and so are the accompanying summer sales. Society tends to place a lot of emphasis on the physical aspects of beauty, whether it be personal or work related. There are so many 'how to ...'s when it comes to make up, accessories, color coordination for clothes, interior decorating, etc. Does God care how you look? Yes! However,

God is more concerned about how your heart or spirit and your soul look. When a person submits to God through our Lord Jesus Christ and humbles themselves before God, God is pleased. Indeed, what God thinks of us should be our first priority. While we each must take good care of our physical bodies, let us make sure our spirit is regenerated and our soul is beautifully adorned in Christ in God.

© By Dr. Sheila Hayford.

July 11
No Age Limit!

Deuteronomy Chapter 34, verse 7:
And Moses was an hundred and twenty years old when he died: his eye was not dim, nor his natural force abated.

Prayer: Dear God; I am excited when I read of Abraham, Isaac, Jacob and those persons of faith in the Bible who did not limit you but used the gift of life you gave them to accomplish great things in you and for your glory. Thank you for using Kalis' swimming accomplishments to challenge young and old alike to press on to greater heights in our spiritual, personal and professional lives. In Jesus' Name. Amen.

95 year old Kalis Rasmussen swimming accomplishments ought to inspire EVERYBODY! Kalis Rasmussen recorded **five World Records** in the 2019 Swim Ontario Masters Provincial Championships in the 95 years to 99 years age group. This Championship is recognized by the Canadian provinces, as well as nationally and internationally. Kalis won the 100 Back, 200 Back, 200 Breast, 100 Breast and 50 Breast swimming events. And she says she started competitively swimming in the year 2000 when she was 76 years old. Wow! So do not go to God with the excuse that you are too old when God still has work for you to do. Embrace life, keep challenging yourself and move on to higher accomplishments with God and in God.

© By Dr. Sheila Hayford.

July 12
Kings, Queens and Priests

Revelation Chapter 1, verses 5, 6:

And from Jesus Christ, who is the faithful witness, and the first begotten of the dead, and the prince of the kings of the earth. Unto him that loved us, and washed us from our sins in his own blood, And hath made us kings and priests unto God and his Father; to him be glory and dominion for ever and ever. Amen.

Prayer: Dear God, thank you for making us kings, queens and priests through your holy Son, our Lord and Savior, Jesus Christ. Help us not to live beneath our God given position in Christ. In Jesus' name, Amen.

Royalty are expected to live and behave in accordance with their royal status. If they misbehave, they may lose their position. From childhood, children born to royal parents are taught how to talk, walk, speak, wave, behave, who to associate with, the roles and responsibilities they are expected to play and fulfill, etc. And for those who marry into royalty, there are certain protocols which must be followed as they attain royal status also. Do you know who you are through our Lord and Savior Jesus Christ? You are part of God's family. That makes you royalty. Through our Lord Jesus, all born again believers are royalty; kings and queens, and are given the priestly assignment. Thus, the Lord Jesus is the King of kings and queens and the High Priest over all he has made priests. Do you know what your role as a king or queen and as a priest entails? You will have to take the time to study the Holy Bible and allow the Holy Spirit to give you understanding and revelation about your role and responsibilities. Royalty not only represent their country at home, they are Ambassadors on the world stage representing their respective countries. Live royally!

© By Dr. Sheila Hayford.

July 13
We Belong To Jesus

1 Corinthians Chapter 6, verses 19-20:

Do you not know that your bodies are temples of the Holy Spirit, who is in you, whom you have received from God? You are not your own; you were bought at a price. Therefore honor God with your bodies. (NIV)

Prayer: Dear Lord Jesus; thank you for redeeming us from sin, satan and hell. We are grateful and blessed and are honored to be a part of your family. Amen.

Yesterday, we were reminded that we are kings, queens and priests through our Lord Jesus Christ. We are Ambassadors of God on this earth representing God and God's kingdom, on public display for the world to see. Thus, it is reasonable to declare that we belong to Jesus. In other words, **the Lord Jesus paid the price that was needed to ransom us from sin, satan and an everlasting hell.** As such, our first and priority allegiance should be to our Lord and Savior, Jesus Christ. Your first allegiance is not to you, not to your family, not to your job, not to your school, not to a denomination, not to a society, as important as these are in your role here on earth. God supersedes all of them. As God's Ambassador, God is expecting us to represent Him well in taking good care of ourselves, our family, on our job, at school, in our church fellowship and worship and in our society. If at any time, anything is said or done that would require a person to compromise their relationship with God or the Word of God, that person must stay true to God. We belong to Jesus Christ!

© By Dr. Sheila Hayford.

July 14
On Time!

Galatians Chapter 4, verses 4, 5:

But when the fulness of the time was come, God sent forth his Son, made of a woman, made under the law, To redeem them that were under the law, that we might receive the adoption of sons.

Prayer: Dear God; we thank you for the gift of life. Help us to plan wisely and not to waste the precious time you have given us. In Jesus' Name, Amen.

God is always on time! God knew he would send the Lord Jesus to redeem mankind from the punishment for sin following the disobedience of Adam and Eve to God. Yet God waited until the right time to send the Lord Jesus to earth to fulfil his God given mission. Think about this. God could have had you born at any time in the existence of humanity on this earth but God chose a specific time for you to be born. You are here to fulfil your God given mission in this generation and to influence eternity to come. You are that important to humankind. It is now a little past midyear and a great time for re-evaluation. Spend time today in prayer and consultation with God for clarification, direction and counsel as you too fulfill your God given mission here on earth.

© By Dr. Sheila Hayford.

July 15
Movie - The Preview

Revelation Chapter 22, verses 12-15:

And, behold, I come quickly; and my reward is with me, to give every man according as his work shall be. I am Alpha and Omega, the beginning and the end, the first and the last. Blessed are they that do his commandments, that they may have right to the tree of life, and may enter in through the gates into the city. For without are dogs, and sorcerers, and whoremongers, and murderers, and idolaters, and whosoever loveth and maketh a lie.

Prayer: Dear God; help us remember that our life is more than we see on this earth for our life continues in eternity to come. Enable us to make wise choices and to live for you in the power of the Holy Spirit. In Jesus' Name, Amen.

Your life here on earth is a preview of your future? So you might ask what I mean by that. In the verses above, the Lord Jesus tells us in the Book of Revelation that he will reward every human being according to how we lived here on earth. Those who received the Lord Jesus as their personal Lord and Savior and lived for God on this earth will have access to the tree of life and to enter through the gates into God's holy city. The sorcerers, whoremongers, murderers, idolaters, those who loved and practiced lying, those who reveled in depravity and thus rejected God on this earth will be condemned to an eternity without God. How will the movie of your life play in eternity? You get to decide.

© By Dr. Sheila Hayford.

July 16
The Half - Time Show

Proverbs Chapter 15, verses 22-23:
Without counsel purposes are disappointed: but in the multitude of counsellors they are established. A man hath joy by the answer of his mouth: and a word spoken in due season, how good is it!

Prayer: Dear God; help us to seek out advice and counsel so that our endeavors and purpose will be established. In Jesus' name, Amen.

It is now time for the Half-Time show of the Year. We have entered the second half of the year and it is time for the half time show for this year of your life. In the beginning of the year when you hopefully wrote down your "Coming Attractions" you wrote down the resolutions and plans you had for this year. You were encouraged to seek out advice and counsel in the specific areas that applied to your aspiring endeavors and to do what was necessary to bring those goals into fruition. The verses here tell us that without counsel some of your goals will not be established but that as you consult with the right people they will be established. Featured Business Resources have been included in this book that may help you. The world is watching your Half-Time of the Year show. How does it look? Take this half time to also give yourself a pep talk with God as you tweak things for the rest of the year. May we bring joy to many and, most importantly, bring joy to our God.

© By Dr. Sheila Hayford.

July 17
What Is In Your Heart?

Luke Chapter 6, verse 45:
A good man out of the good treasure of his heart bringeth forth that which is good; and an evil man out of the evil treasure of his heart bringeth forth that which is evil: for of the abundance of the heart his mouth speaketh.

Prayer: Dear God; you know the hearts of all man and we each must give account of our life to you. Enable us to bring forth good fruit in what we say and in how we live. In Jesus' Name, Amen.

What is in your heart? The Lord Jesus says that what is in your heart will express itself in what you say and how you live. If a person's heart is pure towards God it will show in how they speak and in how they live. If a person is rebellious towards God, that will also show in how they speak and how they live. Why does this matter? It is because we each will have to give account to God for the stewardship of how we lived here on earth. That will, in turn, determine how we will spend the rest of our lives **forever**. Forever is a big deal, so take time to evaluate your life to date and decide how you want your forever life; with God or without God? God respects your free will and has left that choice to you.

© By Dr. Sheila Hayford.

July 18
Wrapped In?

Luke Chapter 2, verse 7:

And she brought forth her firstborn son, and wrapped him in swaddling clothes, and laid him in a manger; because there was no room for them in the inn.

Prayer: Dear God; grant us discernment by the Holy Spirit so that we do not toss out the wrapping paper with your blessing. In Jesus' Name, Amen.

"What is your blessing wrapped in?" The Lord Jesus Christ, God's gift to humanity was wrapped in swaddling clothes and lying in a manger, an unlikely place many would go to looking for a gift. In that lowly manger, Mary gave birth because many had turned her away. The Lord Jesus Christ is the answer to every need humanity would ever face, past, present or future. Wow! So the follow up question to the first question asked in today's devotional is this, "Which of your blessings are you turning away?" Do not throw away your blessing or blessings because they are not wrapped the way you would expect them to be. Your blessing may come in swaddling clothes, not in a suit and a tie. Your blessing may come from a far off place, not where you were looking for it to arrive from. And yes, your blessing may look like an ordinary child, but He is the King of kings and Lord of lords, the everlasting Son of God. He is our Lord and Savior, Jesus the Christ.

© By Dr. Sheila Hayford.

July 19
Fishers Of Men

Mark Chapter 1, verses 16-18:

Now as he walked by the sea of Galilee, he saw Simon and Andrew his brother casting a net into the sea: for they were fishers. And Jesus said unto them, Come ye after me, and I will make you to become fishers of men. And straightway they forsook their nets, and followed him.

Prayer: Dear Lord Jesus; we trust you with our lives. Help us to share you with others in the love and power of the Holy Spirit. Amen.

What was it about the Lord Jesus that made Simon and his brother Andrew immediately give up what they were familiar with in order to follow the Lord Jesus and entrust their future to him? Notice the promise the Lord Jesus gave them. The Lord Jesus did not say their jobs as fishermen were unimportant; the Lord Jesus promised to help them excel in their profession at a higher level and on a higher plane. Wow! If someone made a promise like that to you, would you go for it? Nothing ever done for God is wasted by God. When the Lord Jesus invites us to follow him, it is with our best interests at heart. God knows humankind needs the Lord Jesus for salvation from sin and the consequences of sin, and since God is a God of purpose and of excellence, God's invitation to us is to move us up to a higher level and a higher plane with God. Furthermore, God expands our mission field. We are called to invite those we are know as well as those we are acquainted with at work, in our profession, casually and even strangers to experience the life giving relationship with the Lord Jesus Christ. The foundation of what God gave to us is love and so the foundation when we introduce our Lord and Savior Jesus Christ to others should be love. In love, follow Christ and excel in your God assigned mission.

© By Dr. Sheila Hayford.

July 20
Give Love

1 Corinthians Chapter 13, verses 1-3:

If I speak in the tongues of men and of angels, but have not love (that reasoning, intentional, spiritual devotion such as is inspired by God's love for and in us), I am only a noisy gong or a clanging cymbal. And if I have prophetic powers (the gift of interpreting the divine will and purpose), and understand all the secret truths and mysteries and possess all knowledge, and if I have [sufficient] faith so that I can remove mountains, but have not love (God's love in me) I am nothing (a useless nobody). Even if I dole out all that I have [to the poor in providing] food, and if I surrender my body to be burned or in order that I may glory, but have not love (God's love in me), I gain nothing. (AMPC)

Prayer: Dear God of love, help us to share your love with others, In Jesus Name, Amen.

Give Love; expect love in return
Give Hate; expect hate in return
Give Love; unexpected hate may show up
Give Love Anyway!
© By Dr. Sheila Hayford.

July 21
Busybodies

Luke Chapter 12, verses 13-14:

Someone in the crowd said to him, "Teacher, tell my brother to divide the inheritance with me." Jesus replied, "Man, who appointed me a judge or an arbiter between you?" (NIV)

Prayer: Dear Lord Jesus; thank you for your example. Help us not to be busybodies and to know how to be firm and speak in love when we are tempted with distractions. Amen.

I do not understand why some are so interested in meddling in the affairs of other people; of people they know as family or friends or even of strangers. The issue at hand may be none of their business and most times they are not knowledgeable about the topic and their counsel is carnal. Those interested in gossip may find them amusing but otherwise the actions of a busybody indicate that they have chosen to do nothing better with their time. The Lord Jesus was teaching a large crowd in these verses when right in the midst of his teaching, someone blurted out an uncalled for instruction asking the Lord Jesus to make a statement concerning that person's affairs. That question had nothing to do with the Lord Jesus' teaching, was inappropriate in timing and almost rude in the interruption. The Lord Jesus would not be distracted. In short, the Lord Jesus told him, "That is none of my business." The Lord Jesus did not allow himself to be distracted or to veer off course because someone wanted him to focus on meddling in other people's business. When you are tempted or distracted by what is not part of your assignment or your business, especially when it involves gossip and backbiting, boldly declare that is none of your business and move forward with your God given priorities.

© By Dr. Sheila Hayford.

July 22
Respect God's Man

Matthew Chapter 10, verse 41:
He that receiveth a prophet in the name of a prophet shall receive a prophet's reward; and he that receiveth a righteous man in the name of a righteous man shall receive a righteous man's reward.

Prayer: Dear God; thank you for your true prophets, sent to humanity with their assignment from you. Help us to recognize them and to respect them. In Jesus' Name, Amen.

Respect God's Man! True, it takes the Holy Spirit's gift and empowerment to discern spiritual things. At the same time, with knowledge of the Holy Bible and spiritual growth in your Christian journey through faith in the Lord Jesus, you should be able to recognize when God has brought a prophet, that is, a man or woman of God to you. I used to wonder in the earlier days of my Christian journey when Christian leaders who had walked with God for some time would speak to me about God's special anointing on me and want to partake of that anointing of God. At that time, I was thinking that I was the one that should be looking up at them until I realized they had tapped into the Holy Spirit's discernment and that the seed they were sowing into my life was a seed they were sowing into God's work and anointing. I could not begin to tell you how God has used men and women, true prophets of God to work in my life for good. At the same time, I can also tell you there were many times that the Holy Spirit revealed to me that not all who claimed to be for God or to be speaking for God were of God. Trust the Holy Spirit's discernment and when God sends a prophet or a righteous man or woman to you, respect that person and the anointing of God that they carry. That way you will receive God's prophet's reward and not God's prophet's rejection.

© By Dr. Sheila Hayford.

July 23
Still Living

Psalm 146, verses 1-2:
Praise the Lord. Praise the Lord, my soul. I will praise the Lord all my life; I will sing praise to my God as long as I live.
Prayer: Dear God, I am so happy to be living in Christ in God, on this earth and for all eternity. In Jesus' name, Amen.

The images on television showed the raging wildfires, several acres of parched land, homes destroyed, dramatic rescues of individuals and their pets. What was amazing was that despite all that they had lost, the individuals were just happy to be alive. Some were planning to rebuild when they went back and others may have been planning to move to move to a different area. However, I never heard anyone say they would rather have kept their possessions and lost their life doing so. You see, it all depends on what you value and your perspective in life. Are you happy to be alive? Are you happy with the Lord Jesus' gift of salvation, the Holy Spirit and eternal life? Then boldly and joyfully say so!

© By Dr. Sheila Hayford.

July 24
The Battle Belongs To God

1 Samuel Chapter 17, verses 47-50:

And all this assembly shall know that the Lord saveth not with sword and spear: for the battle is the Lord's, and he will give you into our hands. And it came to pass, when the Philistine arose, and came, and drew nigh to meet David, that David hastened, and ran toward the army to meet the Philistine. And David put his hand in his bag, and took thence a stone, and slang it, and smote the Philistine in his forehead, that the stone sunk into his forehead; and he fell upon his face to the earth. So David prevailed over the Philistine with a sling and with a stone, and smote the Philistine, and slew him; but there was no sword in the hand of David.

Prayer; Dear God, there is no way anyone can fight against you and win. So help us walk in your wisdom and in your power. In Jesus' Name, Amen.

David understood this important fact; the battle is the Lord's battle. You see, Goliath the giant stood out there, decked in full armor for war, hurling insults at God and God's people and challenging God's people to a fight. Sadly for those present then, the people were fearful and none of them thought they could win in a fight against Goliath. That was so until David showed up. David did not go there to fight. In fact, David's job was tending sheep but he had been sent by his father to bring food to his brothers. When David saw and heard Goliath, he could not fathom the cowardice of the people. David did not have a sword, nor a spear but he understood that anyone who insulted God the way Goliath did was in a battle with God and God would ultimately win that battle. And so David offered to fight Goliath and, with God and a stone and a sling, David killed Goliath and the rest is in the history books. Remember, when others come against your God and against you for worshipping your God, they are fighting God and God will ultimately win. Yours is to find out from God what God's battle plan is for that battle and then to obey God. Always leave the results of God's battle up to God. God's battle plan, God's timing, God's way and God's results are best handled by God. So pray, obey God and in accordance with God's Word, allow God to prevail.

© By Dr. Sheila Hayford.

July 25
A Manufactured Crisis

Psalm 101, verses 6,7:
Mine eyes shall be upon the faithful of the land, that they may dwell with me: he that walketh in a perfect way, he shall serve me. He that worketh deceit shall not dwell within my house: he that telleth lies shall not tarry in my sight.

Prayer: Dear God, thank you that you are always with me. I submit to your authority and to your truths. Help me to serve you faithfully. In Jesus' Name, Amen.

How many times have nations gone to war over a manufactured crises? What was presented as truth or fact was later found to be untrue or lies, but in the meantime human lives had were lost. Is God really that concerned with pretenses of any kind? God says that those who practice deceit will not dwell with God. God is looking for those whose hearts are humble towards him and who are willing to submit their lives to the authority of his Son, Jesus Christ. God has also given humanity the faculties to be able to think things out critically and thoroughly before making decisions that could have far reaching consequences and, in some cases, a devastating impact on others. So before you make that company decision, move your entire family out of town for that new job or make those far reaching economic, health, national and political decisions, make sure you are working with God and God's truths.

© By Dr. Sheila Hayford.

July 26
Restoration

Genesis Chapter 40, verse 13:

Within three days Pharaoh will lift up your head and restore you to your position, and you will put Pharaoh's cup in his hand, just as you used to do when you were his cupbearer. (NIV)

Prayer: Dear God of restoration, we believe you. Help us do our part to see your good promises manifest. In Jesus' Name, Amen.

God is a God of restoration and this is so evident in the life and mission of our Lord and Savior Jesus Christ. Adam and Eve were in a wonderful relationship with God with great benefits and they exercised their rightful position on this earth. However, Adam and Eve listened to satan and disobeyed God's instructions to them. With that act, Adam and Eve fell and with them <u>all humanity</u> fell. God could have left it at that! Humanity would forever have remained a spectacle to the universe on the consequences of disobeying God as humanity bore God's punishment for Adam and Eve's sin of disobedience and spent eternity in hell. But God is a God of Restoration and God's restoration is always for the better. God sent His Son, the Lord Jesus Christ to take the punishment of the sins of humanity so that humankind could be restored back to a rightful relationship with God. In doing so, God gives us great privileges and blessings through our Lord Jesus Christ, some of which will only be revealed in eternity to come. The chief cupbearer of Pharaoh had obviously displeased King Pharaoh in some fashion and was thrown into prison. However, God had mercy on him and within three days from his dream he was restored back to his position. That third day was King Pharaoh's birthday and when the king gave a feast to his officials celebrating the occasion, the King restored the cupbearer back to his original position. What has God promised to restore to you? It does not matter how unlikely things may look when it comes to the promised words of God. If God says it will be well with you, believe God and watch God's words come to pass.

© By Dr. Sheila Hayford.

July 27
The Sovereign God

2 Samuel Chapter 7, verses 18-22:

Then King David went in and sat before the Lord, and he said: "Who am I, Sovereign Lord, and what is my family, that you have brought me this far? And as if this were not enough in your sight, Sovereign Lord, you have also spoken about the future of the house of your servant - and this decree, Sovereign Lord, is for a mere human! "What more can David say to you? For you know your servant, Sovereign Lord. For the sake of your word and according to your will, you have done this great thing and made it known to your servant. "How great you are, Sovereign Lord! There is no one like you, and there is no God but you, as we have heard with our own ears. (NIV)

Prayer: O Sovereign God, we are grateful and thankful for your kind words, your goodness, your grace and mercy extended to us through our Lord Jesus Christ, in whose Name we pray. Amen.

We are glad about the Sovereignty of God for if it were not for the grace of God, none of us would be here. You see, God is Sovereign and has the ability to extend mercy and compassion to humankind even when a person is not deserving of it. King David had his challenges and his faults and yet God spoke very kindly to him through the prophet Nathan and gave King David exceedingly great promises. King David was in awe of God's goodness towards him and of God's Sovereignty. He humbled himself before God and accepted God's words to him with humility, gratefulness and worship. What an example for us all! May we live our lives in worship to the Sovereign God.

© By Dr. Sheila Hayford.

July 28
Who Is In Agreement?

Amos Chapter 3, verse 3:
Can two walk together, except they be agreed?
2 Corinthians Chapter 6, verse 16:
And what agreement hath the temple of God with idols? for ye are the temple of the living God; as God hath said, I will dwell in them, and walk in them; and I will be their God, and they shall be my people.

Prayer: Dear Holy Spirit, help us to choose our associations wisely because we want your work in and through us to move forward. In Jesus' Name, Amen.

These verses presupposes that there might be a question about an association between two individuals. A person who worships God will not be involved in idol worship. A person who blesses God will not curse God. Thus, if a person who is a Christian chooses to spend the majority of their time with a person who ridicules and curses their God, one may ask why the person who professes to be a Christian is enjoying the company of one who is mocking their God. If you have a mission or goal for yourself, your company or organization and you have an employee who is always berating you or the company, one might ask why that employee still chooses to work with the company. Who you are in agreement with matters because while a united team moves the entire team forward, discord, strife and differences in beliefs, vision and mission have the potential to limit or destroy the achievements of an entire organization. Who is in agreement with you?

© By Dr. Sheila Hayford.

July 29
All Babies Have Parents!

1 Corinthians Chapter 13, verse 11:

When I was a child, I spake as a child, I understood as a child, I thought as a child: but when I became a man, I put away childish things.

Prayer: Dear God, what a blessing you give to each baby born; the gift of parents. Help each parent look to you for guidance and direction as they raise the children you have placed in their care. In Jesus' Name, Amen.

All babies have parents! Today is National Parent's Day in the United States and reason for us to show love and appreciation for the gift of Parents. The challenge is this. When we look at the state of society today, it is obvious that these can be challenging times for any parent. There is so much good out there and there is also evil that seems to always be in the news. What is a parent to do? If all babies have parents, it becomes obvious that one of the roles of any parent is to raise their children. And that how a person raises their child can influence the way that child lives. What does the Bible say? The Bible encourages parents to raise their children in the fear and knowledge of God. The Bible also encourages parents to ask God for wisdom on how to raise each individual child for each child is unique. The Bible teaches us that parents are stewards entrusted with the care, discipline and teaching of their children, with parents modelling the example of what they teach and speak. As with every human being, God will have the final say in both the parents and the children and God will always do what is right. So hold onto God, Parents. Yours is a great responsibility. Nevertheless, the God who created you is greater and available to help you. Oh! Do your babies grow up so fast! Enjoy them; you will always be their earthly parents. Happy Parent's Day!

© By Dr. Sheila Hayford.

July 30
Happy Father-In-Law Day!

Exodus Chapter 18, verses 13-16, 19-22:

The next day Moses took his seat to serve as judge for the people, and they stood around him from morning till evening. When his father-in-law saw all that Moses was doing for the people, he said, "What is this you are doing for the people? Why do you alone sit as judge, while all these people stand around you from morning till evening?" Moses answered him, "Because the people come to me to seek God's will. Whenever they have a dispute, it is brought to me, and I decide between the parties and inform them of God's decrees and instructions." Listen now to me and I will give you some advice, and may God be with you. You must be the people's representative before God and bring their disputes to him. Teach them his decrees and instructions, and show them the way they are to live and how they are to behave. But select capable men from all the people - men who fear God, trustworthy men who hate dishonest gain - and appoint them as officials over thousands, hundreds, fifties and tens. Have them serve as judges for the people at all times, but have them bring every difficult case to you; the simple cases they can decide themselves. That will make your load lighter, because they will share it with you. (NIV)

Prayer; Dear God, we are indebted to Jethro for the advice he gave to your prophet Moses and are thankful for the humility and grace of your prophet Moses in taking that advice. As we celebrate National Father-in-law Day, we honor you as the greatest Father-in-law for the church body of believers is the bride of your Son, our Lord and Savior Jesus Christ. We are looking forward to that wonderful Marriage Feast. Happy Father-in-law Day! In Jesus' Name, Amen.

Today is Father-in-Law Day in the United States and we are honoring Jethro, the father-in-law of the prophet Moses. When Jethro brought Moses' wife and their two sons and stayed with the prophet

Moses in the wilderness, he noticed Moses was serving as the sole judge for all the people of Israel from morning until evening. Not only did Moses not have much time to spend with his family, if he continued with that heavy schedule he would wear himself out. So Jethro gave the prophet Moses the good advice we read of in these verses. Thankfully, Moses took that advice and by God's grace lived to be one hundred and twenty years of age. Your father-in-law should be your friend. After all, he is also looking out for their son or daughter. So take the time to thank and show your appreciation for your father-in-law. If there has been bad words exchanged in the past between you and your father-in-law and it is possible and wise to do so, seek reconciliation with your father-in-law. For those fathers-in-law that have chosen to make themselves adversarial to their in-laws, confess your sins and ask God and your in-laws if possible for forgiveness. If professional counselling is needed, do your part. God, our heavenly Father-in-law always does His part. It is up to humankind to follow God's example.

© By Dr. Sheila Hayford.

July 31
Your Seat

Luke Chapter 14, verses 7-11:

When he noticed how the guests picked the places of honor at the table, he told them this parable: "When someone invites you to a wedding feast, do not take the place of honor, for a person more distinguished than you may have been invited. If so, the host who invited both of you will come and say to you, 'Give this person your seat.' Then, humiliated, you will have to take the least important place. But when you are invited, take the lowest place, so that when your host comes, he will say to you, 'Friend, move up to a better place.' Then you will be honored in the presence of all the other guests. For all those who exalt themselves will be humbled, and those who humble themselves will be exalted." (NIV)

Prayer: Dear God, help us to humble ourselves before you and to walk in humility towards our fellow human. Let us eschew pride for we want to enjoy your benefits of promotion. In Jesus' Name, Amen.

Your seat in life depends on your humility with God and with man. In this parable, the Lord Jesus is teaching us that the benefits of humility include promotion and the perils of pride include demotion. Which seat do you want to be seated in?

© By Dr. Sheila Hayford.

August 1
Raised Up

Ephesians Chapter 2, verses 4-7:

But God, who is rich in mercy, for his great love wherewith he loved us, Even when we were dead in sins, hath quickened us together with Christ, (by grace ye are saved;) And hath raised us up together, and made us sit together in heavenly places in Christ Jesus: That in the ages to come he might shew the exceeding riches of his grace in his kindness toward us through Christ Jesus.

Prayer: Our heavenly Father, we are so touched by your goodness and favor to us. Help us not to take your grace for granted but to walk with you in the process of living a sanctified life in Christ. So help us, in the power of the Holy Spirit. In Jesus' Name, we pray. Amen.

Wow! What a promotion! To be raised up and made to sit in heavenly places through our Lord and Savior Jesus Christ! How does that happen? It happens just as these verses tell us; when we were dead in sin, God sent his Son, the Lord Jesus Christ to earth to die for our sins and for us to receive the righteousness of our Lord and Savior Jesus Christ in return. With the righteousness we receive in Christ we become part of the family of God and with that comes many benefits, on this earth and in the ages to come. Anyone who acknowledges their sin, accepts the finished work of the Lord Jesus on the cross of Calvary on their behalf and accepts the Lord Jesus as their Lord and Savior is born again in Christ in God. And that is just the beginning of an eternity with our Lord Jesus. There is much more grace, goodness and kindness to come!

© By Dr. Sheila Hayford.

August 2
Revenge – God's Prerogative

Romans Chapter 12, verse 19:
Do not take revenge, my dear friends, but leave room for God's wrath, for it is written: "It is mine to avenge; I will repay," says the Lord. (NIV)

Ephesians Chapter 4, verses 26-27:
Be ye angry, and sin not: let not the sun go down upon your wrath: Neither give place to the devil.

Prayer: Dear God, we do not want to give any place to the devil. So help us trust you to take care of us and to be the righteous Judge, exacting vengeance on our behalf. In Jesus' Name, Amen.

Vengeance is God's prerogative. Offenses come to all because of the sins of humankind. With offenses, real or perceived, especially when an injustice is perceived, comes the tendency to become angry. However, the Bible warns a person not to sin when they are angry and not to go to bed angry; neither should a person give the devil or satan a place or foothold in their life. You see, when a person is angry about a real or perceived wrong they may want to exact revenge on the person who caused the wrong. In their anger they may end up doing the wrong thing themselves, cause more harm than they thought and put themselves in position to be tempted by the devil to commit further acts of revenge. In the process their soul is poisoned, they may become preoccupied with their adversary, they may become bitter, their mind, will and emotions may become contaminated with evil thoughts and thus they negatively impact many who may be unrelated to the offense. Consider God's better plan. God who is the Sovereign God knows everything and everyone COMPLETELY. God knows the motives and intentions of every heart, the rights or wrongs of every action and the different scenarios that could occur. Moreover, God does not want his children distracted by being drawn into unnecessary fights, or living with unforgiveness and bitterness. So God says to his children, "Let me handle the situation on your behalf." I know from experience that when God is done exacting vengeance in God's time and in God's way on my behalf I look in amazement and say to God, "you mean this little thing they did to me got you so upset." Yes, God can mete righteous judgement on your behalf. So, if you are tempted to hand out immediate revenge in a matter, seek God's counsel first and remember these words of Scripture, Vengeance is mine; I will repay, saith the Lord.

© By Dr. Sheila Hayford.

August 3
The Ground Rules

Numbers Chapter 23, verse 19:
God is not a man, that he should lie; neither the son of man, that he should repent: hath he said, and shall he not do it? or hath he spoken, and shall he not make it good?

Prayer: Dear Holy Spirit, I love being in your class. Help me to apply the lessons you teach me where needed. In Jesus' Name I pray, Amen.

It is the month of August and this month we are going to be in God's summer school. Yes, by all means enjoy the nice weather but make sure you have your personal study time with God as priority. Today we are going to start with the Ground Rules for God's summer school.

Ground Rules:

1. God's Word is Ultimate Truth.
2. The Holy Bible is written for the instruction of humanity and will always have the final word.
3. The lessons taught are intended to be applied where indicated.
4. The warnings given in the lessons are intended to be heeded.
5. The recipient of the lesson is the one who must first make the changes where indicated.
6. Love is the foundation of all that is taught and applied in this school.
7. Courtesy to your fellow students is required; no bullying, no foul talk, no cheating, no lying, treat others with love and respect, considering how you would like to be treated.
8. Respect for your Instructor is required, no rude talking back to the Holy Spirit, the Instructor, discipline to the student may be applied by God if necessary.
9. Tuition is free to humankind with the understanding that it cost the Lord Jesus Christ the shedding of his blood on the Cross of Calvary, death, burial and ultimately resurrection to pay the price for the sins of humanity and to give the Holy Spirit as a gift to humankind.
10. The goal of the lessons are personal and spiritual growth and maturity in Christ in God. Your grades will be given by God and God has the final say in everything.

© By Dr. Sheila Hayford.

August 4
True Science

1 Timothy Chapter 6, verse 20:

O Timothy, keep that which is committed to thy trust, avoiding profane and vain babblings, and oppositions of science falsely so called:

Romans Chapter 1, verses 19-21:

Because that which may be known of God is manifest in them; for God hath shewed it unto them. For the invisible things of him from the creation of the world are clearly seen, being understood by the things that are made, even his eternal power and Godhead; so that they are without excuse: Because that, when they knew God, they glorified him not as God, neither were thankful; but became vain in their imaginations, and their foolish heart was darkened.

Prayer: Dear Holy Spirit; continue to teach us more of your truth for you are the Ultimate Authority in truth. In Jesus' name, Amen.

True Science never contradicts God. When it appears as if Science is contradicting the Holy Bible it is because the study of Science has not yet caught up with the truth of God or because some have made a deliberate decision to go against the word of God and are trying to justify their theories. For years it seemed to humankind that the earth was flat and that if a person went far enough they would fall off the earth, only to find out that the Bible is true when it says the earth is round. So the true study of Science becomes a study of the works of God. The innovative ideas and products that are continually being developed by humankind reflect the creative abilities God has given to humanity and should be used to benefit humanity, not for society's destruction. True Science reveals the truths of a True God.

© By Dr. Sheila Hayford.

August 5
God's Calculus I - Loss Versus Gain

Luke Chapter 17, verse 33:

Whosoever shall seek to save his life shall lose it; and whosoever shall lose his life shall preserve it.

Prayer: Dear Holy Spirit; we wholeheartedly submit ourselves to your instruction. Help us to be good students as we learn, apply what you need us to apply and share what you teach us with others. In Jesus' Name, Amen.

Calculus can be a difficult subject for many although it comes easy to some. The interesting thing about God's calculus is that it goes against the natural tendencies of a carnal mind. In other words, a person needs the Holy Spirit to give them understanding and illumination of God's calculus. It is not a subject to be feared; it is a subject to be learned, applied and which provides great benefits when applied. The principles involved in God's calculus involve what may appear to be a loss or a minus which actually work out to become a gain or a plus. In this verse, the Lord Jesus is saying that the person who is willing to give his life in submission to God and for the service of God does not lose his life, he actually gains his life. This is because everybody born on earth since Adam and Eve sinned is under the curse of the sins of Adam and Eve and that includes an everlasting hell that was originally created for satan and those angels who followed satan. When Adam and Eve followed satan's advice and disobeyed God, Adam and Eve condemned humanity to hell and separation from God. The Lord Jesus came to earth to pay the punishment for the sins of humanity when he died on the cross and rose again and offers this good news of salvation freely to anyone who will repent of sin and invite him into their heart and life as Lord and Savior. Anyone who receives the Lord Jesus in this way becomes part of God's family, receives the gift of the Holy Spirit and the gift of everlasting life. Thus, that person actually preserves their life, gaining their life back in the way God intended. Your homework is to apply God's calculus I in your own life by giving your life to God even if it means you lose some relationships or what seems to be a loss and see how God restores and preserves you. In God's calculus I the first thing you give to God is you!

© By Dr. Sheila Hayford.

August 6
God's Calculus II – Always Give God First

Proverbs Chapter 3, verses 9-10:

Honour the Lord with thy substance, and with the firstfruits of all thine increase: So shall thy barns be filled with plenty, and thy presses shall burst out with new wine.

Prayer: Dear Heavenly Father, you bless us with so much. Help us to be good stewards of what you entrust to us and to always give you to you first. In Jesus' Name, Amen.

In God's Calculus I we learned that we must first give our lives to God through our Lord Jesus Christ. When we do so, we do not lose out on life, we gain everlasting life. God's Calculus II has to do with the understanding the difference between Ownership and Stewardship. When God created Adam and Eve, the first of humankind, God gave Adam and Eve dominion and authority on the earth subject to the limitations God gave them and placed them as stewards in the Garden of Eden. Thus, when God would come in the cool of the day to chat with them, I am sure God would be looking and inspecting the garden to see how things were going. Everything good thing we have on this earth, including the finances we have worked for, those things we have purchased and those items received as gifts are all given to us from God. It is God who gave us the strength, intellect, ability, talent and sound mind to do what we do and who gave us the favor to receive whatever we receive, whether in our finances or in kind, so we ought to show God honor, appreciation and thankfulness and contribute to the advancement of God's kingdom. Yes, God wants you to take good care of you. Yes, God wants you to take good care of your family. And yes, you should honor your God with the first fruits of your increase. In God's Calculus II when you give to God you do not lose, instead you receive from God greater in return. So your homework is to list the different ways you receive from God and the projected wages, bonuses and rewards you are expecting to receive and then write down how and what you will contribute to God's work as you show God gratitude and honor in your life. Then follow up by writing all the wonderful ways God gives you back greater and share with others how God's Calculus II works.

© By Dr. Sheila Hayford.

August 7
God's Calculus III – Reciprocity

Luke Chapter 6, verse 38:
Give, and it shall be given unto you; good measure, pressed down, and shaken together, and running over, shall men give into your bosom. For with the same measure that ye mete withal it shall be measured to you again.

Prayer: Dear God, thank you for teaching us the principle of reciprocity. Help us not let the actions of others deter us from obeying your God given principles. In Jesus' Name, Amen.

In God's Calculus II we learned about always giving to God first. God's Calculus III involves reciprocity. What you do for others will generally come back to you. Many who have much wealth are some of the most generous in what they give out to benefit their fellow man and for the benefit of society as a whole. They have tapped into God's Calculus III which will generally work for those who apply it. However, we recognize we live in a sinful world and not all good acts will receive good in return. And so I say:
- If one gives good, expect good in return
- If one gives hate, expect hate in return
- If one gives good, unexpected hate may show up
- Give Good Anyway

© By Dr. Sheila Hayford.

August 8
God's Calculus IV - The Law of Eternal Rewards

1 Corinthians Chapter 2, verse 9:

But as it is written, Eye hath not seen, nor ear heard, neither have entered into the heart of man, the things which God hath prepared for them that love him

Prayer: Dear God; we are trusting you with our eternal rewards. Help us to work on God's Calculus I, God's Calculus II and God's Calculus III while we are on this earth, in the power of the Holy Spirit. In Jesus' Name we pray. Amen.

God's Calculus IV is the recognition of the human limitations in fully comprehending how, when and where God apportions individual human rewards. As we read in Scripture, God has so many rewards for us in eternity to come, on the other side of this earth. It is true how we live on this earth will determine those rewards, but there is no human algorithm we could use to ascertain what those rewards will be. So God's Calculus IV is to leave the calculations of your eternal rewards to God. Work on God's Calculus I, God's Calculus II and God's Calculous III while you are on this earth and trust God with God's Calculus IV.

© By Dr. Sheila Hayford.

August 9
History is His Story

Hebrews Chapter 1, verses 1-4:

God, who at sundry times and in divers manners spake in time past unto the fathers by the prophets, Hath in these last days spoken unto us by his Son, whom he hath appointed heir of all things, by whom also he made the worlds; Who being the brightness of his glory, and the express image of his person, and upholding all things by the word of his power, when he had by himself purged our sins, sat down on the right hand of the Majesty on high: Being made so much better than the angels, as he hath by inheritance obtained a more excellent name than they.

Prayer: Dear Lord Jesus, we thank you for our redemption. Thank you for the privilege of becoming a part of your story. Amen.

The History class we are studying is unlike any other history lesson. This is because most History is the study of what has taken place in the past. In God's school, the History class is about His Story; the story of the Lord Jesus Christ. You see, even before God created the foundations of the earth, God knew the risk involved in creating humanity with a free will to determine their destiny based on the choices they made and knew the predicament Adam and Eve would place humanity in. So way back then, God the Father, made the decision that his only begotten Son, the Lord Jesus Christ would come to earth to die on the cross and save humanity from sin, satan and separation from God. This same Lord and Savior, Jesus Christ, would rise again and is seated at God's Right hand of authority. However, His story is ongoing. The Lord Jesus will come to earth again. The Lord Jesus will reign and rule forever and will receive his bride, the church of all born again believers who have received the Lord Jesus Christ as Lord and savior. So the Holy Bible is our introduction to His Story and our lives will become a part of His Story. Isn't it exciting to get to be a part of God's history, as a part of His Story? Wouldn't you like others to be a part of His story? We need to share His story with others. Your assignment given to you by the Lord Jesus Christ himself is to share His story.

© By Dr. Sheila Hayford.

August 10
Critical Thinking

Isaiah Chapter 1, verse 18:

Come now, and let us reason together, saith the Lord: though your sins be as scarlet, they shall be as white as snow; though they be red like crimson, they shall be as wool.

Prayer: Dear God; we confess our sins to you, asking for your forgiveness through the finished work of your Son, our Lord Jesus Christ. Empower us by the Holy Spirit to live for you. In Jesus' Name, Amen.

This class is to encourage us to apply critical spiritual evaluation and understanding when it comes to us as individuals and humankind at large. If a person had a very large debt to pay but had no way of paying it and someone offered to pay that debt for them, the person who had the debt would want to find out what would be the conditions under which the other person would satisfy their debt. If it was agreeable for both of them, the debt would be satisfied. Every human being, by virtue of being born on this earth after Adam and Eve has a debt to God we can never repay on our own and that debt is called sin. The punishment for that debt is hell and eternal separation from God. God, our heavenly Father, has provided humanity with a benefactor in the person of our Lord and Savior Jesus Christ. The Lord Jesus has died on the cross for the sins of humanity of all ages, once and for all. All a person has to do to receive the Lord Jesus offer to pay their sin debt in full for all time is to repent of sin, confess their sins to God asking for forgiveness and to accept the Lord Jesus Christ as their personal Lord and Savior. Their sins will be wiped away by God and the person will receive the gift of the Holy Spirit and be saved in Christ in God. Critical spiritual thinking is involved here as the choice determines one's eternal future and one only gets to make that choice while here on earth. A person's choice is sealed once that person departs from this earth. So consider the conditions of your benefactor, the Lord Jesus Christ. Consider what a person stands to gain with God and what a person will lose without God. The assignment for each person today is to make the right decision with the eternal implications of their choice in mind and to lead others, by God's grace and power, to consider the eternal implications for their lives and to make the right decisions.

© By Dr. Sheila Hayford.

August 11
English - God's Question Demands An Answer

Mark Chapter 11, verse 33:

The baptism of John, was it from heaven, or of men? answer me. And they reasoned with themselves, saying, If we shall say, From heaven; he will say, Why then did ye not believe him? But if we shall say, Of men; they feared the people: for all men counted John, that he was a prophet indeed. And they answered and said unto Jesus, We cannot tell. And Jesus answering saith unto them, Neither do I tell you by what authority I do these things.

Prayer: Heavenly Father, help us to be honest with ourselves and with you and to always answer your questions. In Jesus' Name, Amen.

In this English class, we learn that God's questions demand an answer. The Lord Jesus Christ asked a question of those who had come to him. When they refused to answer the Lord Jesus' question, the Lord Jesus Christ refused to give them an answer to their question. Many times some will go to God with a question. In reply to their question, God will ask the person a very pertinent question. We know God knows the heart of every human being and even our thoughts before they are formed. Thus, when God asks an answer of us, it is to get us to acknowledge the truth about ourselves and the truth about God. Some get offended by God's question and walk off, others refuse to answer God's question. In either case, as a result of not answering God's question, God does not answer their question. Your homework today is to answer God's question with regard to the questions you have asked him. Indeed, the lesson for everyone is this: Answer God's questions.

© By Dr. Sheila Hayford.

August 12
Languages

Acts Chapter 2, verses 4-11:

All of them were filled with the Holy Spirit and began to speak in other tongues as the Spirit enabled them. Now there were staying in Jerusalem God-fearing Jews from every nation under heaven. When they heard this sound, a crowd came together in bewilderment, because each one heard their own language being spoken. Utterly amazed, they asked: "Aren't all these who are speaking Galileans? Then how is it that each of us hears them in our native language? Parthians, Medes and Elamites; residents of Mesopotamia, Judea and Cappadocia, Pontus and Asia, Phrygia and Pamphylia, Egypt and the parts of Libya near Cyrene; visitors from Rome 11 (both Jews and converts to Judaism); Cretans and Arabs - we hear them declaring the wonders of God in our own tongues!" (NIV)

Prayer: Dear Holy Spirit; it amazing that you give to us so many gifts. May we use all your gifts as wise stewards for the glory of God. In Jesus' Name, Amen.

The class today is on the study of Languages and in this case, on Foreign Languages. Many have heard of various ways to study other languages; by text, visually, via audio, etc. In God's school, Foreign Languages may be spoken without study. What did you say? You mean one could speak in a foreign language without learning to speak that language? Yes, and that is true in God's school because the Holy Spirit gives the gift of speaking in other languages without studying those languages to born again believers. With this Holy Spirit given gift you can speak fluently in another language without studying that language and like those in the verses above, those whose native tongue is in the foreign language you are speaking will understand what you are saying. Moreover, the Holy Spirit also gives to born again believers the gift of interpreting what is spoken in a foreign language, even though that person may not have studied that language. If you have any questions about this Foreign Languages summer class, refer to the ground rules of God's Summer School. Ask God your questions and answer God's questions when God asks questions of you. Then be prepared to take God's Word as your final word.

© By Dr. Sheila Hayford.

August 13
Sewing Class

Revelation Chapter 7, verses 9-10:
After this I beheld, and, lo, a great multitude, which no man could number, of all nations, and kindreds, and people, and tongues, stood before the throne, and before the Lamb, clothed with white robes, and palms in their hands; And cried with a loud voice, saying, Salvation to our God which sitteth upon the throne, and unto the Lamb.

Matthew Chapter 22, verses 11-13:
And when the king came in to see the guests, he saw there a man which had not on a wedding garment: And he saith unto him, Friend, how camest thou in hither not having a wedding garment? And he was speechless. Then said the king to the servants, Bind him hand and foot, and take him away, and cast him into outer darkness, there shall be weeping and gnashing of teeth.

Prayer: Dear God; we are living in times of grace on this earth when anyone who chooses to do so may receive the Lord Jesus Christ as Lord and Savior and receive the white robe of salvation through the righteousness of the Lord Jesus Christ. May every person professing Christianity make sure they have the right clothes on for the Lord Jesus' marriage feast. In Jesus' Name, Amen.

Today we are going to attend Sewing Class and the topic of study is the difference between a ready-made dress and one sewed at home or as a hobby. A ready-made dress is usually sewn by someone other than the wearer to certain specifications. In the case of dresses that are manufactured for mass production and retail, the specifications are usually those recognized by the major retailers and customers go to the store or shop online to buy the garment based on what they feel will fit or look good on them. A ready-made dress may also be custom tailored. In other words, measurements for the person who will wear the attire are taken and the garment design is sewed to their specific measurements. Alterations may also be done to a mass-produced garment in order to better fit the wearer. A hand-crafted dress sewed by the wearer is one done according to the likes, preferences or whims of the wearer. In the verses we read today, someone showed up at the feast without the right attire. When a person receives salvation through Jesus Christ, that person receives the righteousness of the Lord Jesus Christ and a white robe sewn to God's specifications in exchange for their sin stained garment. Only those with the white robe of Jesus' salvation have the proper attire to be at the wedding banquet of the Lord Jesus. Some assume that just because they attend church and do commendable acts such as feeding the poor and fighting for social justice, they will be given a seat at God's banquet. When the master found the improperly dressed person trying to sneak in, the person was removed and cast out into everlasting hell. The lesson today is: Make sure you have the right attire on when the Lord Jesus comes to take his own with him to the feast.

© By Dr. Sheila Hayford.

August 14
Art Class

John Chapter 19, verses 34, 36-37:
But one of the soldiers with a spear pierced his side, and forthwith came there out blood and water. For these things were done, that the scripture should be fulfilled, A bone of him shall not be broken. And again another scripture saith, They shall look on him whom they pierced.

Prayer: Dear Lord Jesus, thank you for taking such brutal punishment in order to pay the price for my sins. I confess my sins to you, asking for forgiveness and resolve to live for you. Come into my life as my Lord and Savior and grant me your gift of the Holy Spirit who now dwells in me. I am filled with joy and look forward to your Second Coming. Amen.

Today in Art Class we are going to behold a picture, hang up for us to see with a study of the picture and what it represents. In the verses above we read of a person who has been pierced in his side by a spear by soldiers, with blood and water gushing from his side. We are told that this person has no bones broken. Moreover, many are looking at him. Of whom does this verse speak of? It describes our Lord and Savior Jesus Christ, hanging on the cross at Calvary for the sins of humanity. God had revealed in the Holy Scriptures the way the Lord Jesus would die on the cross and the Scripture was being fulfilled by the Lord Jesus in perfect detail. The lesson here is that whatever God says comes to pass. God sent his Son, the Lord Jesus to earth to save humanity from their sins. The Bible says this same Lord Jesus Christ, who is resurrected and seated at the right hand of God the Father, is coming back to earth again to take those who have received him as Lord and Savior back with him. At that time the Lord Jesus will come through the clouds and every eye will look up and behold this wondrous living picture. Will you be happy on that day? Those who have rejected the Lord Jesus Christ will be sad. The lesson today is this: Make the eternally wise decision to receive the Lord Jesus Christ as your Lord and Savior if you have not already done so today.

© By Dr. Sheila Hayford.

August 15
Reading Class

Deuteronomy Chapter 17, verses 18-20:

And it shall be, when he sitteth upon the throne of his kingdom, that he shall write him a copy of this law in a book out of that which is before the priests the Levites: And it shall be with him, and he shall read therein all the days of his life: that he may learn to fear the Lord his God, to keep all the words of this law and these statutes, to do them: That his heart be not lifted up above his brethren, and that he turn not aside from the commandment, to the right hand, or to the left: to the end that he may prolong his days in his kingdom, he, and his children, in the midst of Israel.

Prayer: Dear God; help us to be faithful in reading the Holy Bible daily and to do what you command us to do therein. In Jesus' Name, Amen.

These verses tell us the instructions that were to be given to the king. He was to have and keep a copy of the laws of God and was to read it <u>all the days of his life.</u> The purpose of the reading was to ensure that the king was God fearing, read and understood what God required of him and obeyed God in whatever God said the king should do. Reading God's Word and applying it would ensure that the king's heart would not be prideful and as the king, in turn, taught his children, God would grant the king longevity. The required reading book for this class is the Holy Bible and we are to read it every day. Not only must we read the Bible, we must do what God tells us to do in the Bible and God will reward our obedience. Your assignment: Have your own Bible and read a Chapter a day, starting with the gospel of John. Allow God the Holy Spirit to be your Teacher and to guide and direct you as you live for God.

© By Dr. Sheila Hayford.

August 16
Cooking

Genesis Chapter 6, verses 21-22:

You are to take every kind of food that is to be eaten and store it away as food for you and for them." Noah did everything just as God commanded him.

Prayer: Dear God, thank you that you have given us so many choices when it comes to what we will eat. Help us take the responsibility for those you have placed under our care seriously. In Jesus' Name, Amen.

In the cooking class today, we will focus on food supply and food storage. I like to buy food in bulk because it is usually cheaper and I like to buy food on sale. I also clip and use coupons to save money so my money goes a long way when it comes to food purchases. Noah was going to be living in the ark for forty days and forty nights. Noah would be in the ark with his family, two each of various birds and animals and God told Noah to make sure he had enough food stored to feed all on board the ark because when the flood came, no one would be able to go out to get any food. So, Noah did everything God told him to do. And because Noah obeyed God, the human race did not become extinct. Some of you may enjoy cooking, others may enjoy eating out. The lesson here is to make sure that we have enough food for not only for us but for those who are under our care. It is a shame to see the way food is wasted by some when the food thrown away could be used to feed many. It is also heartwarming to see the many organizations that are working to bring an end to food hunger. Do your part when it comes to your food supply and storage. Many lives may be depending on you.

© By Dr. Sheila Hayford.

August 17
Physical Education: Play By The Rules

2 Timothy Chapter 2, verses 4-5:
No one serving as a soldier gets entangled in civilian affairs, but rather tries to please his commanding officer. Similarly, anyone who

competes as an athlete does not receive the victor's crown except by competing according to the rules. (NIV)

Prayer: Dear Holy Spirit, we need your enablement to run our life's race according to God's rules so help us submit to your authority and leadership. In Jesus' Name, Amen.

We finished the Cooking class and so it is appropriate to ask what happens after a person eats their food. The person might begin to feel sleepy. If the person spends a lot of their time eating, sitting on the couch and not doing much exercise, their lifestyle could be a factor when it comes to their health. So our class today is on Physical Education. One of the ways a person may exercise is to play a sport. There are so many sports; Football, Soccer, Hockey, Basketball and more. Today we will focus in our Physical Education class on the Rules. What is the first thing you have to know if you want to be successful in any sport? The answer is: the Rules of the Sport. We sometimes see athletes perform great feats, only to be disqualified because they failed to play by the rules. That athlete trained and put in all those hours of rigorous training, was careful when it came to what they ate, sacrificed their personal time and then during or after the competition, they were disqualified for failing to play by the rules. Their hard work coming into the game seemingly wasted. When it comes to our spiritual life, we have to play by God's rules. God is the Creator of humanity and if we liken life to a race, then we must run by God's rules. God's rules pertain to life and godliness and are written for our instruction and correction in the Holy Bible. In our Reading class we were asked to read a Chapter of the Bible a day. Your assignment today is to write down the play book God wants you to execute or practice based on the Chapter you read in the Bible each day and then do what God instructs you to do.

© By Dr. Sheila Hayford.

August 18
Geography

For since the creation of the world God's invisible qualities - his eternal power and divine nature - have been clearly seen, being understood from what has been made, so that people are without excuse. (NIV)

Hebrews Chapter 1, verse 3:

Who being the brightness of his glory, and the express image of his person, and upholding all things by the word of his power, when he had by himself purged our sins, sat down on the right hand of the Majesty on high:

Prayer: Dear God; thank you for your amazing creation. We are in awe of you and worship you, the Creator. In Jesus' Name, Amen.

In Geography class today we will discuss how the study of Geography gives humankind no excuse. The verse above tells that since God created the world, and that includes the oceans, the seas, the land, the creatures, the plants and all the beauty we behold, it is obvious that a divine Power, God, who has been in existence before the creation of humankind, has created what we see. Such complex creations did not just show up but they function according to God's divine instructions. In fact, God tells us in the book of Romans that the Lord Jesus upholds all things by His word of power. So as you behold the wonderful creations of an awesome God, and explore and study the complexities of God's creative genius, let us be careful to worship God and to give God praise, thanks and honor. For Geography gives humankind no excuse when it comes to the divine nature, genius and eternal power of God.

© By Dr. Sheila Hayford.

August 19
Music

Psalm 150, verses 1-6:

Praise ye the Lord. Praise God in his sanctuary: praise him in the firmament of his power. Praise him for his mighty acts: praise him according to his excellent greatness. Praise him with the sound of the trumpet: praise him with the psaltery and harp. Praise him with the timbrel and dance: praise him with stringed instruments and organs. Praise him upon the loud cymbals: praise him upon the high sounding cymbals. Let every thing that hath breath praise the Lord. Praise ye the Lord.

Revelation Chapter 4, verses 8-11:

Each of the four living creatures had six wings and was covered with eyes all around, even under its wings. Day and night they never stop saying: "'Holy, holy, holy is the Lord God Almighty,' who was, and is, and is to come." Whenever the living creatures give glory, honor and thanks to him who sits on the throne and who lives for ever and ever, the twenty-four elders fall down before him who sits on the throne and worship him who lives for ever and ever. They lay their crowns before the throne and say: "You are worthy, our Lord and God, to receive glory and honor and power, for you created all things, and by your will they were created and have their being." (NIV)

Prayer: Revelation Chapter 7, verse 12: "Amen! Praise and glory and wisdom and thanks and honor and power and strength be to our God for ever and ever. Amen!" (NIV)

In our Music Class today, we will study Psalm 150, a song of Praise to God. It starts with an appropriate command to praise the Lord. That is our rightful duty for how dare any human enjoy all the wonderful things God has given to us and endowed us with and not offer praise and worship to God. Notice how the Psalmist subtly reminds us of the distinction between God and man. God who inhabits eternity also has his

Holy Sanctuary where he is worshipped continually as we read in the book of Revelation. As human beings we are encouraged to praise God in song and with musical instruments; the trumpet, the harp, the guitar, the organ, the cymbal, whatever musical instrument there is or is yet to be created. We are also encouraged to praise God in the dance. Indeed everything that is alive ought to praise and worship the Almighty God. And so ends our Summer school; however, our praise and worship to God continues; on this earth and in eternity to come. Hallelujah!

© By Dr. Sheila Hayford.

August 20
Guidance

Psalm 32, verse 8:
I will instruct thee and teach thee in the way which thou shalt go: I will guide thee with mine eye.

Prayer: Dear God; you know I am indebted to you for your continual faithfulness. Thank you for your keeping power. May I bring you much joy, through my Lord and Savior, Jesus Christ. Amen.

This verse is one of the verses that I anchored my life and my hope on when I received the Lord Jesus as my Lord and Savior in my teenage years. I needed God's guidance and wisdom in everything. And God promised to instruct me, teach me and guide me. God kept that promise then, God is keeping that promise now and God will be faithful to keep this promise in the future. What is it that you need guidance about? The many choices we have these days could be overwhelming but the God we have is never stressed out. Take God at His Word and allow Him to prove Himself faithful.

© By Dr. Sheila Hayford.

August 21
Age Is Not Just A Number

Psalm 90, verse 12:
So teach us to number our days, that we may apply our hearts unto wisdom.

Prayer: Dear God; every life has value to you and each person comes to earth packaged with your purpose and plan for each of us. Help us to diligently seek you and your wisdom and to fulfil your good plans for us and in us. In Jesus' Name, Amen.

Sometimes you hear people talk about age as being just a number. To me, that minimizes the fullness of a person's life. Age is to be celebrated, age is to be valued, life is to be live fully. In this verse, we are encouraged to take into consideration, with thoughtful planning and wisdom, our life here on earth. No matter how long a person lives on this earth, this earth is not their permanent home. Thus it behooves us to plan and to fill our lives with things of value on this earth and to look ahead when it comes to matters of eternal value. When we submit to God the Holy Spirit and apply ourselves to God's wisdom, age is not just a number, it becomes a testimony of the faithfulness of our God.

© By Dr. Sheila Hayford.

August 22
Work and Leisure

Philippians Chapter 2, verses 13-15:
For it is God which worketh in you both to will and to do of his good pleasure. Do all things without murmurings and disputings: That ye may be blameless and harmless, the sons of God, without rebuke, in the midst of a crooked and perverse nation, among whom ye shine as lights in the world;

Prayer: Dear God, help us to be careful how we live, whether at work or in our leisure, so we will please you in all things. In Jesus' Name, Amen.

Work and Leisure. Note that the title did not say 'Work; Not Pleasure' because some seem to feel they must hate their job but enjoy their leisure. Everything that we do, whether at work, on the job or at leisure should be done as unto the Lord God. Your job may not be your dream job, but if you work at it with a good attitude and do a good job, God may have you promoted at that company, God may cause you to start your own company, God may lead you to work for a different company or move you in an entirely different direction. When God blesses you with leisure time, that time is also to be valued as you have the opportunity to be refreshed in spirit, soul and body. The challenge is not to confuse the two. Some will give their job less than their best and spend a whole year planning in intricate detail every aspect of their summer vacation. Others might work exceedingly well at their job and refuse to take time off for themselves and their families to be rejuvenated. God wants us to be whole in every aspect. Please God at work and in your leisure!

© By Dr. Sheila Hayford.

August 23
Hershey Park – Here We Come!

Nehemiah Chapter 1, verses 10-11:
"They are your servants and your people, whom you redeemed by your great strength and your mighty hand. Lord, let your ear be attentive to the prayer of this your servant and to the prayer of your servants who delight in revering your name. Give your servant success today by granting him favor in the presence of this man." I was cupbearer to the king. (NIV)

Prayer: Dear God; thank you for answering our prayers beyond our imagination. You give us so much joy. In Jesus' Name, Amen.

I travel a lot and when people request prayer, I offer to pray with them right there and then. On one of my travels, I met a woman crying. She was a stranger and feeling God's compassion for her I asked her why she was crying. She gave the reasons and I offered to pray with her. She agreed and so we did. I knew God had answered our prayers and I did not get her contact information. Well, it so happened that about five months later, I was in the same area. I saw this happy lady waving at me, trying to get my attention. She told me she had been looking for me to let me know how God answered our prayer. I would never have recognized her as the same person; she looked so happy! She then told me the specific ways God had answered our prayers, some beyond human imagination and that as we spoke someone had paid for her and her children to visit Hershey Park. It was an AMAZING testimony. Just as Nehemiah asked God for an unusual favor from the king and God granted his request, so God answered our prayers even better than we imagined. What do you need God to do for you that seems to be beyond human imagination? As God's servants, we should seek God earnestly in prayer. And allow God to provide the answers.

© By Dr. Sheila Hayford.

August 24
The Tongue Of The Learned

John Chapter 6, verse 45:
It is written in the prophets, And they shall be all taught of God. Every man therefore that hath heard, and hath learned of the Father, cometh unto me.

Prayer: Dear God, help us to be teachable students when we study the Word of God and to accurately share our Lord and Savior Jesus

Christ with others; by the enablement of the Holy Spirit and in Jesus' Name we pray, Amen.

How a person presents themselves to others matters. What is even more important is how a person presents their God to others. The Lord Jesus makes it clear that God's desire is to teach humankind. When we study the Holy Bible, we read and hear God speaking to us and we learn of God the Father. Since the Holy Bible is a revelation to humanity of the Lord Jesus Christ and God's mission and plans for humanity are `through our Lord and Savior Jesus Christ, those who receive God's teaching regarding the salvation available through His Son in faith receive the Lord Jesus Christ. There is a confidence that comes when a person is speaking about a topic with which they are familiar or have experience with. How would you describe your relationship with God? Are you a teachable student of the God's Word? Are you a learned teacher when it comes to sharing the Lord Jesus Christ with others?

© By Dr. Sheila Hayford.

August 25
God Proved Himself

Malachi Chapter 3, verse 10:
Bring ye all the tithes into the storehouse, that there may be meat in mine house, and prove me now herewith, saith the Lord of hosts, if I will not open you the windows of heaven, and pour you out a blessing, that there shall not be room enough to receive it.

Prayer: Dear God, you are God and yet you choose to favor humanity when we submit ourselves to you. Thank you for your faithfulness and your goodness. In Jesus' name, Amen.

I had received funds from a project and decided to tithe in obedience to God. Moreover, my heart is filled with gratitude for God's goodness and so I decided to add an offering with that tithe to God. I was not giving in order to get from God. I was giving knowing that God's Word is true. Well, as God had it, a company was offering random free travel for the customers. I had seen the promotion earlier and I did not get any of those free seats, but their promotion had been extended for another two months. When I went to book my travel, the date I wanted was unavailable. The date they had was not what I wanted but the Holy Spirit asked me not to brush off that date. So I looked at the times for that date, choose my time and, voila, I had a free seat! It was totally miraculous, a gift from God to me and a penny less than my tithe and offering amount. God proved himself! Are God's blessings always monetary? No! God's blessings to humankind start with the Lord Jesus Christ and the Lord Jesus Christ can never be bought with money. In fact, the Lord Jesus is the one who purchased our salvation. However, God knows that in order to live on this earth we have to deal with monetary matters and God meets our financial needs as well. When God asks us to prove Him, God is not asking an individual to arrogantly put God to the test. What God wants us to do is to allow God to prove Himself faithful to us. Thank you, dear Lord Jesus, for so great a salvation!

© By Dr. Sheila Hayford.

August 26
All Hands On Deck

1 Chronicles Chapter 28, verse 21:

And, behold, the courses of the priests and the Levites, even they shall be with thee for all the service of the house of God: and there shall be with thee for all manner of workmanship every willing skilful man, for any manner of service: also the princes and all the people will be wholly at thy commandment.

Prayer; Dear God, thank you for the different gifts each person brings in your service. May we be faithful in the use of our gifts and be united in working for the advancement of your kingdom. In Jesus' Name, Amen.

When it comes to service for God, especially when it comes to service in the congregation of Christian believers God wants all hands on deck. Some believe that God's work is only for those who are involved in full time Christian ministry. That is not so. When King David was speaking to his son, Solomon, who would be building God's physical building for the worship and service of God, the priests were obviously on board. However, in addition to the priests, all willing skillful men and women in whatever profession or trade or study were welcome to participate. The princes, leaders and all the people who were willing to be a part were also welcome to participate. Does that mean we are to be indiscriminate when it comes to the work of God? No! If a person is skilled in a particular trade but what they bring to the table or their mission will not align with what God has said concerning a particular project, they should not be allowed to cause dissension and strife and thus should not be involved in that particular project. God may have a different project for them to be involved with. So, when it comes to God's Service it should be: All United Hands On Deck!

© By Dr. Sheila Hayford.

August 27
Play By Play!

2 Samuel Chapter 6, verse 21:
And David said unto Michal, It was before the Lord, which chose me before thy father, and before all his house, to appoint me ruler over the people of the Lord, over Israel: therefore will I play before the Lord.

Prayer: Dear God; thank you for reminding us that we ought to be God pleasers first. In Jesus' Name, Amen.

Why do some curse themselves by their own acts? What should have been a day of great rejoicing for Michal, the daughter of Saul, turned out to be to her detriment. The Ark of God was being returned to the City of

David after being in the house of Obededom and David was overjoyed, especially since he heard how God had blessed the house of Obededom. As the Ark of God was being brought to the City of David, when those carrying the Ark of God had gone every six paces, David offered sacrifices to God. David danced before God with all his might during the procession and brought in the Ark of God with shouting and the sound of the trumpet. Then David gave every man and woman in attendance a cake of bread, some meat, some wine in celebration and blessed the people. Afterwards, David returned to bless his house. One would have thought that Michal would be happy! No, she was not. Michal despised David for dancing before God and when David came to bless his house, Michal told David that he was dancing in order to attract the attention of the women there. David, a man using his gift of praise and worship to God, as we read of in so many of the Psalms in the Bible, was being accused by someone who did not have fellowship with God. So how did that happen? Michal, King Saul's daughter loved David. King Saul told David that in order to marry Michal, David would have to bring him the foreskin of one hundred Philistines, thinking that David, of whom King Saul was jealous, would be killed in the process. David lived, fulfilled King Saul's request and so King Saul gave Michal to David as wife with the hope that she would snare him. So be careful who you allow close to you when it comes to the sacred things of God. No one should want to have what should have been their blessing replaced with a curse.

© By Dr. Sheila Hayford.

August 28
Rahab's Roof

Joshua Chapter 2, verses 8-9, 12-13, 18-19:
And before they were laid down, she came up unto them upon the roof; And she said unto the men, I know that the Lord hath given you the land, and that your terror is fallen upon us, and that all the inhabitants of the land faint because of you. Now therefore, I pray you, swear unto me

by the Lord, since I have shewed you kindness, that ye will also shew kindness unto my father's house, and give me a true token: And that ye will save alive my father, and my mother, and my brethren, and my sisters, and all that they have, and deliver our lives from death. Behold, when we come into the land, thou shalt bind this line of scarlet thread in the window which thou didst let us down by: and thou shalt bring thy father, and thy mother, and thy brethren, and all thy father's household, home unto thee. And it shall be, that whosoever shall go out of the doors of thy house into the street, his blood shall be upon his head, and we will be guiltless: and whosoever shall be with thee in the house, his blood shall be on our head, if any hand be upon him.

Prayer: Dear God of love and restoration; how beautiful that you would use Rahab, one who was despised by many and labelled as a harlot, to become an example of faith in God. May we faithfully serve you, by the power of the Holy Spirit. In Jesus' Name, we pray. Amen.

Never write a person off because they might surprise you when you meet with them in God's heaven. Rahab was a harlot, yet when the lives of the two men Joshua had sent to check out the land of Canaan were in danger, Rahab protected those two men in her roof. Rahab believed God would keep His promise to give the land of Canaan to the people of Israel and had faith that God would reward her for saving their lives. In in the process Rahab and her entire family were saved from destruction and she is mentioned in the book of Hebrews as a person of faith. Sometimes serving God is risky, especially in places where some are persecuted if they openly profess to be of the Christian faith. What should we do to help persecuted Christians? We must, first, pray for them. No doubt, Joshua must have prayed for and with the two men who were sent and those prayers were crucial in Rahab's decision to protect them. Secondly, give godly wisdom as indicated. Rahab gave the men specific instructions on what to do to return back to their people safely and it was after they obeyed all of them that their lives were spared. If they had obeyed one or the other but not all of Rahab's instructions, their lives may have been lost. Thirdly, leave the final result to God. God already knows those who will be martyred for Christ and in the book of Revelation, God has specific rewards for them. So, share salvation through our Lord and Savior Jesus Christ with others and allow them to respond in faith. God's favor be with you!

© By Dr. Sheila Hayford.

August 29
Let Your Yes Be Yes

Matthew Chapter 5, verses 34-35:

But I say unto you, Swear not at all; neither by heaven; for it is God's throne: Nor by the earth; for it is his footstool: neither by Jerusalem; for it is the city of the great King.

James Chapter 5, verse 12:

But above all things, my brethren, swear not, neither by heaven, neither by the earth, neither by any other oath: but let your yea be yea; and your nay, nay; lest ye fall into condemnation.

Prayer: Dear God; profanity is not acceptable to you. Help us to be mindful of the words we speak. In Jesus' name, Amen.

In the society we live in, some swear and use profanity in their everyday conversation as if it were an acceptable form of conversation. However, as professing Christians, we must ask ourselves if such conversation is acceptable to God. The Lord Jesus in the book of Matthews says we must not swear at all. And the Apostle James tells us not to swear, not by any person, place or oath. When a person starts to swear, they are prone to say things that may lead them into sin and since we know the words we speak are important, we must all be mindful of our words. So what should a person who struggles with profanity and swearing do? The first would be to acknowledge their problem and their need for God's help. Help is available for humanity through our Lord Jesus Christ and the Holy Spirit is given freely to all who receive the

Lord Jesus as Lord and Savior. The Holy Spirit indwells every born again believer and is our help as we live the Christian life. God's work in each of us is an ongoing process on this earth and thus we must be patient with ourselves and with God as we allow God's Word to change and transform our lives.

© By Dr. Sheila Hayford.

August 30
Jacob: Dressed In Deceit

Genesis Chapter 27, verses 15-19:

And Rebekah took goodly raiment of her eldest son Esau, which were with her in the house, and put them upon Jacob her younger son: And she put the skins of the kids of the goats upon his hands, and upon the smooth of his neck: And she gave the savoury meat and the bread, which she had prepared, into the hand of her son Jacob. And he came unto his father, and said, My father: and he said, Here am I; who art thou, my son? And Jacob said unto his father, I am Esau thy first born; I have done according as thou badest me: arise, I pray thee, sit and eat of my venison, that thy soul may bless me.

Prayer: Dear God, help us not to fall for the deceitfulness of satan. In Jesus' Name, Amen.

Why would Rebekah do that to her sons? Why would she dress Jacob in such a manner as to deceive his father into thinking that Jacob was Esau? Her actions resulted in a huge rift between the two brothers with unnecessary heartache and pain. In fact, if God had not intervened in the life of Jacob, who knows what would have happened? The good news is that Jacob subsequently had many encounters with God and repented towards God. God, however, allowed Jacob's children to lie to Jacob and to deceive Jacob about their brother Joseph, whom his brothers mistreated by selling him into slavery after changing their initial plan to kill Joseph, and Jacob lived for years in agony thinking that Joseph was dead. Eventually Jacob and his family were reunited with Joseph and God changed Jacob's Name from Jacob the deceiver to Israel, a prince. Each human being since Adam and Eve is born into this earth dressed in the garment of sin because Adam and Eve allowed the deceiver, satan, to cause them to disobey God. However, when a person receives the Lord Jesus Christ as Lord and Savior, they become born again believers and children of God Almighty through Christ and thus become princes and princesses. Glory to God!

© By Dr. Sheila Hayford.

August 31
August Company

Joshua Chapter 5, verses 13-15:
Now when Joshua was near Jericho, he looked up and saw a man standing in front of him with a drawn sword in his hand. Joshua went up to him and asked, "Are you for us or for our enemies?" "Neither," he replied, "but as commander of the army of the Lord I have now come." Then Joshua fell facedown to the ground in reverence, and asked him, "What message does my Lord have for his servant?" The commander of the Lord's army replied, "Take off your sandals, for the place where you are standing is holy." And Joshua did so. (NIV)

Prayer: Dear Lord Jesus, it is amazingly marvelous and wonderful that we are blessed and favored to have God as our heavenly Father and to be in the company of those of the household of faith who believe and put their faith in you; past, present and future. Thank you so very much. Amen.

When a person is in distinguished company, they may be referred to as being in august company. When the prophet Moses met God though the burning bush encounter, God asked the prophet Moses to take off his sandals for the prophet Moses was on holy ground. Billions in humanity will never have that experience. However, in these verses, Joshua was favored in God's mercy to have a similar experience. Joshua met someone in the likeness of a man with a sword drawn. And so, Joshua asked the man a question, seeking to know on whose side the man was fighting. To Joshua's amazement, the Man was a commander of the army of the Lord and Joshua fell before him in reverence. The Man asked Joshua to take off his sandals, for Joshua was standing on holy ground. In the next chapter we are told the LORD then gave Joshua specific instructions on how they would win Jericho. The fighting men with Joshua were to march around the walls of Jericho with the priests blowing the trumpets once a day for six days with the fighting men in silence and on the seventh day they were to march seven times with the priests blowing the trumpets. When the entire army heard the long blast of the trumpet, they were to give a loud shout, the walls of Jericho would fall and God would give them victory. Joshua and the people obeyed God and God did exactly as He promised, with Rahab and her entire family being spared because of her act of kindness towards the two men Joshua had earlier sent to Jericho. What august company; the prophet Moses and Joshua, favored to be with God on holy ground. Through our Lord Jesus Christ, we now can have audience with this Great and Awesome God.

© By Dr. Sheila Hayford.

September 1
Everlasting Light

Revelation Chapter 21, verse 23:
And the city had no need of the sun, neither of the moon, to shine in it: for the glory of God did lighten it, and the Lamb is the light thereof.
Prayer: Dear God; I joyfully reflect on this verse as I imagine how glorious it will be in that city that needs no sun nor moon. We thank you that through our Lord Jesus Christ, you are always with us. Hallelujah! In Jesus' Name, Amen.

I enjoy the summer days filled with long daylight hours! When the seasons change, I do not like to see those shorter daylight hours. How glorious it will be in that wonderful city, described in the book of Revelation, where we will have no need of the sun, nor of the moon. The glory of God and the Eternal Lamb of God, King of kings and Lord of lords, the Light of the World, Jesus Christ, will be the light. Human words could not begin to describe that experience. We are trusting God's keeping power and look forward to being in that city. Shout for joy!!

© By Dr. Sheila Hayford.

September 2
Flocks Have Responsibilities Too!

Ezekiel Chapter 34, verse 2:
Son of man, prophesy against the shepherds of Israel, prophesy, and say unto them, Thus saith the Lord God unto the shepherds; Woe be to the shepherds of Israel that do feed themselves! should not the shepherds feed the flocks?

2 Timothy Chapter 2, verse 15:
Study to shew thyself approved unto God, a workman that needeth not to be ashamed, rightly dividing the word of truth.

Prayer: Dear God; help us spend time in your Word and enable us, by the Holy Spirit, to discern truth from error. In Jesus' Name, Amen.

I enjoy hearing from God. However, I do not always agree with what I hear said by some to be the interpretation of Scripture when I compare what some say with the written word of God. Many times that might be due to a misunderstanding or misinterpretation of the grammar of the English language. At other times, it is plainly a false representation of Scripture. So, one time I went to God upset after I heard what I knew was wrong teaching being preached to a large number of people, some ignorant about what God's Word says. I asked God how he could stand to see the Preacher mislead God's people. I was so hurt for the people listening and wondered why God would let that go on … and I told God how I felt. Pastors and Preachers are described as Shepherds of the flocks in Scripture and the congregation are described as the flocks. Calmly, God responded and told me the flock had a responsibility too. God is absolutely right. You see, no one can go to God and blame another person for leading them in the wrong direction, especially if the person doing the blaming failed to do their part in studying the Bible for themselves to see if what was said was in agreement with what the Holy Bible says. Pastors have their responsibility before God and flocks have their responsibilities too!

© By Dr. Sheila Hayford.

POWER UP 4 SUCCESS
510 Duncan Road, Wilmington, DE 19809
Phone: (302) 898-4013
Email: Bryant.met@gmail.com

We offer Training, Certifications & Coaching

Start Where You Are - We help you get there!

September 3
When You Are Ready

Revelation Chapter 3, verse 20:

Behold, I stand at the door, and knock: if any man hear my voice, and open the door, I will come in to him, and will sup with him, and he with me.

Prayer: Dear Lord Jesus, we invite you in. Work with and in us as we face the challenges and tests in life. You are our perfect example and our hope and trust is in you. Amen.

He was a stranger and came to me asking for help and so we began talking. Turns out he had two small children so I asked him about his future goals. His response was "it isn't that deep!" and added that all he wanted was a one-time help, just for that particular time. It was obvious he was not ready to work towards change that would improve things for his betterment and so I did not pursue that conversation. The Lord Jesus tells us in the verse above that He stands knocking at the door of every heart. When a person is ready to change for the better and opens the door to invite the Lord Jesus into their life as their Lord and Savior, the Lord Jesus will come in and have conversations and fellowship with them. God is always willing and ready to come in when genuinely invited. Whatever the challenge or issue may be, when you are ready, invite God in. God is not only willing; God is more than able to work on your behalf.

© By Dr. Sheila Hayford.

September 4
Regular Or Premium

Psalm 37, verse 4:

Delight thyself also in the Lord: and he shall give thee the desires of thine heart.

Prayer: Dear God, we desire to grow in our relationship with you. Help us to be good disciples of our Lord Jesus Christ and to please you in all things. In Jesus' Name, Amen.

It used to be that most people would buy their coffee from the store, restaurant or fast food place. Then the custom flavored coffee became very popular. Some did not think many would be willing to pay that much for premium coffee till Starbucks showed up. Now premium coffee is almost commonplace. When it comes to your automobile, you can use regular gasoline to run your automobile or you may use the more superior premium gasoline to run it. The same principles holds true when it comes to our spiritual life. A person may be happy to invite the Lord Jesus into their heart as Lord and Savior and to escape a burning hell, as well they should. However, for those who want to grow in their relationship with God and who spend time in conversation, praise and worship with God, study Scripture and obey God, their relationship with God moves to a higher level. God desires more of us; do we desire more of God? Is your relationship with our Lord Jesus at the basic regular level or are you striving towards premium level?

© By Dr. Sheila Hayford.

September 5
Walking With The Wise

Proverbs Chapter 13, verse 20:
He that walketh with wise men shall be wise: but a companion of fools shall be destroyed.

Prayer: Dear Holy Spirit, we value your wisdom at all times. Help us to be quick to hear you speak to us and to obey your promptings right away. In Jesus' Name, Amen.

You can tell a lot about a person by the people they associate with. I once saw a student in a Tee shirt that said, "Speak nerdy to me." She had decided she wanted to associate with those with whom she had certain characteristics in common. If you associate closely with the wise, it suggests you enjoy their company and are more like to consult with them and make wise choices. The reverse is also true. Some have gotten into trouble just by being in the company of those practicing mischief. Walk with the wise and seek the All-wise Holy Spirit's counsel in all things.

© By Dr. Sheila Hayford.

September 6
Your Good Name

Proverbs Chapter 22, verse 1:

A good name is rather to be chosen than great riches, and loving favour rather than silver and gold.

Mark Chapter 8, verse 36:

For what shall it profit a man, if he shall gain the whole world, and lose his own soul?

Prayer: Dear God; thank you for the righteousness of our Lord Jesus Christ which we receive when we invite the Lord Jesus Christ into our heart and life as Lord and Savior. Nothing can compare with the Lord Jesus' good Name for it is through him and in his Name we pray. Amen.

Your Good Name is worth more to God than riches or any material wealth. You see, what God says about a person here on earth matters for all eternity. What will it profit a person if they have material wealth but, in the process, lose their soul? Furthermore, will a person be truly able to enjoy their riches on this earth if they acquired them improperly? When a person receives the Lord Jesus into their life as Lord and Savior their sins are forgiven, the slate of their past life of sin is washed clean and the person receives the righteousness of the Lord Jesus Christ. In other words, when a person receives the Lord Jesus Christ, they are born again and their name is now good with God. They may still have to deal with some of the earthly consequences of their past, but their future from the time of salvation onwards is eternally secure in Christ in God. Remember, a forever heaven or a forever hell is at stake in every person's life. Make sure your name is good with God.

© By Dr. Sheila Hayford.

September 7
God Is For Us

Jeremiah Chapter 30, verses 19-20:

From them will come songs of thanksgiving and the sound of rejoicing. I will add to their numbers, and they will not be decreased; I will bring them honor, and they will not be disdained. Their children will be as in days of old, and their community will be established before me; I will punish all who oppress them. (NIV)

Prayer: Dear God; we praise and thank you for your immense goodness to us. Indeed, you are for us through our Lord and Savior, Jesus Christ. Hallelujah! Amen.

When God is for a person, that person is forever blessed. Sometimes when a person faces challenges, those looking from the outside may not realize that test may be so that God can promote that person when they pass the test. However, when God's good promises are openly fulfilled, there is no mistaking that God is for us. With that comes God's warning. Those who try to oppress God's blessed will be punished by God. Let us come to God in worship with loud songs of rejoicing and thanksgiving, for our God continues to deal bountifully with us. Increase is in God's provision for us and not lack. Great progression is in God's plans for us. Hallelujah!

© By Dr. Sheila Hayford.

September 8
Peace With Thanksgiving

Colossians Chapter 3, verses 15-16:

Let the peace of Christ rule in your hearts, since as members of one body you were called to peace. And be thankful. Let the message of Christ dwell among you richly as you teach and admonish one another with all wisdom through psalms, hymns, and songs from the Spirit, singing to God with gratitude in your hearts. (NIV)

Prayer: Philippians Chapter 4, verse 7:

And the peace of God, which passeth all understanding, shall keep your hearts and minds through Christ Jesus. In Jesus' Name, Amen.

It is such a joy to be at peace with God and at peace with your fellow man. Does that mean everyone is in agreement with you all the time or that you are in agreement with others all of the time? No! It means that you have allowed the peace of God to **_rule_** in your heart. In other words, do not depend on your circumstances to decide how you will feel towards God and towards others. Instead, allow God's peace which is within you to have rule in you and to influence your attitude towards others and to your circumstances. Thus, you can remain thankful to God; thankful for God's peace and thankful for God's rule in your life. So, in your worship of God and in your ministry to others, allow God's peace to rule in you <u>with</u> thanksgiving.

© By Dr. Sheila Hayford.

September 9
Chosen!

1 Thessalonians Chapter1, verse 4:

Knowing, brethren beloved, your election of God.

Romans Chapter 9, verses 24-26:

Even us, whom he hath called, not of the Jews only, but also of the Gentiles? As he saith also in Osee, I will call them my people, which were not my people; and her beloved, which was not beloved. And it shall come to pass, that in the place where it was said unto them, Ye are not my people; there shall they be called the children of the living God.

Prayer: Dear God; I find myself in awe of the fact that we are your beloved children for even before we were born into this world, you accepted us through our Lord Jesus Christ. We are thankful and grateful to you. We love you dearly. In Jesus' name, Amen.

There is the glow of the bride and the joy of the bridegroom at the wedding. Her glow and his joy reflect the fact that they have been chosen! Of all the women in the world, he chose her to be his bride and of all the men in the world she chose him to be her husband. So it is with our bridegroom, our Lord and Savior, Jesus Christ. And we, his bride, are glowing! Before we were even born into this world, God had chosen us to be his. Amazing! So then, if you say we are chosen, do you mean some have not been chosen to be part of God's family? No! A person's acceptance or rejection of God depends on that person's free-will. However, the All-knowing, Almighty God knows in advance those who will choose to receive the Lord Jesus as Lord and Savior on this earth and has accepted us into His beloved. How awesome is that!

© By Dr. Sheila Hayford.

September 10
The Rewards Of Ownership

1 Corinthians Chapter 3, verses 11-15:
For other foundation can no man lay than that is laid, which is Jesus Christ. Now if any man build upon this foundation gold, silver, precious stones, wood, hay, stubble; Every man's work shall be made manifest: for the day shall declare it, because it shall be revealed by fire; and the fire shall try every man's work of what sort it is. If any man's work abide which he hath built thereupon, he shall receive a reward. If any man's work shall be burned, he shall suffer loss: but he himself shall be saved; yet so as by fire.

Prayer: Dear God; help us as we grow in and live our Christian life. May we experience the rewards of ownership. In Jesus' name, Amen.

Oh! The Joys of Ownership! You worked hard and bought that new home or new car. You own it, as long as you make those timely loan payments or have paid for your home or car in full. Now you get to enjoy it. Nice! Is that the kind of ownership we are discussing today when it comes to the Rewards of Ownership? No! The Rewards of Ownership in these verses are based on your ownership of the works you accomplished while you are here on earth and are given on what is referred to as the Day of the Lord when the works of each individual person are judged by God. God says each person's work on that day will be tested by fire. If their work remains intact through the fire, that person will receive a reward from God. If the person's work is burned and they are a born again believer, they will still have escaped hell's fire but they will not receive a reward for their work. Remember, the foundation we each get to build on is our Lord Jesus Christ. Yes, the Lord Jesus Christ saves us, but we have to *work out our salvation*, that is, take ownership of how we grow and the works we do in our relationship with the Lord Jesus Christ. May we be in place to receive God's rewards!

© By Dr. Sheila Hayford.

September 11
A New Era

Daniel Chapter 6, verses 26-27:

I make a decree, That in every dominion of my kingdom men tremble and fear before the God of Daniel: for he is the living God, and stedfast for ever, and his kingdom that which shall not be destroyed, and his dominion shall be even unto the end. He delivereth and rescueth, and he worketh signs and wonders in heaven and in earth, who hath delivered Daniel from the power of the lions.

Prayer: Dear God, we thank you for your mighty power at work in the lives of humanity. Thank you for the gift of your Son, the Lord Jesus, to humanity and the gift of the Holy Spirit who ushered in a New Era for the kingdom of God is now God with us and God within us. Hallelujah! In Jesus' name, Amen.

Life before that September 11th day was simpler. It was not that things were necessarily easier. It was that people were more trusting and many could not imagine that such hatred for a fellow human being could exist. And so a new era of anticipated harmful acts, fear, increased anxiety and distrust was ushered in. In an effort to ease the fears of many, a lot of changes were made. When the Lord Jesus came to earth and began preaching and teaching, many of those living at the time were familiar with the Scriptures of the Old Testament. However, the Lord Jesus was and is the fulfillment of those Scriptures and promises made by God and so he ushered in a New Era. No longer was the kingdom of God *at hand* as preached by John the Baptist, the kingdom of God is here. How wonderful! We can boldly come to God's throne in the name of the Lord Jesus and have an audience with God. Are you taking the Lord Jesus at his word or are you still depending on man's traditions such as humanly defined good works and sacrifices to get you into God's presence? A new decade has begun. Move forward in God's New Era!

© By Dr. Sheila Hayford.

September 12
Depravity? Remember Lot's Rescue

2 Peter Chapter 2, verses 7-9:
and if he rescued Lot, a righteous man, who was distressed by the depraved conduct of the lawless (for that righteous man, living among them day after day, was tormented in his righteous soul by the lawless deeds he saw and heard) - if this is so, then the Lord knows how to rescue the godly from trials and to hold the unrighteous for punishment on the day of judgment. (NIV)

1 Corinthians Chapter 10, verse 13:

There hath no temptation taken you but such as is common to man: but God is faithful, who will not suffer you to be tempted above that ye are able; but will with the temptation also make a way to escape, that ye may be able to bear it.

Prayer: Dear God; thank you that you will not allow any of your children to be tempted beyond their ability, through the power of the Holy Spirit. So let us have faith in you and trust you for we are overcomers in Jesus Christ, in whose Name we pray. Amen.

Have you heard some cursing and using profanity when they should have known better? I have stood with others to take a stand not to participate in what we viewed as disrespectful to our Lord Jesus, even when some did not find that necessary. So what does a person do when increasingly faced with an environment that is hostile to their faith? In addition to prayer and seeking God's wisdom, one must remember Lot's rescue. To be fair, Lot was partly to blame for his situation because he chose the place where he would live based on how it looked externally. Maybe if Lot had consulted with God on that matter, Lot might have chosen a different area to live. Nevertheless, Lot had to put up with the depravity in his environment; until God said, "Enough!" and sent his angel to rescue Lot and Lot's family. It was a miraculous intervention by God and a lesson to us that God knows when enough is enough and will not allow a person to be tempted beyond what they can bear. If God trusts you to be able to withstand the temptation by God's grace and power, you must trust God also for your rescue. When God says, "Enough!" so it is!

© By Dr. Sheila Hayford.

September 13
Taught By The Lord

Isaiah Chapter 54, verse 13:

And all thy children shall be taught of the Lord; and great shall be the peace of thy children.

Prayer: Dear God; Your Family Protection Plan comes with wonderful promises! We receive your great promises, In Jesus' Name. Amen.

Yesterday, we read of God's dramatic rescue of Lot and Lot's family from evil. Today we read of what I call God's Family Protection Plan. How does this work? It is put in motion when children are brought up in the reverence and knowledge of God. By that I do not mean forceful church services attendance as if attendance at church services was a form of punishment, nor do I mean telling children how they ought to live godly lives when the parents are not modelling godly living to their children. While church service attendance is good and godly living is to be desired, teaching children, by God's help, about the love, strength and power of God and to love the Lord Jesus because of what God has done for us in Christ is very important. Teaching a child right from wrong and helping each child develop their personal relationship with God puts the child in a position of peace and security and under the protection of the Almighty God. So do not be timid when it comes to raising your children with God's principles. Great will be their peace, as well as your peace of mind in knowing that with God's help you raised your children right.

© By Dr. Sheila Hayford.

September 14
Long Term and Long Range

Jeremiah Chapter 29, verse 11:
For I know the plans I have for you," declares the Lord, "plans to prosper you and not to harm you, plans to give you hope and a future. (NIV)

Prayer: Dear God; enable us to choose your long-term eternal plans for us with their far-reaching implications on this earth and throughout eternity. I Jesus' Name, Amen.

Long term versus long range; is there a difference? Yes, there is. When a person plans long term they are planning for an extended period of time. However, when a person plans long range, it may not necessarily be for a long period of time but it has far reaching effects, that is, the effects span a wide area. The Holy Spirit wants us to have both; long term and long-range planning, effectiveness and influence. Long term planning involves planning for this earth and for eternity to come. Long range planning involves effecting God's plans and purpose here on earth as we share the good news of salvation with others and allow the far reaching power and influence of the Holy Spirit, working in and through us, to effect change. By God's power, may we achieve both!

© By Dr. Sheila Hayford.

September 15
Antique or Outdated?

John Chapter 4, verses 28-29, 41-42:
The woman then left her waterpot, and went her way into the city, and saith to the men, Come, see a man, which told me all things that ever I did: is not this the Christ? And many more believed because of his own word; And said unto the woman, Now we believe, not because of thy saying: for we have heard him ourselves, and know that this is indeed the Christ, the Saviour of the world.

Prayer: Dear God, we thank you for the written Word of God and the living Word of God, your Son and our Lord and Savior, Jesus Christ. You are always relevant, never outdated. In Jesus' Name, Amen.

I love antiques! I enjoy history and love to see artifacts and antique items representing different times. It can be very fascinating. At the same time, I also care about things being relevant to the times we live in.

Antique cars are sometimes restored by their owners, not only to show us how those cars looked and the way they were designed to function, they are sometimes restored to be able to be driven on the roads. Sometimes a person may hold onto clothes they have not worn in a long time or that they never wore. With time, those clothes become out of fashion or outdated. The Word of God is relevant for all times. Thus the Holy Bible is not meant to be an antique item on the shelf in your home or given to others as an antique keepsake. The Holy Bible is intended by God to be read by humanity and applied. Are you living according to the applied Word of God?

© By Dr. Sheila Hayford.

September 16
Trucks

1 Timothy Chapter 2, verse1:
I urge, then, first of all, that petitions, prayers, intercession and thanksgiving be made for all people -
Prayer: Dear God, prayer is vitally important in our relationship with you. Help us, by the Holy Spirit, to pray to you sincerely and in truth. In Jesus' Name, Amen.

I am fascinated by tires. And not just any tires? I am fascinated by large tires, the ones used by farmers and on large trucks. I did not grow up on a farm, and find it is interesting to watch the farm machines at work, not minimizing all the hard work that entails. However, larger is not necessarily better. In the gospels the Lord Jesus chided the scribes for their long prayers. They were making a pretense of their prayers by praying long prayers in order to impress people and not God. God was not equating their sincerity to the length of their prayers but to the condition of their heart. If you have a large truck that needs those large tires to function, that is well and good. If you pray long sincere prayers as you commune with God, that is well and good. However, we must all make sure that whatever we do, our priority should be to do everything in sincerity towards God and in truth.

© By Dr. Sheila Hayford.

September 17
Games; Productive or Non-Productive?

Romans Chapter 6, verse 22:
But now being made free from sin, and become servants to God, ye have your fruit unto holiness, and the end everlasting life.

Prayer: Dear God; May pleasing you be the primary focus of our lives, with our eternal destiny in mind. In Jesus' Name, Amen.

I enjoy Sports; Basketball, football, soccer, track and more. I am not, however, into video games. I like the discipline and training of the athletes as they perform their skills and abilities, especially in competition. Many are focused in their mind, on a rigorous diet, a strict schedule and are trained to face and overcome challenges in the sport. The question for me becomes, when is a game or sport productive as a hobby or profession and when does it become non-productive? Why the question? I personally do not know anyone who does not like the famed basketball player, Michael Jordan. I admired him on the court when he came to play in my home state, I admired his grace under pressure and his civility to the opposing team. On the other hand, there are times we read of an athlete who became overwhelmed by their success and turned to illicit drug abuse, gambling or infidelity. The game that once had provided provision and success had now become non-productive because of the way the athlete was handling it and it was ruining their life. That athlete needed some time off to re-evaluate their life and get things in proper focus. The Bible says whoever or whatever rules a person is who or what a person serves. Does God have rule in your life?

© By Dr. Sheila Hayford.

September 18
Suited For God's Battle

Ephesians Chapter 6, verses 13-17:

Wherefore take unto you the whole armour of God, that ye may be able to withstand in the evil day, and having done all, to stand. Stand therefore, having your loins girt about with truth, and having on the breastplate of righteousness; And your feet shod with the preparation of the gospel of peace; Above all, taking the shield of faith, wherewith ye shall be able to quench all the fiery darts of the wicked. And take the helmet of salvation, and the sword of the Spirit, which is the word of God:

Prayer: Our Heavenly Father, you have provided humanity with everything we need to win in life through our Lord and Savior, Jesus Christ. Help us to follow your plan. In Jesus' Name, Amen.

As soldiers of the Lord Jesus Christ's army, we are engaged in God's battle against the devil and all the evil that follows with the devil. Every soldier depends on his or Commander-In-Chief as to how the battle is to be waged, what to wear, etc. If the soldier puts on only a part of the necessary armor and goes to war, they may get hurt. In these verses we are told what armor what God want us to put on. Each part of the armor is important. Negligence in one part may cause the armor to be lopsided and ineffective. Let us make sure that with God's help, we are properly suited for God's battle.

© By Dr. Sheila Hayford.

September 19
Don't Limit Yourself

John Chapter 9, verse 4:

I must work the works of him that sent me, while it is day: the night cometh, when no man can work.

Prayer: Dear Heavenly Father; help us make full use of the time you have given us here on earth. In Jesus' Name, Amen.

There have been many times I have seen untapped potential in a person, just waiting to come forth. I may take the initiative and have a discussion about their abilities and talents and the way those could impact others for good. Many times, the individual is already waiting for confirmation or a way to express their gift. However, there have been others whose first response is surprise, followed by doubt that their talent or ability is of any significance. Some even doubt their own self-worth. God brought us into this worth intricately woven with talents, gifts and abilities and we each have a part to play in unwrapping those gifts, talents and abilities; in ourselves and in others. Remember, there are some talents and abilities that are only useful in this earth realm arena so don't leave earth with your earth talents and abilities unwrapped.

© By Dr. Sheila Hayford.

September 20
Forthright Diplomacy

Proverbs Chapter 8, verse 6, 7:
Hear; for I will speak of excellent things; and the opening of my lips shall be right things. For my mouth shall speak truth; and wickedness is an abomination to my lips.

Prayer: Dear God; we look to you in all things. Help us as we speak your uncompromising truths in love. In Jesus' Name. Amen.

I have a personality that does not like to beat around the bush. I say what I mean. The Bible tells us to be quick to hear, slow to speak and slow to ager. Which means, I have to reflect on my words before I speak. I like to ask God what or how God would have me speak so that what I say is in accordance with what God wants. Sometimes God will say to be quiet, other times God will let me speak. The challenge comes when what God says may not be what the person wants to hear. Then comes the need for forthright diplomacy; speaking God's truths forthrightly, without being obnoxious. The verses here give guidelines in such circumstances; speak of excellent things, speak right, speak truth and do not speak lies, gossip, profanity, backbiting or with wicked intentions. God wants us to yield to the Holy Spirit's promptings in what to say and how we say it and to leave the results to God.

© By Dr. Sheila Hayford.

September 21
The Finished Product

Philippians Chapter 1, verse 6:
Being confident of this very thing, that he which hath begun a good work in you will perform it until the day of Jesus Christ:
Prayer: Dear God, we are trusting your finishing power to complete the assignments you have given us. In Jesus' Name, Amen.

In the first Morning Glory we had a devotional entitled, "It Looks A Mess Right Now!" In that devotional, I discussed construction workers working on a commercial building project. Well, there was a particular construction building project I saw from the start to finish in the downtown area. It wasn't even in an area one would have thought had enough space for an apartment complex with adjacent parking areas and it looked a mess when construction started and in the earlier stages of the building project. Now take a look at the finished product. It is a marvel! Expensive apartments with luxury amenities, easy parking on site and access to a lot of places. The owners were forward thinkers, seeing and recognizing what others may have missed and used that opportunity to develop the area for the benefit of many. God is the Ultimate Forward Planner and God's plans span eternity. We are God's "Work in Progress" right now but in God's timing, our "Finished" product will show. Bless and thank God!

© By Dr. Sheila Hayford.

September 22
The Legendary Architect: Phil Freelon

James Chapter 2, verse 22:
Seest thou how faith wrought with his works, and by works was faith made perfect?
Prayer: Dear God; help us put some works with our faith and thus bring you glory. In Jesus' Name, Amen.

I have tremendous respect and admiration for Phil Freelon, the lead Architect of The National Museum of African American History and Culture (NMAAHC) which is part of the Smithsonian Museums in Washington, D.C. One of the things I really admire about Phil Freelon is that he did not rest on his laurels after completing many successful projects. Nurtured by his wonderful family, Phil studied and excelled in Architecture. He founded an Architectural Firm, taught, designed many buildings and won numerous awards. In North Carolina, he was the architect for the Durham Ballpark, as well as a Raleigh-Durham International Airport Terminal, Public Libraries, Government and University buildings. He designed many other notable buildings including the Center for Civil and Human Rights in Atlanta, Georgia and the Emancipation Park Conservancy in Houston, Texas. His crowning pinnacle of success is, of course, The National Museum of African American History and Culture. All these works continue to still bear testimony to his hard work ethic. Phil was a wonderful husband, father and grandparent and a fine example of a commitment to use the gifts and talents received from our Creator for the good of humanity. What are we building with the gifts and talents we have received from God?

© By Dr. Sheila Hayford.

September 23
Do You Remember When ...?

Hebrews Chapter 10, verse 17:
And their sins and iniquities will I remember no more.
Prayer: Dear God; thank you for the gift of forgiveness that you extend to us. Help us to extend the gift of forgiveness to ourselves and to others and to live victoriously. In Jesus' Name, Amen.

This elderly group were having a nostalgic conversation. The lady said, "Remember those cookies [and then she said the name of those cookies] that we used to buy. They were so sweet! They were better than the Oreo Cookies!" She looked at one of the guys and he said, "No, I don't remember!" They all laughed! That is what God says when you go to him talking about the past sins God forgave you. God does not remember them. So why do you? The devil wants you to walk in condemnation. God wants you to walk in victory. Move on with God!

© By Dr. Sheila Hayford.

September 24
I'm Grown Up Now

Hebrews Chapter 5, verse 14:
But strong meat belongeth to them that are of full age, even those who by reason of use have their senses exercised to discern both good and evil.
Prayer: My Heavenly Father; the more I know you, the more I want to grow in you. So help me, In Jesus' Name, Amen.

I had known him when his mother would bring him to church. He loved the Lord and we were overjoyed when he went to college. In his first year of college his mother would pick him up and he would spend the weekends at home. Well, his mother moved and when I saw him at church I asked about college and he said he had one semester remaining. It seemed like that time went by fast. I also asked about his family and whether he had been home for the weekend. He said he had not been home that weekend. And then after a brief pause he added, "Unless there is a holiday or something special, I don't go home for the weekend." I was impressed! He was essentially saying, "I'm grown up now!" Wow! Isn't that what we want for our children? That they grow up. God wants that for His children; that they grow up. So it is time to feast on strong meat from God's table; the milk is good but it is for babies. God wants to bring the filet mignon!

© By Dr. Sheila Hayford.

September 25
Take Care

Hebrews Chapter 2, verse 1:
Therefore we ought to give the more earnest heed to the things which we have heard, lest at any time we should let them slip.

Prayer: Dear God; help us never to take you and our relationship with you through our Lord Jesus Christ for granted. Yes, we are secure in you in Christ and we are very thankful. In Jesus' Name, Amen.

Why should we take care? It is because in any relationship, when people take each other for granted they can become less appreciative of what they have and allow the relationship to stagnate or grow cold. When a person takes God and God's grace for granted, they may become less appreciative of all they have in Christ in God instead of being diligent and growing in their relationship with our Lord Jesus Christ and in the power of God the Holy Spirit. They might even become dull of hearing to the plans and purposes of God for their life. So the verse warns us to pay attention and earnestly heard the Word of God. The highway sign on the road of life each day is "Take Care! Extreme Caution Needed!

© By Dr. Sheila Hayford.

September 26
Abundance

Matthew Chapter 6, verse 31-33:

Therefore take no thought, saying, What shall we eat? or, What shall we drink? or, Wherewithal shall we be clothed? (For after all these things do the Gentiles seek:) for your heavenly Father knoweth that ye have need of all these things. But seek ye first the kingdom of God, and his righteousness; and all these things shall be added unto you.

Prayer: Our heavenly Father, we come to you with our desire to have our priorities right. So help us to meet your needs and the needs of your kingdom and we will have plenty or far more than enough. In Jesus' Name, Amen.

Why worry? Yes, God knows we have needs and that is why God promises to take care of our needs. However, God's promise of provision is conditional. We have to seek the good of God and the good of God's kingdom and then what we need and desire from God will be given by God to us. What does God need or desire of us? What do we need or desire of God? Let us, by the power of God the Holy Spirit, make it happen.

© By Dr. Sheila Hayford.

September 27
Pressing On

Philippians Chapter 3, verse 14:

I press toward the mark for the prize of the high calling of God in Christ Jesus.

Prayer: Dear God; enable us by your power to keep moving forward, striving for excellence in all that we do for we want to hear those precious words, 'Well Done!" In Jesus' Name, Amen.

As a person grows in their Christian walk and meets people of different races and cultures, there may be the temptation to compare themselves with others. However, the Christian journey is not a comparative race, it is a "finish your race" marathon. Every person has their life's journey planned out for them by God and the goal of every individual should be to discover and run that race. So throw aside hindrances and unnecessary burdens that are designed to keep you in the same position year after year. If a person is not moving forward, they may get left behind. There is a prize waiting for those who complete their race according to God's specifications. Press on towards the finish line!

© By Dr. Sheila Hayford.

September 28
Woven:

Ephesians Chapter 2, verse 22:
And in him you too are being built together to become a dwelling in which God lives by his Spirit. (NIV)

Prayer: Dear God; you are an awesome Creation. I marvel at your works and your infinite wisdom. Help us to make our bodies worthy temples of the Holy Spirit. In Jesus' Name we pray. Amen.

We know we are collectively a part of the body of believers through the salvation we received from our Lord and Savior Jesus Christ. It is also wonderful to know that individually we are houses or temples of God the Holy Spirit. So while God, the Master Designer, has designed the church body with many parts meant to function as a collective unit, God has intricately woven our parts and designed us to house God the Holy Spirit within us. So our focus should be to make sure that as God's temple, the Holy Spirit within us is comfortable, is free to move anywhere and at all times and is not grieved. So help us, dear Holy Spirit. In Jesus' Name, Amen.

© By Dr. Sheila Hayford.

September 29
Hold Fast

Hebrews Chapter 2, verses 23-24:
Let us hold fast the profession of our faith without wavering; (for he is faithful that promised;) And let us consider one another to provoke unto love and to good works:

Prayer: Dear Holy Spirit, help us to hold fast in our profession and confessions of faith in Christ Jesus. We love you. In Jesus' Name, Amen.

Hold fast! When it seems like you are the only one who is hopeful, hold fast! When it seems like you are the one doing all the work, hold fast! When it seems like you are the only one rejoicing in Christ in God, hold fast! When it seems like you are the only one who is serving God, hold fast! Do not lose your joy and do not lose your drive. Keep loving others with God's love and encouraging others as you serve your God. Our faithful God sees and our faithful God rewards!

© By Dr. Sheila Hayford.

September 30
If You Know God, Say So

Revelation Chapter 1, verse 2:
Who bare record of the word of God, and of the testimony of Jesus Christ, and of all things that he saw.

Prayer: Dear God, help us not to be stingy in sharing our Christian faith with others. In Jesus' Name, Amen.

The Apostle John, the disciple of our Lord and savior Jesus Christ, wrote down his knowledge of and experience with the Lord Jesus Christ in the gospel of John and shared that with others in the hope that they might also believe in the Lord Jesus. In the Book of revelation, the Lord Jesus Christ trusted the Apostle John to share with humanity the Revelation the Lord Jesus Christ gave him. What do you know about the Lord Jesus Christ? What is your experience with the Lord Jesus Christ? What has God done for you? Share God with the hope that many will be encouraged and that many will have faith and believe on the Lord Jesus Christ.

© By Dr. Sheila Hayford.

October 1
Live Long

Psalm 91, verses 14-16:
Because he hath set his love upon me, therefore will I deliver him: I will set him on high, because he hath known my name. He shall call upon me, and I will answer him: I will be with him in trouble; I will deliver him, and honour him. With long life will I satisfy him, and shew him my salvation.

Prayer: Dear God, we thank you for the gift of life. Help us to use our time on this earth wisely. In Jesus' Name, Amen.

Thank God for giving us light or illumination when it comes to long life. There are many promises in the Bible God gives us when it comes to long life, understanding God's conditions and recognizing the unique life God has for each individual.

Here are three of God's conditions for long life:
- Unswervable in our love for God

- Know the "I AM" God in God's various names – Lord, Savior, Healer, Provider, Protector, Deliverer, and more where needed
- Call on God; in prayer, in song, in shout, in cry, in praise, in worship, in posture, in life

Rewards that God promises us include:
- Answers to our prayers
- God's presence in the midst of our challenges
- God's deliverance
- God's honor and promotion
- Long life

Of course, when we know God as Lord, we serve and honor God by taking good care of our bodies, eating right, exercising and living for God. Live long and live strong in Christ.

© By Dr. Sheila Hayford.

October 2
God's Show And Tell

Hebrews Chapter 11, verses 17-23:

By faith Abraham, when he was tried, offered up Isaac: and he that had received the promises offered up his only begotten son, Of whom it was said, That in Isaac shall thy seed be called: Accounting that God was able to raise him up, even from the dead; from whence also he received him in a figure. By faith Isaac blessed Jacob and Esau concerning things to come. By faith Jacob, when he was a dying, blessed both the sons of Joseph; and worshipped, leaning upon the top of his staff. By faith Joseph, when he died, made mention of the departing of the children of Israel; and gave commandment concerning his bones. By faith Moses, when he was born, was hid three months of his parents, because they saw he was a proper child; and they were not afraid of the king's commandment.

Prayer: Dear God, we are honored to read about your choice children of faith; choice because they chose to believe in you and in your Word. Help us to be godly examples in our generation and to influence generations to come for good. In Jesus' Name, Amen.

What an encouragement this chapter of God's Show and Tell is to humanity. We read of 'ordinary' people believing God's promises in spite of the challenges they were facing and in the process receiving amazing rewards from God. Abraham had waited for about a century to have the child God promised, Isaac. So when God asked Abraham to sacrifice his son, Isaac, it seemed a contradiction of sorts. But not to Abraham. Abraham believed God could raise his son Isaac from the dead. Moreover, Abraham told his son, Isaac as they were going up in what seemed a sacrifice of Isaac, that God would provide himself the ram to be sacrificed and told his servants that he and Isaac would both return back from the mountain. Indeed, God told Abraham not to sacrifice Isaac in what was a test of Abraham's faith and God did himself provide humanity with his Son, the Lord Jesus Christ who sacrificed his life for the sins of humanity and rose from the dead. Wow! Are you in God's Show and Tell book? Remember, your story is still being written. Rahab had messed up before she got in God's Show and Tell chapter. Joseph went through a lot of hard times before God made it up to him on this earth with promotion, power and plenty and he is in God's Show and Tell chapter. What will be your story to future generations?

© By Dr. Sheila Hayford.

October 3
The Miracle Of Multiplication

Genesis Chapter 24, verses 34-36:
And he said, I am Abraham's servant. And the Lord hath blessed my master greatly; and he is become great: and he hath given him flocks, and herds, and silver, and gold, and menservants, and maidservants, and

camels, and asses. And Sarah my master's wife bare a son to my master when she was old: and unto him hath he given all that he hath

Luke Chapter 6, verse 38:

Give, and it will be given to you. A good measure, pressed down, shaken together and running over, will be poured into your lap. For with the measure you use, it will be measured to you." (NIV)

Prayer: Dear God; we can never outdo you; we wouldn't even try to. Thank you for your goodness and faithfulness to us, through Jesus Christ our Lord, in whose Name we pray. Amen.

God is a God of plenty. God has an abundance of all things good so when God gives us this promise in the book of Luke, God is able to make it good. We read of Abraham in the Bible as the Father of faith and he is. As Abraham obeyed God and gave to God willingly and obediently, God blessed Father Abraham so much that Abraham's servant had this testimony to say about Father Abraham, "… the Lord hath blessed my master greatly; and then went on to list some of the blessings God had given Abraham. Remember, the Miracle of Multiplication not only applies when you give to others, it also applies when you give to God. Bless God! God is looking for an opportunity to show Himself faithful.

© By Dr. Sheila Hayford.

October 4
The Miracle Of Healing: Do Something!

Mark Chapter 2, verses 3-5, 8-12:

And they come unto him, bringing one sick of the palsy, which was borne of four. And when they could not come nigh unto him for the press, they uncovered the roof where he was: and when they had broken it up, they let down the bed wherein the sick of the palsy lay. When Jesus saw their faith, he said unto the sick of the palsy, Son, thy sins be forgiven And immediately when Jesus perceived in his spirit that they so reasoned within themselves, he said unto them, Why reason ye these things in your hearts? Whether is it easier to say to the sick of the palsy, Thy sins be forgiven thee; or to say, Arise, and take up thy bed, and walk? But that ye may know that the Son of man hath power on earth to forgive sins, (he saith to the sick of the palsy,) I say unto thee, Arise, and take up thy bed, and go thy way into thine house. And immediately he arose, took up the bed, and went forth before them all; insomuch that they were all amazed, and glorified God, saying, We never saw it on this fashion.

Prayer: Dear Lord Jesus; Yours is the Name that is above all names and before you every knee must bow. The knees of sickness bow to you, the knees of sin bow to you. The knees of satan bow to you. Thank you for redeeming humanity from the curse of sin. We love you and we worship you. Amen.

The miracle of healing is not a passive act. If a person desires something from God, that person has to do something. The person may call on God in prayer and study God's Word to find out what God has to say on the issue. When it comes to healing, it is no different. A person has to bring God some faith. Look at the faith of the four friends who brought the sick man to Jesus to be healed. When they realized there were too many people for them to walk through the crowd, they brought the Lord Jesus some determination. They uncovered part of the roof and then let their friend down through the roof! The Lord Jesus was so impressed he not only healed the sick man but forgave the man's sins. Could the man's sins have something to do with his sickness? We are not told. However, we do know that Jesus did not hold his sins against him when he came to the Lord Jesus for help; the Lord Jesus healed him and forgave his sins. And so with the faith and determination of his friends and the faith of the sick man, the Lord Jesus gave the sick man a multiplication of miracles. What miracles do you need from God? Do something!

© By Dr. Sheila Hayford.

October 5
The Miracle of Deliverance: Do Not Panic!

Daniel Chapter 6, verses 19-23:

Then the king arose very early in the morning, and went in haste unto the den of lions. And when he came to the den, he cried with a lamentable voice unto Daniel: and the king spake and said to Daniel, O Daniel, servant of the living God, is thy God, whom thou servest continually, able to deliver thee from the lions? Then said Daniel unto the king, O king, live for ever. My God hath sent his angel, and hath shut the lions' mouths, that they have not hurt me: forasmuch as before him innocency was found in me; and also before thee, O king, have I done no hurt. Then was the king exceedingly glad for him, and commanded that they should take Daniel up out of the den. So Daniel was taken up out of the den, and no manner of hurt was found upon him, because he believed in his God.

Prayer: Dear God, you are our Strong Deliverer! We thank you and we praise you! Enable us to always trust you, knowing that you will always do what is best for us. In Jesus' Name. Amen.

Daniel had been unfairly put in the lions' den because his adversaries hated the fact that he was about to be promoted and so they tricked the king into signing a law that would punish Daniel for praying to God as was Daniel's habit. What was Daniel to do? Do what Daniel did. Daniel did not panic. Daniel did not change his Christian stance to save himself from the lions' den. Daniel entrusted himself to God's deliverance. And God came through for Daniel. God sent his angel to shut up the mouth of the lions. That was a miracle! So in the midst of lions, Daniel stayed calm. When the king who had been concerned about Daniel all night came in the morning to check on Daniel, Daniel was safe. And so God answered King Darius' question with a resounding, "Yes!" God is able to deliver his faithful servants, in God's way, and in God's timing.

Do not panic; trust God! © By Dr. Sheila Hayford.

October 6
The Miracle Of New Life

John Chapter 11, verses 21-27, 39-45:

Then said Martha unto Jesus, Lord, if thou hadst been here, my brother had not died. But I know, that even now, whatsoever thou wilt ask of God, God will give it thee. Jesus saith unto her, Thy brother shall rise again. Martha saith unto him, I know that he shall rise again in the resurrection at the last day. Jesus said unto her, I am the resurrection, and the life: he that believeth in me, though he were dead, yet shall he live: And whosoever liveth and believeth in me shall never die. Believest thou this? She saith unto him, Yea, Lord: I believe that thou art the Christ, the Son of God, which should come into the world. Jesus said, Take ye away the stone. Martha, the sister of him that was dead, saith unto him, Lord, by this time he stinketh: for he hath been dead four days. Jesus saith unto her, Said I not unto thee, that, if thou wouldest believe, thou shouldest see the glory of God? Then they took away the stone from the place where the dead was laid. And Jesus lifted up his eyes, and said, Father, I thank thee that thou hast heard me. And I knew that thou hearest me always: but because of the people which stand by I said it, that they may believe that thou hast sent me. And when he thus had spoken, he cried with a loud voice, Lazarus, come forth. And he that was dead came forth, bound hand and foot with graveclothes: and his face was bound about with a napkin. Jesus saith unto them, Loose him, and let him go. Then many of the Jews which came to Mary, and had seen the things which Jesus did, believed on him.

Prayer: Dear Lord Jesus; thank you for the gift of New Life. We believe you and we trust you for our today and our future forever. Amen.

What an amazing miracle Lazarus experienced! Lazarus had been dead for four days and yet when the Lord Jesus called for Lazarus to come out of the grave, Lazarus immediately experienced the miracle of new life. Many of those who were there and witnessed this miracle of new life believed on the Lord Jesus Christ. The Lord Jesus is the Resurrection and the life and he makes a very bold statement: "... **he that believeth in me, though he were dead, yet shall he live: And whosoever liveth and believeth in me shall never die."** You see, when we receive the Lord Jesus Christ as our personal Lord and Savior, we receive <u>New Life</u> in Christ in God. With our salvation we receive the gift of the Holy Spirit and the gift of eternal life. That means that our lives continue on a different level when we leave this earth for the Lord Jesus is and will always be with us. And so, here comes the Lord Jesus' follow up question, "Believest thou this?"

© By Dr. Sheila Hayford.

October 7
The Miracle of God's Reversal

Deuteronomy Chapter 29, verse 5:

Yet the Lord says, "During the forty years that I led you through the wilderness, your clothes did not wear out, nor did the sandals on your feet.

Isaiah Chapter 43, verses 12-13:

I have revealed and saved and proclaimed - I, and not some foreign god among you. You are my witnesses," declares the Lord, "that I am God. Yes, and from ancient days I am he. No one can deliver out of my hand. When I act, who can reverse it?" (NIV)

Mark Chapter 16, verse 18:

They shall take up serpents; and if they drink any deadly thing, it shall not hurt them; they shall lay hands on the sick, and they shall recover.

Prayer: Dear God; thank you for your divine reversals on behalf of your children and for the new life we now have in you. Help us to always take you at your Word. In Jesus' Name. Amen.

That was miraculous! Moses, in speaking with the people, reminded them that in all the forty years the people were in the wilderness, neither their clothes nor sandals wore out! God reversed what would have been the natural course of their sandals and extended the use of those shoes. Before he was taken up into heaven, the Lord Jesus told his disciples that whoever believes in the Lord Jesus for salvation will experience God's divine reversal. They will receive new life instead of hell's fire, the sick will be healed in Jesus' name, and if, perchance, they consume any harmful food they will be harmed. God is saying to us through the prophet Isaiah that when God reveals, saves and delivers, no one can fight against God and win. Let us allow God's miraculous reversals to work on our behalf.

© By Dr. Sheila Hayford.

October 8
Blessed As You Come In And Go Out

Deuteronomy Chapter 28, verses 1-6:

And it shall come to pass, if thou shalt hearken diligently unto the voice of the Lord thy God, to observe and to do all his commandments which I command thee this day, that the Lord thy God will set thee on high above all nations of the earth: And all these blessings shall come on thee, and overtake thee, if thou shalt hearken unto the voice of the Lord thy God. Blessed shalt thou be in the city, and blessed shalt thou be in the field. Blessed shall be the fruit of thy body, and the fruit of thy ground, and the fruit of thy cattle, the increase of thy kine, and the flocks of thy sheep. Blessed shall be thy basket and thy store. Blessed shalt thou be when thou comest in, and blessed shalt thou be when thou goest out.

Prayer: Dear God, we receive your blessings with appreciation and joy. Help us to do our part in keeping our great covenant with you, through our Lord and Savior Jesus Christ. Amen.

Wow! Let us take time to meditate on these wonderful promises of God. Yes, they are conditional; we have our part to uphold. However, it is a blessing to even be in great covenant with God, trusting the Holy Spirit to enable us live for God. There is no place for fear when God, the Almighty God, is taking care of His children. Enjoy the blessings of God in your comings and goings as you diligently hearken to and obey God.

© By Dr. Sheila Hayford.

October 9
New Homes

Zechariah Chapter 8, verses 16-21:

These are the things that ye shall do; Speak ye every man the truth to his neighbour; execute the judgment of truth and peace in your gates: And let none of you imagine evil in your hearts against his neighbour; and love no false oath: for all these are things that I hate, saith the LORD. And the word of the Lord of hosts came unto me, saying, Thus saith the Lord of hosts; The fast of the fourth month, and the fast of the fifth, and the fast of the seventh, and the fast of the tenth, shall be to the house of Judah joy and gladness, and cheerful feasts; therefore love the truth and peace. Thus saith the Lord of hosts; It shall yet come to pass, that there shall come people, and the inhabitants of many cities: And the inhabitants of one city shall go to another, saying, Let us go speedily to pray before the Lord, and to seek the Lord of hosts: I will go also.

Prayer: Dear God: Thank you for our homes as well as for our neighbors. May we live with our neighbors in accordance with your word. In Jesus' Name, Amen.

We all know how it is when a person moves into a new home. You are eager to become acquainted with your neighbors. Do your neighbors matter to God, or is your new home just about you? What does God say? God tells us in these verses that we are to walk in truth and at peace with our neighbors. We are not to imagine evil concerning our neighbors. We should be examples of God's joy and gladness and celebrate joyful occasions with our neighbors. And God promises there will come a time when our neighbors and us will go together to others, encouraging them to come with us to pray and seek God and to worship God together. So as you pray about your new homes, keep your neighbors in prayer. We are looking forward to times of great rejoicing!

© By Dr. Sheila Hayford.

October 10
Something Old; Something New

2 Corinthians Chapter 5, verse 17:
Therefore if any man be in Christ, he is a new creature: old things are passed away; behold, all things are become new.

Prayer: Dear God, help us live at our new creation level in Christ in God, and not give place to carnality, by the power of the Holy Spirit. In Jesus' Name. Amen.

Something old and something new? Who does that describe? You! And every born again believer in our Lord Jesus Christ! The sin nature of humanity as a result of the sins of Adam and Eve is referred to as the carnal or old nature in the Bible. When a person receives the Lord Jesus as their Lord and Savior they are born again as a new creation with a regenerated spirit and become part of the family of God. The old nature is at odds with the things of God but God gives us the indwelling Holy Spirit to help us overcome sin and live for God. When we sin, we should be quick to confess our sins to God, ask God for and receive God's forgiveness and move forward in our Christian faith and walk with God. So do not feed your carnal nature by deliberately putting yourself in places where you know you struggle with temptation, especially when you are new in your Christian faith. And for those who have walked this Christian walk for a while, live with God's wisdom looking to yourself so you do not place yourself in compromising situations. Remember, your true nature is now your new nature in Christ in God. Live at God's new creation level for you!

© By Dr. Sheila Hayford.

October 11
The Blessedtitudes

Matthew Chapter 5, verses 1-12:

And seeing the multitudes, he went up into a mountain: and when he was set, his disciples came unto him: And he opened his mouth, and taught them, saying, Blessed are the poor in spirit: for theirs is the kingdom of heaven. Blessed are they that mourn: for they shall be comforted. Blessed are the meek: for they shall inherit the earth. Blessed are they which do hunger and thirst after righteousness: for they shall be filled. Blessed are the merciful: for they shall obtain mercy. Blessed are the pure in heart: for they shall see God. Blessed are the peacemakers: for they shall be called the children of God. Blessed are they which are persecuted for righteousness' sake: for theirs is the kingdom of heaven. Blessed are ye, when men shall revile you, and persecute you, and shall say all manner of evil against you falsely, for my sake. Rejoice, and be exceeding glad: for great is your reward in heaven: for so persecuted they the prophets which were before you.

Prayer: Dear Lord Jesus, I so love you. We know your blessings to us are first and foremost spiritual and that they also include soul blessings, physical blessings and material blessings for you came to make us whole. We worship and reverence you and seek to please you in all things. You are our Blessing, our Lord, our Savior and our God. All we have is in you. Thank you. Amen.

In these times, when some are quick to equate the blessings of God with only material things, such as a new car or a new home, let us reflect on what I call the Blessedtitudes, those who the Lord Jesus calls blessed.

Wow! Blessed are those who are sorrowful over sin? Blessed are those who are made fun of for serving God? And then how does the Lord Jesus end this Sermon. He says to us, "Rejoice, and be exceeding glad: for great is your reward in heaven: for so persecuted they the prophets which were before you." So take heart. When God is in us and for us, we are truly blessed!

© By Dr. Sheila Hayford.

October 12
New Discoveries

Acts Chapter 2, verse 3:
After sighting Cyprus and passing to the south of it, we sailed on to Syria. We landed at Tyre, where our ship was to unload its cargo.

2 Timothy Chapter 3, verses 15-17:
And that from a child thou hast known the holy scriptures, which are able to make thee wise unto salvation through faith which is in Christ Jesus. All scripture is given by inspiration of God, and is profitable for doctrine, for reproof, for correction, for instruction in righteousness: That the man of God may be perfect, thoroughly furnished unto all good works.

Prayer: Dear God, thank you for your Holy Scriptures, intended for the benefit of humanity. May we grow in our relationship with you and in our desire to learn more of you, through Jesus Christ, our Lord and Savior, Amen.

Columbus Day is the Day when the discovery of the Americas by Christopher Columbus is celebrated. As with any discovery, the benefits of that discovery may benefit some and impoverish others. Christopher Columbus was eager to give Spain dominance over the region and in the process some of the indigenous natives may have become impoverished. The thing about many of the new discoveries, whether they be of a place or a people is that they were already in existence; they just happened to be discovered. Discovering what already exists is different from creating what originally did not exist. When a person first discovers their need for God and invites the Lord Jesus to be their Lord and Savior, that discovery may be new to them, but the Lord Jesus, was already there, waiting to be found by them. As the new Christian reads the Bible, he or she discovers truths about the Lord Jesus they did not know before and grows in their Christian faith. God's discoveries as we read and study Scripture and grow in God are intended for the benefit of humanity. However, unlike Christopher Columbus' discovery, the final destination of a born again believer is not on this physical earth. The Lord Jesus is preparing wonderful places for us that are yet to be discovered by us. Come on board!

© By Dr. Sheila Hayford.

October 13
Joseph: Promotion, Power, Plenty.

Genesis Chapter 31, verses 39-49:

And Pharaoh said unto Joseph, Forasmuch as God hath shewed thee all this, there is none so discreet and wise as thou art: Thou shalt be over my house, and according unto thy word shall all my people be ruled: only in the throne will I be greater than thou. And Pharaoh said unto Joseph, See, I have set thee over all the land of Egypt. And Pharaoh took off his ring from his hand, and put it upon Joseph's hand, and arrayed him in vestures of fine linen, and put a gold chain about his neck; And he made him to ride in the second chariot which he had; and they cried before him, Bow the knee: and he made him ruler over all the land of Egypt. And Pharaoh said unto Joseph, I am Pharaoh, and without thee shall no man lift up his hand or foot in all the land of Egypt. And Pharaoh called Joseph's name Zaphnathpaaneah; and he gave him to wife Asenath the daughter of Potipherah priest of On. And Joseph went out over all the land of Egypt. And Joseph was thirty years old when he stood before Pharaoh king of Egypt. And Joseph went out from the presence of Pharaoh, and went throughout all the land of Egypt. And in the seven plenteous years the earth brought forth by handfuls. And he gathered up all the food of the seven years, which were in the land of Egypt, and laid up the food in the cities: the food of the field, which was round about every city, laid he up in the same. And Joseph gathered corn as the sand of the sea, very much, until he left numbering; for it was without number.

Prayer: Dear God, thank you for the encouragement you give us through the example of Joseph. Help us to remain steadfast and true to you. In Jesus' Name, Amen.

Does it seem that God has overlooked you? Does it seem like God has forgotten his good promises to you? You know, when those who seem to be flouting evil seem like they are prosperous. Joseph was a teenager when God gave him the wonderful dreams regarding his future. However, it seemed everything that followed next was evil, despite Joseph's continued stand for God. So where was God? God was right there with Joseph. Every time Joseph passed God's test, check marks were being ticked that moved Joseph closer to God's pay day for Joseph. And at thirty years of age, God rewarded Joseph with Promotion, Power and Plenty. As a result of Joseph's faithfulness to God, the entire known world was saved, Joseph was able to bring his family including the brothers who wronged Joseph into prosperity and protection and God received great glory. So "No!" you have not been overlooked by God. You have been set up by God. Stay true to God, in God's strength and power, and allow God to reward you with Promotion, Power and Plenty on the day God chooses. Your reward may be on this earth like Joseph; it certainly will be in eternity to come when you receive your overcomer's reward. Lives here on earth are depending on you so don't fail God.

© By Dr. Sheila Hayford.

October 14
No Distractions Here

Nehemiah Chapter 6, verses 2-3:

That Sanballat and Geshem sent unto me, saying, Come, let us meet together in some one of the villages in the plain of Ono. But they thought to do me mischief. And I sent messengers unto them, saying, I am doing a great work, so that I cannot come down: why should the work cease, whilst I leave it, and come down to you?

Prayer: Dear God, help us be prepared for the detractors but not distracted by our detractors. Help us to complete our assigned tasks with joy. In Jesus' Name, Amen.

Have you noticed some who are always talking to you only when you are busy at work? When you are on your lunch break they hardly say anything to you. But when you are steeped in concentration at work, they are ready for some small talk. That is a distraction. Nehemiah and the people were hard at work rebuilding God's temple. However, not everyone was happy about that and some sought to distract them and others sought to harm them. Nehemiah's response was: Why should he stop his great work to cater to their distractions? In other words, his response was, "No Distractions Here." Nehemiah continued the work until he completed his task. We, also, have work to do for God and there are some who would try to throw us off course. Be prepared for them but do not be distracted by them. Ask God the Holy Spirit for wisdom, grace and power. And let your response to your detractors be, "No Distractions Here."

© By Dr. Sheila Hayford.

October 15
Make God Bigger

Psalm 34, verse 3:
O magnify the Lord with me, and let us exalt his name together.

Prayer: Dear God; you are God, bigger than every challenge, the Ultimate in Authority. We worship you! Thank you for our Lord Jesus

Christ, before whom every knee will bow in submission. We praise you, we bless you and we magnify your holy Name. In Jesus' Name, Amen.

Why make God bigger? It is because sometimes your problems may appear to be bigger. It is because some in society may want you to think that they are bigger than your God. It is because we need to remind ourselves of the awesomeness of our God. It is because we would love for others to join us in the praise and worship of our God. Whatever the reason, please join me as we lift up the Name of our Lord Jesus Christ, the Name that is above every name, to whom all knees **will** eventually bow. Let us exalt His Name <u>together!</u>

© By Dr. Sheila Hayford.

October 16
Generational Blessings

Isaiah Chapter 44, verse 3:
For I will pour water upon him that is thirsty, and floods upon the dry ground: I will pour my spirit upon thy seed, and my blessing upon thine offspring:

Prayer: Dear God, thank you for your promise of generational blessings, through our Lord and Savior, Jesus Christ. In whose Name we pray. Amen.

There are many things money cannot and could not buy, God's generational blessings included. So you seek God and obey him. You faithfully serve God with joy and seek to share God with others. Are your blessings from God just for you? No! God is blessing you, your family and your descendants. How awesome is that! That is cause for eternal praise, eternal worship and forever thankfulness to our God.

© By Dr. Sheila Hayford.

October 17
Let God Work It Out

Proverbs Chapter 16, verses 3-4:

Commit to the Lord whatever you do, and he will establish your plans. The Lord works out everything to its proper end - even the wicked for a day of disaster.

Prayer: Dear God; you are always good. So we yield to your direction and submit to your authority. In Jesus' Name, Amen.

I love that God works things out both ways; in our individual lives and in the lives of others. And I love that God works on God's timetable, the way God chooses and has the final authority in all things. No human can compete with God at that level. So let us bring our plans to God in prayer and in consultation with the Word of God and the Holy Spirit and trust God to work things out for our good. So what if you were unfairly treated? God knows how to handle that too. Let God do God's part and let us do the seeking God, believing God, trusting God and obeying God part.

© By Dr. Sheila Hayford.

October 18
I Will Rejoice

Habakkuk Chapter 3, verse 18:

Yet I will rejoice in the Lord, I will joy in the God of my salvation.

Prayer: Dear God: My joy is in you. My salvation is in you. My hope is in you and my eternal future is in you. How wonderful! In Jesus' name, Amen.

We note the "I will" in this verse. It suggests a predetermined attitude. This is part of the song written by the prophet Habakkuk to the chief singer on his stringed instruments. The prophet reminds us that we have great reason to be joyful because the Lord Jesus has saved us and blessed us in Christ in God. We have hope and our hope is eternal. Hallelujah! So we have made up our minds to rejoice in our God and to let God and the world know how happy we are. We are not boastful, we are not praising God for show, we are appreciative and grateful to God for who God is and what God has and continues to do in our lives. To God be all the glory!

© By Dr. Sheila Hayford.

October 19
Wisdom's Instruction

Proverbs Chapter 15, verse 33:
Wisdom's instruction is to fear the Lord, and humility comes before honor. (NIV)

Prayer: Dear God, help us to learn from and to apply the wisdom of the Holy Spirit. In Jesus' Name, Amen.

Yes, wisdom is instructing us to reverence God. We should come to God with reverence for God is a holy God. And we should come before God in humility for we are fully dependent on God for everything, including our very life. God always has time to respond to a person who sincerely humbles themselves before God. It is interesting that wisdom is also teaching us that humility should precede honor. In other words, do not promote a proud or arrogant person. Let us walk in humility before God and in our relationships with our fellow man and allow God's wisdom to manifest in us.

© By Dr. Sheila Hayford.

October 20
God's Mission Accomplished

Isaiah Chapter 55, verse 11:

So shall my word be that goeth forth out of my mouth: it shall not return unto me void, but it shall accomplish that which I please, and it shall prosper in the thing whereto I sent it.

Prayer: Dear God, Thank you that your word will never come back to you void. Help us to share you with others. In Jesus' name, Amen.

How does God's Mission Accomplished look like? This verse shows us what it looks like with regards to the Word of God. The Lord God makes this profound statement. Every word God speaks will not come back to God without accomplishing what God intended that word to do. Wow! If God's preached word is sent out in the Sermon on salvation through the Lord Jesus Christ people will be saved. Does that mean everyone hearing will be saved, knowing that God respects each person's free will? It means that for some, that word will act as a judge if they chose to reject God because they were given that opportunity. For some, that same word will convict them of their sins and they may then come to God at a later time. Still for some who may already have accepted the Lord Jesus as Lord and Savior, it may provide insight they had not yet had. So share God's words and leave the results to God. The Mission of God's Words will be accomplished.

© By Dr. Sheila Hayford.

October 21
The Mind Of Christ

Philippians Chapter 2, verses 4-7:
Look not every man on his own things, but every man also on the things of others. Let this mind be in you, which was also in Christ Jesus: Who, being in the form of God, thought it not robbery to be equal with God: But made himself of no reputation, and took upon him the form of a servant, and was made in the likeness of men:

Prayer: Dear Lord Jesus, our perfect example. Thank you for all that you suffered for the sake of humanity and for bringing us to God. Help us to live in the power of the Holy Spirit, having the mind of Christ. Amen.

As we study Scripture, one might ask, "What was the mind of Christ." These verses give us the answer. The mind of Christ was a mind that was submissive to the will of God. When God the Father sent the Lord Jesus to earth to come and die on the cross for sinners the Lord Jesus Christ did not consider that an insult because while the Lord Jesus is God, he not only willingly submitted to the will of God, he made the will of God his own. Secondly, the mind of Christ was an unselfish mind. The Lord Jesus came to earth because he cared about the wellbeing of others and the salvation of sinners. Thirdly, the mind of Christ was one of humility. Yes, the Lord Jesus is God the Son. And yet he did not call his holy angels to destroy those who wanted to kill him, the Lord Jesus allowed himself to be beaten, tortured and killed by humankind in order to bear the punishment of the sins of humankind and to bring all who receive him, and that includes us, into God's family. Finally, the mind of Christ is the mind of God. The Lord Jesus will fulfill all that our heavenly Father has said and will judge and reign over all. Our finite human minds could not fathom everything the mind of Christ entails. However, God wants us to start with what God has taught us about the mind of Christ and to have the same submissive to God, unselfish, humble, knowing who are, whose you are, knowing and fulfilling your assignment from God, mind of Christ.

© By Dr. Sheila Hayford.

October 22
The Restorer of Life

Ruth Chapter 4, verse 14-15:

And the women said unto Naomi, Blessed be the Lord, which hath not left thee this day without a kinsman, that his name may be famous in

Israel. And he shall be unto thee a restorer of thy life, and a nourisher of thine old age: for thy daughter in law, which loveth thee, which is better to thee than seven sons, hath born him.

Prayer: Dear Lord Jesus, the Restorer of life; we thank you for the gift of salvation, the gift of the Holy Spirit and for eternal life. Amen.

In these verses we read the blessing the women gave to Naomi when her daughter in law gave birth to Obed. One of these blessing was the restorer of Naomi's life. Naomi had some hurdles to overcome in her past but when Ruth came into her life and she was blessed to have Obed, Naomi was filled with joy and had much to live for. The Lord Jesus is the Restorer of Life to anyone who will receive him. Each person, since the times of Adam and Eve, has the punishment for sin which includes death and hell against them. That would be sad if that was the end of the story. The good news is this: The Lord Jesus Christ has come and has paid the price for all the sins of all of humanity once and for all. All who receive the Lord Jesus Christ as Lord and Savior will be restored to eternal life. Do you know the Lord Jesus Christ as the Restorer of your life?

© By Dr. Sheila Hayford.

October 23
God's Youth

1 Timothy Chapter 4, verse 12:
Let no man despise thy youth; but be thou an example of the believers, in word, in conversation, in charity, in spirit, in faith, in purity.

Prayer: Dear God, you and I know the joys of being saved in my youth as well as the challenges. It was a challenging, exciting and enjoyable time and we loved sharing you with others. Help our youth as they face the pressures of their times, for you are always relevant and you will never fail. In Jesus' Name, Amen.

I know from personal experience that the Lord Jesus is able to save us in our teenage years all the way through adulthood and throughout eternity. So to the youth I say: Do not let anyone tell you otherwise. Remember, the Lord Jesus is our example and our standard. Yours is to be the example of a disciple of the Lord Jesus Christ in what you say, how you speak, sharing God's love with others, living a pure life in the power of the Holy Spirit and growing in faith. Don't allow another person's opinions, hang-ups, misperceptions about you or their experience with other youth cause you to become discouraged or to give up. God has made you strong because he has much work for you to do. And have fun growing in your relationship with god and living with God. Serving the devil may look like fun but the devil destroys from the inside out. I honor your commitment to God. Now share your love for and relationship with God with your fellow youth, and allow God to lead you, to speak through you and to use you. Blessings!

© By Dr. Sheila Hayford.

October 24
Show Jesus Love

John Chapter 14, verse 23:
Jesus answered and said unto him, If a man love me, he will keep my words: and my Father will love him, and we will come unto him, and make our abode with him.

Prayer: Dear Lord Jesus, help us show you by our obedience that we love you. Amen.

Many times we tell the Lord Jesus that we love him, but how can we <u>show</u> the Lord Jesus that we love him? It is by our obedience in doing what he says we should do. It is that simple! Are there challenges at times? Yes, because a person who loves God may do things that do not please God. However, when we sin and confess our sins to God and ask for forgiveness, we are forgiven because the Lord Jesus has paid the price for all sin. We then continue in our Christian faith. When we obey the Lord Jesus and show the Lord Jesus we love him, we make God happy and enjoy fellowship with God the Father, God the Son and God the Holy Spirit. Priceless!

© By Dr. Sheila Hayford.

October 25
FACT: Faith Is An ACT

James Chapter 2, verses 18-24:

Yea, a man may say, Thou hast faith, and I have works: shew me thy faith without thy works, and I will shew thee my faith by my works. Thou believest that there is one God; thou doest well: the devils also believe, and tremble. But wilt thou know, O vain man, that faith without works is dead? Was not Abraham our father justified by works, when he had offered Isaac his son upon the altar? Seest thou how faith wrought with his works, and by works was faith made perfect? And the scripture was fulfilled which saith, Abraham believed God, and it was imputed unto him for righteousness: and he was called the Friend of God. Ye see then how that by works a man is justified, and not by faith only.

Matthew Chapter 7, verses 16-17:

Ye shall know them by their fruits. Do men gather grapes of thorns, or figs of thistles? Even so every good tree bringeth forth good fruit; but a corrupt tree bringeth forth evil fruit.

Prayer: Dear Lord Jesus; we love you and we reverence you! Let us not make a show of faith, but rather show our faith in you in our words and in our deeds for **F**aith is an **ACT**. Amen.

FACT: **F**aith is an **ACT**. In other words, many believe the Lord Jesus is the Son of God. Even the devils recognize Jesus as the Son of God. However, to have faith in the Son of God requires action. When a person invites the Lord Jesus to be their personal Lord and Savior, that person does not only believe in the Lord Jesus they put some action with their faith. They agree with the Holy Bible that all humanity has sinned and therefore they confess their sins to God in prayer. They believe the Lord Jesus has paid the price for their sin and so they ask God for forgiveness from sin. They believe they received the free gift of the Holy Spirit when they invited the Lord Jesus to be their Lord and Savior and so ask the Holy Spirit for guidance. They renew their minds with the Word of God which in turn affects the way they live and so their actions begin to show the power of God at work in their life. It is by our words and our works that we share our faith authentically with others for the Lord Jesus says we will be known by our fruits. What do our words and our works say about our Lord Jesus Christ?

© By Dr. Sheila Hayford.

October 26
God's Open Door

Revelation Chapter 3, verse 8:

I know thy works: behold, I have set before thee an open door, and no man can shut it: for thou hast a little strength, and hast kept my word, and hast not denied my name.

Prayer: Dear Lord Jesus; thank you for God's open doors in our lives. Help us, in the power and strength of the Holy Spirit, recognize those doors and to walk through them in order to fulfill God's plans and purpose for our lives. Amen.

What is God's Open Door? It is God's door of opportunity, God's provision, God's ordained projects that he makes available to us through our Lord Jesus Christ. The thing about an open door is that you have to enter or go through the door in order to experience the opportunity, provision, project, whatever is in there or whomever God has for you to meet in order to experience the benefit of the open door. If you do not go through God's open door, you have essentially chosen to forfeit that benefit. What the Holy Spirit is teaching us in these words of our Lord

Jesus Christ is that when God has opportunities and projects that are God ordained for us, no man can fight God's work in us and win. So with God's victory guaranteed on our behalf through our Lord and Savior Jesus Christ, no one can blame another person for their refusal to go through God's open door, whether they do that out of fear, laziness, procrastination, unbelief, persecution or for whatever reason. God has open doors for you. Go through God's open doors with God and the wisdom of God. You need those doors open to fulfil your God given purpose.

© By Dr. Sheila Hayford.

October 27
He Is The Rock

Deuteronomy Chapter 32, verse 4:
He is the Rock, his works are perfect, and all his ways are just. A faithful God who does no wrong, upright and just is he. (NIV)
Prayer: Dear God, our solid rock. We thank you that we are safe and secure in you, through our Lord and Savior, Jesus Christ. In Jesus' Name, Amen.

God is our Rock. What does that entail? When we think about a rock, we think of something solid, something strong, something that can withstand storms. A rock may have some sharp or rough edges that may cause harm to a ship or to a person if they interact with the rock in the wrong way. So, as we study this verse closely we see that God is our sure, strong and solid foundation. God is just and does no wrong and thus, God will treat all who interact with him justly, whether they are obedient to God or not. God is upright, so all God does is holy. Moreover, God is faithful; there is no deficiency with God. Since God is our Rock with all His glorious attributes, we should move forward in our Christian journey with full assurance, knowing that our Rock will never fail us.

© By Dr. Sheila Hayford.

October 28
God's Faithful People

Psalm 145, verses 10-11:
All your works praise you, Lord; your faithful people extol you. They tell of the glory of your kingdom and speak of your might, (NIV)
Prayer: Dear Holy Spirit, help us to be faithful to God in how we live and enable us to be faithful stewards of all God has entrusted us with. In Jesus' Name, Amen.

God is faithful and God has faithful people. Yes, God's nature shows in those who have been redeemed by the Lord Jesus. Through the salvation that comes through the Lord Jesus Christ, we are now sons and daughters in the family of God. So what are the characteristics of God's faithful people? They are faithful in their service to God in the power of the Holy Spirit and they share God with others. They magnify and praise God and they tell others of the good news of salvation through our Lord Jesus Christ. They share the power of God to save, heal and deliver and invite others to experience God as well. Does God call you faithful?

© By Dr. Sheila Hayford.

October 29
Blessed By Association

Genesis Chapter 30, verse 27:
And Laban said unto him, I pray thee, if I have found favour in thine eyes, tarry: for I have learned by experience that the Lord hath blessed me for thy sake.
Prayer: Dear God; we thank you for extending your favor to us and to others. In Jesus' Name, Amen.

Laban had been deceitful to Jacob when it came to the way he handled the wages of Jacob. That was very wrong. What was smart about Laban in this verse is that Laban recognized that he was blessed by God because Jacob had come into his household. That was wise. If a person is blessed of God and you are associated with them in right standing, it is possible that your association with them will cause you to experience blessing as well. However, Laban wanted Jacob to stay with him for as long as possible for selfish reasons; so that Laban could continue to be blessed instead of asking Jacob to do what God wanted Jacob to do. So blessed one, others should recognize the benefit of rightly associating with you, right because God says so. Are you blessed by association?

© By Dr. Sheila Hayford.

October 30
This Earth As We Know It

Mark Chapter 13, verse 31:
Heaven and earth shall pass away: but my words shall not pass away.

Prayer: Dear Lord Jesus, you are seated in victory at God's right hand and of your kingdom there is no end. We are eternally grateful and thankful to you for saving us. Blessing and glory, salvation and honor be yours, now and forevermore, Amen.

Sometimes people will say things like "you can't take it with you" to stress the fact that temporal things are temporal. No one can use temporal things outside this earth realm. The Lord Jesus Christ and the Words of the Lord Jesus Christ will outlast this earth as we know it. For the Bible tells us that this earth will pass away. And so while we must not use that as an excuse to shirk earthly stewardship responsibility, it is important that we make plans for our eternal future that will outlast this temporal earth as we know it. Place your faith and trust in the One who is forever, our Lord, our God and our Savior, Jesus the Christ.

© By Dr. Sheila Hayford.

October 31
What is Truth?

Psalm 85, verse 11:

Truth shall spring out of the earth; and righteousness shall look down from heaven.

Prayer: Dear Lord Jesus: May our lives reflect your truths. Amen.

Pilate asked the Lord Jesus, "What is truth?" The Lord Jesus says in John Chapter 14, verse 6 that He is The Way, The Truth and The Life. So truth is personified in the Lord Jesus Christ. You see, truth is an attribute of God, in whom there is no falsehood. And so when the verse says truth shall spring forth from the earth, it implies that God's people are expressing God's truths in the earth when the righteous God looks down from his abode at the activities of humankind. What does God see when he looks down on our lives? Does God see God's truth springing out? Do our words and actions acknowledge God's truths? Do we bring glory to God?

© By Dr. Sheila Hayford.

November 1
Desert or Dessert Mentality

Deuteronomy Chapter 1, verses 2, 19-21, 26-27, 34-38:

(It takes eleven days to go from Horeb to Kadesh Barnea by the Mount Seir road.) Then, as the Lord our God commanded us, we set out from Horeb and went toward the hill country of the Amorites through all that vast and dreadful wilderness that you have seen, and so we reached Kadesh Barnea. Then I said to you, "You have reached the hill country of the Amorites, which the Lord our God is giving us. See, the Lord your God has given you the land. Go up and take possession of it as the Lord, the God of your ancestors, told you. Do not be afraid; do not be discouraged." But you were unwilling to go up; you rebelled against the command of the Lord your God. You grumbled in your tents and said, "The Lord hates us; so he brought us out of Egypt to deliver us into the hands of the Amorites to destroy us. When the Lord heard what you said, he was angry and solemnly swore: "No one from this evil generation shall see the good land I swore to give your ancestors, except Caleb son of Jephunneh. He will see it, and I will give him and his descendants the land he set his feet on, because he followed the Lord wholeheartedly." Because of you the Lord became angry with me also and said, "You shall not enter it, either. But your assistant, Joshua son of Nun, will enter it. Encourage him, because he will lead Israel to inherit it.

Prayer: Dear God; you are always good; that is your character. Help us to work with you to achieve your desired outcome for our lives. In Jesus' Name, Amen.

We celebrate National Cinnamon Day in the United States and with that you would think of something sweet or something that is fun. However, today we are going to learn lessons from a group of people who grumbled and complained just about anything. They complained about the food, they complained about the prophet Moses, they pressured Aaron into making an image of a golden cow for them to worship, they even complained that God who had so miraculously delivered them from Egypt and wrought mighty signs in order to deliver and protect them and which they had seen and experienced, hated them. You mean they said, God *"hated"* them? When God heard that, God decided none of them except Caleb and Joshua and the little ones would enter the land God promised them. So what should have been an eleven-day journey spanned over several years and those that did the complaining, murmuring, stirred up strife, blamed and disobeyed God and worshipped the manmade golden calf died in the wilderness. How did that happen? They settled for what I call a desert mentality in which they focused on what they did not have instead of what they did have. They were not thankful for the manna and quail but murmured and complained because, in today's vernacular, they did not have filet mignon. When you have what I call a dessert mentality, you are appreciative and enjoy what you have with the expectation that you will have more than enough and be able to enjoy some dessert. When the people in these Scripture verses disobeyed God and began to falsely accuse and blame God, they forfeited God's blessing. Sobering! Do not allow a seeming lack in one area to obscure your perspective on all the good God graciously gives you. You might only be eleven days away from your blessing!

© By Dr. Sheila Hayford.

November 2
Mob Rules? Aaron And The Golden Calf

Exodus Chapter 32, verses 1-9:

And when the people saw that Moses delayed to come down out of the mount, the people gathered themselves together unto Aaron, and said unto him, Up, make us gods, which shall go before us; for as for this Moses, the man that brought us up out of the land of Egypt, we wot not what is become of him. And Aaron said unto them, Break off the golden earrings, which are in the ears of your wives, of your sons, and of your daughters, and bring them unto me. And all the people brake off the golden earrings which were in their ears, and brought them unto Aaron. And he received them at their hand, and fashioned it with a graving tool, after he had made it a molten calf: and they said, These be thy gods, O Israel, which brought thee up out of the land of Egypt. And when Aaron saw it, he built an altar before it; and Aaron made proclamation, and said, To morrow is a feast to the Lord. And they rose up early on the morrow, and offered burnt offerings, and brought peace offerings; and the people sat down to eat and to drink, and rose up to play. And the Lord said unto Moses, Go, get thee down; for thy people, which thou broughtest out of the land of Egypt, have corrupted themselves: They have turned aside quickly out of the way which I commanded them: they have made them a molten calf, and have worshipped it, and have sacrificed thereunto, and said, These be thy gods, O Israel, which have brought thee up out of the land of Egypt. And the Lord said unto Moses, I have seen this people, and, behold, it is a stiffnecked people:

Prayer: Dear God; it is sad that Aaron succumbed to the mob in doing what was evil in your sight. We resolve to stand for you and your holy principles, in the power of the Holy Spirit and through our Lord and Savior, Jesus Christ for it is in Jesus' Name that we pray. Amen.

This is an election year in the United States and as we hear every election, this may be the most important election. Voters will be at the polls and God is asking those who profess to be born again Christians to remember who saved and delivered them from sin, and to whom their primary allegiance ought to be in the lesson of Aaron the priest and the golden calf. How could Aaron the priest, called by God to accompany the prophet Moses to Pharaoh with the message from God to release God's people and who had witnessed the miraculous signs God did to bring about their deliverance, fashion a golden calf from the people's jewelry and even worse, refer to the calf as the god who brought them out of Egypt? The answer is very simple; Aaron yielded to the mob rules and brought evil and disastrous consequences to an entire people. It was so bad God was ready to wipe out all the people, except for Moses. So what happened? Moses was up on the mountain with God, hearing from God and receiving instruction from God for the people. While Moses was away, the people were under Aaron the priest. When the people felt Moses was taking too long in coming down from the mountain, they asked the prophet Aaron to make them gods to go before them. One would have thought that Aaron would remind the people of their first allegiance to God, the God who had delivered them. Instead Aaron succumbed to the pressure of the mob, built a golden image in direct disobedience to the commands of God, built an altar to the image Aaron called a god and then tried to justify his evil act by declaring they would feast unto the Lord when in fact the people were worshipping their own deceptive image; God was nowhere in that mix. And so, each child of

God must remember our primary citizenship is of God's kingdom. We are ambassadors of God representing the Lord Jesus Christ on this earth and we each will have to give account to God for what we do. The mob may not necessarily be right. What does God say?

© By Dr. Sheila Hayford.

November 3
Vote Your Christian Conscience

1 Timothy Chapter 4, verses 1-2:
Now the Spirit speaketh expressly, that in the latter times some shall depart from the faith, giving heed to seducing spirits, and doctrines of devils; Speaking lies in hypocrisy; having their conscience seared with a hot iron;

Acts Chapter 24, verses 15-16:
and I have the same hope in God as these men themselves have, that there will be a resurrection of both the righteous and the wicked. 16 So I strive always to keep my conscience clear before God and man. (NIV)

It is time to vote your Christian conscience; not just on this very important day, but every day of the year. There are many issues at hand, some in agreement with the word of God, others contrary to the word of God. The Apostle Paul says it succinctly; there are deceptive or seducing spirits and doctrines of devils in society, seeking to cause some who profess to be Christians to compromise and lose their Christian faith. Do not fall for evil. The Apostle Paul who knows that every one of us will ultimately give an account to God for our individual actions, says he strives to always have a clear conscience before God and before humankind. So vote with God on any issue, whether it is popular in the eyes of society or not. Every election is very important as it will shape decisions with far reaching implications. Vote your Christian conscience!

© By Dr. Sheila Hayford.

November 4
Take Time To Reflect

Psalm 67, verses 3-5:

Let the people praise thee, O God; let all the people praise thee. O let the nations be glad and sing for joy: for thou shalt judge the people righteously, and govern the nations upon earth. Selah. Let the people praise thee, O God; let all the people praise thee.

Prayer: Dear God; Government is a God created institution for you are the Ultimate in authority and your governance is forever. Yes, you have given humanity responsibilities on this earth but each person has to answer to you for their stewardship on this earth. This merits sober consideration so let us make time to spend in reflection with you. Amen.

With the whirlwind of politics and elections, it is wise to take some time for reflection. In the Psalm above, David asks us to pause and remember that the Lord God, our God, is the Righteous Judge who will judge all people righteously and who will govern all the nations of the earth. That is cause for great celebration! So when things do not seem to go the way you would have wanted, because God respects the free-will of humankind, pause and reflect that every one's time on this earth is temporary and God in the end will make things right. All individuals and the nations will come under God's governance. Selah!

© By Dr. Sheila Hayford

November 5
All Food? Yes, No Condemnation!

Genesis Chapter 8, verse 3:

Everything that lives and moves about will be food for you. Just as I gave you the green plants, I now give you everything. (NIV)

1 Corinthians Chapter 8, verses 7-9:

Howbeit there is not in every man that knowledge: for some with conscience of the idol unto this hour eat it as a thing offered unto an idol; and their conscience being weak is defiled. But meat commendeth us not to God: for neither, if we eat, are we the better; neither, if we eat not, are we the worse. But take heed lest by any means this liberty of yours become a stumblingblock to them that are weak.

Romans Chapter 14, verse 23:

And he that doubteth is damned if he eat, because he eateth not of faith: for whatsoever is not of faith is sin.

Prayer: Dear God; we thank you for all the things you freely give us to enjoy. In Jesus' Name, Amen.

We are free to eat anything! Seriously? Yes! I would say I would eat anything and then I heard some enjoyed muskrat (no offense to muskrat lovers) and other delicacies and so I now say I can eat anything but prefer not to eat the muskrat example. In other words, we should not be condemned by any man in what we eat, because the Almighty God, who is holy and righteous, gave all to us for food. So what if a person or an organization has a different opinion? Ask yourself if you will go with a man's tradition over what the Word of God says. Or what if a person's conscience bothers them if they eat certain foods? Then that person should not eat those foods because if they do without faith that they are doing the right thing, they sin. However, they must not project their "weak" conscience and judge others in what they eat. Enjoy *your* food!

© By Dr. Sheila Hayford.

November 6
Announce It

Psalm 68, verse 11:

The Lord announces the word, and the women who proclaim it are a mighty throng: (NIV)

Prayer: Dear God; enable me, by the Holy Spirit, to announce my faith filled words and bring you glory when they manifest. In Jesus' Name, Amen.

It was close to the holidays and the Speaker had a gift. It was a large, elegant tower with different layers of boxed Christmas items wrapped elegantly. It was beautiful! The speaker was going to give it as a gift to one of the attendees and to 'tease' us he passed it around. As it came my way, I was about to say, "Let me take a look at what I will be getting!" I hesitated and soon it was on to the next attendee. When I was announced as the winner, I was ecstatic! As I got up and gave thanks for my gift, I told the attendees the announcement I had planned to make but did not and how the gift I received was confirmation I should have made that announcement. Afterwards one lady came to me and said she was moved by what I had planned to say ahead of receiving that gift. You see, I should have spoken in faith ahead of time. That way, the testimony would be obvious. God still honored my faith, but sharing my faith ahead of the gift would have brought God glory when the manifestation took place. You may never know the full impact of your faith filled words. Announce them and bring God glory!

© By Dr. Sheila Hayford.

November 7
The Good LORD

Psalm 86, verse 5:
For thou, Lord, art good, and ready to forgive; and plenteous in mercy unto all them that call upon thee.

Prayer: Dear God; we thank you that you are really truly good, always good and you extend your goodness to humankind, through your Son, the Lord Jesus Christ. We appreciate you and are grateful for your great mercy towards us. In Jesus' Name, Amen.

Sometimes we hear the expression, "The Good Lord" almost as a cliché or as a preamble to a speech in which God is not otherwise mentioned. However, this verse reminds us that God is **really** good and then lists some of the ways God expresses his goodness towards humanity. One of the expressions of God's goodness to us is that God is always ready to forgive us when we come to God sincerely confessing our sins, repenting of our sins and asking God to forgive us because His Son, the Lord Jesus has taken the punishment of the sins of humanity. In fact, when we believe God and receive the Lord Jesus as our Lord and Savior, God welcomes us into the family of God and gives us the gift of the Holy Spirit and the gift of eternal life. Thus, God is and forever will always be with His children, Awesome! Another expression of God's goodness to us is the abundance of mercy God shows to humankind. If you were God, would you cause the sun to shine on those who insulted you or spoke bad about you? That is why God is God. God, in God's mercy, causes the sun to shine on the just and the unjust, gives free air to those who serve him and those who do not serve him and is more than ready to meet us where we are when we come to him sincerely. So, when we say, "The good LORD" we really mean it. Thanks be to God!

© By Dr. Sheila Hayford.

November 8
Jesus Christ – Our Great Intercessor

Psalm 68, verse 19:

Praise be to the Lord, to God our Savior, who daily bears our burdens. (NIV)

Prayer: Dear Lord Jesus, I love you! You and I know the special times you have come to me with great promises and words of encouragement when I shared my concerns with you. Everything you promised took place just as you said and extended beyond my human imagination. It is with great joy that I recommend you to others. Thanks again, Amen.

Aren't we glad that when we receive the Lord Jesus Christ into our heart as Lord and Savior, we are not left to live our Christian faith by ourselves? I am eternally grateful that the Lord Jesus came and <u>lived among</u> humankind. Whatever we may go through or may be going through, the Lord Jesus Christ has experienced. We cannot go to the Lord Jesus with our burdens and say to the Lord Jesus, "You just don't know" because that is not so; the Lord Jesus knows entirely. And isn't it great to know that our Risen Lord Jesus, seated at the right hand of Almighty God the Father, is our Priest who is interceding to our Father God on our behalf? Yes, the Lord Jesus is available to us and invites us to bring him our daily burdens and concerns. We will, in turn, experience His peace, His intercession on our behalf and God's intervention in our lives. Why wait? Share your burdens, cares and concerns with the Lord Jesus now.

© By Dr. Sheila Hayford.

November 9
Celebrating Freedom

John Chapter 8, verse 36:
If the Son therefore shall make you free, ye shall be free indeed.
Prayer: Dear Lord Jesus; I know I am a sinner and am grateful that you died on the cross for my sins. I confess my sins to you, asking for forgiveness. I choose to live a new life with you and invite you now into my heart and life to be my Lord and Savior. Thank you for the gift of the Holy Spirit you give me now, as a born again child of God, to enable me live for you. Lead and direct me and enable me to share my faith with others. Help me to have conversations with you daily for you are so happy. I am happy too! Amen.

In the United States, World Freedom Day is celebrated to commemorate the fall of the Berlin Wall. I vividly recall watching on the television in November, 1989 when West Germany opened the Berlin

Wall so that East Germans could walk across freely to West Berlin. Families that had not seen each other in decades were reunited. There was so much joy and happiness as many crossed the wall. As we watched history unfolding we were all so happy! The peoples of the world rejoiced. So much so that in December of 1989, work began to officially tear down the Berlin Wall and that was completed in 1990. Today the people of East Germany and West Germany peacefully live together. The Lord Jesus came to earth to bring humanity the ultimate in freedom. How so? This is because the Lord Jesus came to earth to set us free from sin, satan and death. When the Lord Jesus died on the cross it was to take the punishment of the sins of humanity and when the Lord Jesus rose from the dead, the Lord Jesus defeated death for humanity so we all will rise again. However, this freedom in Jesus Christ is a gift that may be accepted or rejected because God values your free will. We sincerely hope you will choose to receive the Lord Jesus into your life as your personal Lord and Savior. If so, pray the prayer for today. Start to read the Bible beginning with the gospels and share your new found faith with others. Look for a church where the Bible is preached to help you grow in your Christian faith journey. We will rejoice with you and God's angels will rejoice with you in heaven. It is such a big deal with God. Make today your celebrating God's Freedom Day!

© By Dr. Sheila Hayford.

November 10
God's Test

Proverbs Chapter 17, verse 3:
The crucible for silver and the furnace for gold, but the Lord tests the heart. (NIV)
Prayer: Dear God; enable us, in the power of the Holy Spirit to live for you and to pass your tests. In Jesus' Name, Amen.

There are tests for almost anything in society. If you are in school, you generally have to study and pass tests in order to be promoted to the next class. Some companies ask you to take a test when you apply for a job with them. Doctors will sometimes ask their patients to have tests done. Silver is tested with the silver crucible and gold is tested with heat. So, what does God test when it comes to humanity? This verse teaches us that God tests the heart. God not only knows out thoughts and our words before we speak them, God tests our motives, our intents, our biases and since God is God, words would not be adequate to describe in full all God tests when God tests our hearts. If we work hard to pass our earthly tests in school and on the job and want to make sure that priced possessions have the exact amount of gold or silver claimed, shouldn't we make every attempt to pass God's test? How would we do that? By depending on the Holy Spirit to help us; for the Holy Spirit knows the mind of God and enables humankind to live for God. The Lord Jesus gives the gift of the Holy Spirit to every person who confesses and repents of sin, decides to live for God and receives the Lord Jesus into their heart and life as their Lord and Savior. Invite the Lord Jesus into your heart as your Lord and Savior today and receive the gift of the Holy Spirit today. God's desire is for you to pass God's test.

© By Dr. Sheila Hayford.

November 11
Veterans

Ezekiel Chapter 27, verse 9:

Veteran craftsmen of Byblos were on board as shipwrights to caulk your seams. All the ships of the sea and their sailors came alongside to trade for your wares. (NIV)

Prayer: Dear God; thank you for giving us the ability to work hard and to excel at what we do. We salute the veterans of the faith as well as those veterans working honorably in our society and in our country. In Jesus' Name, Amen.

A veteran is usually very experienced in their particular field of expertise, has worked in their field for a relatively long time and is generally valued for his or her contributions to society. So, as we celebrate Veteran's Day in the United States, we should ask ourselves if veterans are really appreciated for their service to humanity. Our appreciation and thanks should go to all who have served with honor; veterans of the faith, skilled veterans in their respective disciplines and veterans who have served honorably and continue to serve their country well. Happy Veteran's Day!

© By Dr. Sheila Hayford.

November 12
It Is Working For My Good

Romans Chapter 8, verse 28:
And we know that all things work together for good to them that love God, to them who are the called according to his purpose.

Prayer: Dear Sovereign God; we trust you and willingly submit to your words and your authority. Thank you for working all things out for our good. In Jesus' Name, Amen.

Have you heard a person say, "I wonder what good can come out of this?" That should never be said by a born again believer of our Lord Jesus Christ. No situation is hopeless when God is involved because God says in His Word that he will work all things in conjunction for our good. So, do not fret if you are done wrong, or if you are facing what looks like an impossible situation. God does not lie and God cannot fail. Trust God and let your words and your actions correspond with your faith in God. God says all things will work in conjunction for our good. Let us believe God!

© By Dr. Sheila Hayford.

November 13
Don't Be Envious

Proverbs Chapter 27, verse 4:

Wrath is cruel, and anger is outrageous; but who is able to stand before envy?

Prayer: Dear God; envy is nothing to flout or to be proud of. Help us, as children of God and disciples of the Lord Jesus Christ, to reflect your character in all that we do. In Jesus' Name, Amen.

Wow! This verse shows the gravity and depravity of envy. We know that being angry to the point of wrath can cause people to act cruelly and that prolonged unrestrained anger can cause a lot of harm. Envy is deplorable and this verse suggests may be even worse than anger. So why does envy seem to be acceptable to some, and why do some even flout their envy. Some will rob or worse in order to have somebody else's pair of sneakers, car or home, with no consideration as to the toil and work it took the other person. A person is essentially telling God that God did not do a good job with the abilities, gifts and talents God gave them when they are envious and covet what belongs to others. Every person has something good to offer because we are uniquely created by God. Love God, love you and love others. Love your neighbor as yourself!

© By Dr. Sheila Hayford.

November 14
I Found It

Luke Chapter 15, verse 9:

And when she hath found it, she calleth her friends and her neighbours together, saying, Rejoice with me; for I have found the piece which I had lost.

Prayer: Dear God: Thank you for helping me find what I had lost. Help me share the good news of salvation with others so lost sinners will find new life in Jesus Christ. In Jesus' Name, Amen.

I had spent most of the day running errands and in the evening I noticed one of my pair of earrings was missing. It was a nice pair and I prayed I would find it. Then I thought that would be ridiculous because I did not want to have to go out of my way just to find that one earring. So I thought that was it. Several weeks later, I had just left the house and 'happened' to look down. There was my 'lost' earring! The metal ring for the earlobe was missing but could be replaced. The earring itself was intact. I found it! Glory to God! God and God's angels rejoice over each sinner who was lost in sin but found new life in Jesus Christ. Rejoice!

© By Dr. Sheila Hayford

November 15
The Gift Of Appreciation

1 Corinthians Chapter 12, verse 18:
But in fact God has placed the parts in the body, every one of them, just as he wanted them to be. (NIV)

Prayer: Dear God, thank you for the different gifts you have given to humanity. Help us to use our gifts for the glory of God. In Jesus' Name, Amen.

I am so glad I have the opportunity to enjoy the various gifts, talents and abilities God has given to me and to others. I do not play the violin but I get to appreciate and enjoy Yo Yo Ma's performances. I say, I have the gift of appreciation. When I have opportunity, I thank the artists or musician for allowing others to experience their gift and allowing society to be enriched by their presence. God specifically gave you the gifts and abilities you have. Use them for the glory of God and the benefit of humanity.

© By Dr. Sheila Hayford

November 16
Seedtime And Harvest

Genesis Chapter 8, verse 22:
While the earth remaineth, seedtime and harvest, and cold and heat, and summer and winter, and day and night shall not cease.
Prayer: Dear God; help us to live our lives with eternity to come in mind. In Jesus' Name, Amen.

Seedtime and Harvest; that is a Biblical principle. A farmer plants corn in expectation of a harvest of corn. You sow time in study and reap the benefits of a good job. You sow friendliness to your fellow man and you reap friendliness in return. The important thing of note is this; there is time in between the sowing and the harvesting and what you do with the time in between will determine the quality of the harvest or if you will reap the expected harvest. You must water the ground, weed and fertilize, protect the growing crops and have good weather for a good harvest. The full harvest for what we sow here on earth is in eternity. Let us be careful how we sow, what we sow and what we do with the time we have.

© By Dr. Sheila Hayford

November 17
Jesus Sums It Up

Luke Chapter 10, verse 27:

And he answering said, Thou shalt love the Lord thy God with all thy heart, and with all thy soul, and with all thy strength, and with all thy mind; and thy neighbour as thyself.

Prayer: Dear Holy Spirit; enable us to truly love and serve God and to extend God's love in action to our neighbor. In Jesus' Name, Amen.

The Christian life is simple; not easy, but not complicated. How should we live? The Lord Jesus sums it up. We should love God with our entire being and love our neighbor as we love ourselves. When we have mastery of that, we can talk with God about what's next. In the meantime, let us ask and depend on the Holy Spirit to love God with all that we are and in all that we have and do and to love ourselves enough to be able to truly love our neighbor.

© By Dr. Sheila Hayford

November 18
Apostle Paul Expounds

Romans Chapter 13, verse 9:
For this, Thou shalt not commit adultery, Thou shalt not kill, Thou shalt not steal, Thou shalt not bear false witness, Thou shalt not covet; and if there be any other commandment, it is briefly comprehended in this saying, namely, Thou shalt love thy neighbour as thyself.

Prayer: Dear Lord Jesus; you did not leave us ignorant of our responsibilities towards our neighbors. So help us glorify you in our relationships. Amen.

The Lord Jesus summed up how we should treat our neighbor. In this verse, the Apostle Paul expounds on our responsibility towards our neighbor as revealed in the Ten Commandments. So in effect, our responsibilities towards our neighbor are summed up in one word, love. If you truly love God, you will love your neighbor.

© By Dr. Sheila Hayford

November 19
Intercessors

Exodus Chapter 34, verse 9:

"Lord," he said, "if I have found favor in your eyes, then let the Lord go with us. Although this is a stiff-necked people, forgive our wickedness and our sin, and take us as your inheritance." (NIV)

Prayer: Dear God; you are willing and able to intervene in the affairs of men when your children call on you. Let us come boldly to your throne of grace, through our Lord Jesus Christ, in whose Name we pray, Amen.

Oh, how we need more intercessors! As we look at the state of affairs, it is obvious that we need more intercessors; people in relationship with God who will plead with God for their fellow men, women and children and for their communities and nations without compromising their relationship with God or their godly standards. Moses knew he was highly favored of God and could have enjoyed God's blessings with no guilt. However, he had a heart of compassion for his people and pleaded with God on their behalf. Do we?

© By Dr. Sheila Hayford

November 20
See What God Sees

Numbers Chapter 22, verse 31:

Then the Lord opened Balaam's eyes, and he saw the angel of the Lord standing in the road with his sword drawn. So he bowed low and fell facedown. (NIV)

Prayer: Dear Holy Spirit; grant us discernment in our daily living. Help us to depend on you for guidance and instruction and to heed your promptings. In Jesus' Name, Amen.

Balaam was beating his donkey in the natural realm because he could not discern the angel of the Lord standing in the road. When Balaam's spiritual eyes were opened, he saw God's angel. How many have been fighting the wrong people or the wrong battles because they could not discern who or what God had placed in front of them? The Holy Spirit gives us the discernment to see what God wants us to see and empowers us to live victoriously. We must ask God the Holy Spirit for wisdom, discernment and guidance and then follow through with what God instructs us to do. Ask!

© By Dr. Sheila Hayford

November 21
Whose Wisdom?

Proverbs Chapter 3, verse 7:
Be not wise in thine own eyes: fear the Lord, and depart from evil.
Prayer: Dear God; we reverence you as God and we humbly submit to your authority. In Jesus' Name, Amen.

God places a high value on wisdom and we all need wisdom for daily living. So what does this verse mean? This verse exhorts us to fear God and depart from evil. Scripture tells us that the fear or reverence of God is the beginning of wisdom so a person who is wise in their own eyes is one who does not acknowledge the wisdom of God. Such thinking is arrogant and prideful, two characteristics God hates. Let us submit ourselves to God and God's authority and walk humbly with God.

© By Dr. Sheila Hayford

November 22
Let God Do The Fighting

Deuteronomy Chapter 1, verse 30:

The Lord your God, who is going before you, will fight for you, as he did for you in Egypt, before your very eyes, (NIV)

Prayer: Dear God; you always know what is best for us. Help us to obey you in all things, in the power of the Holy Spirit. In Jesus' Name, Amen.

Have you ever been in a situation where you wanted to get even but God said not to? It is like a parent who realizes that if their child tried to fight a particular person, their child might end up getting hurt and so they ask the child to allow the parent to handle the situation. God is our heavenly Father and he knows that sometimes when we try to seek immediate revenge it will spiritually be to our detriment so God asks us to allow Him to fight for us. When God speaks, obey God and let God do the fighting.

© By Dr. Sheila Hayford

November 23
Are You In The Book?

Revelation Chapter 21, verse 27:
And there shall in no wise enter into it any thing that defileth, neither whatsoever worketh abomination, or maketh a lie: but they which are written in the Lamb's book of life.

Prayer: Dear Lord Jesus, we thank you that you have written our names in your Book of Life. We know your desire is that all will be saved. Help us to do our part in sharing your love and the good news of salvation through you with others. Amen.

Which book are we talking about here? It is the Lamb's book of Life. It is the book in which the Lord Jesus has written the names of all who have received the finished work of the Lord Jesus Christ, described as the Lamb of God, and have invited the Lord Jesus into their heart as Lord and Savior. Yes, the Lord Jesus is preparing an exclusive, amazing place for us. And who gets to decide who can be there? You get to choose! However, you can only choose while you are living on this earth so do not delay. It is going to be a beautiful place, more beautiful than words can describe or the human mind can fathom. We would love to see you there. Accept God's gift, the Lord Jesus Christ as your Lord and Savior today!

© By Dr. Sheila Hayford

November 24
The Coming Judge

Revelation Chapter 19, verses 15-16:

And out of his mouth goeth a sharp sword, that with it he should smite the nations: and he shall rule them with a rod of iron: and he treadeth the winepress of the fierceness and wrath of Almighty God. And he hath on his vesture and on his thigh a name written, King Of Kings, And Lord Of Lords.

Prayer: Dear Lord Jesus; thank you for paying the price for the sins of humanity, sins that came as a result of the sins of Adam and Eve's disobedience to God, and for giving humanity the opportunity to receive your free gift of salvation. We bless you and willingly submit to your authority. Amen.

In the month of December, we will be celebrating the coming of the Lord Jesus Christ as a baby to this earth, sent by God for the salvation of humanity. However, we must remember that the Lord Jesus now sits at the right hand of authority of God the Father and has been given the Name above all names. He will judge the nations with righteous judgment and it will not be pleasant for those who choose to reject him. The Lord Jesus did not come to the earth the first time to condemn humanity, he came to save humanity. We are living in times of grace when all who choose to have the opportunity to receive the Lord Jesus Christ as their Lord and Savior. Everyone can accept the Lord Jesus while they are still living on earth. Take advantage of God's grace and goodness and willingly submit to the Lordship of the Lord Jesus Christ today.

© By Dr. Sheila Hayford

November 25
Did God Hear You?

Exodus Chapter 15, verse 1:
Then sang Moses and the children of Israel this song unto the Lord, and spake, saying, I will sing unto the Lord, for he hath triumphed gloriously: the horse and his rider hath he thrown into the sea.

Prayer: Dear God, thank you for being our wonderful heavenly Father who only desires the best for his children. We appreciate you. In Jesus' Name, Amen.

Each of us has a unique song that we can sing to God. We do not have to have musical talent to sing to God. We can sing to God anywhere and at any time. We can sing loudly or softly, with or without instruments. What God desires is a sincere song sang from the heart. What has God done for you? Who is God to you? How has God helped you? How has God saved, delivered and protected you? We read in this verse that Moses and the children of Israel sang to God when God wrought a mighty deliverance as they safely passed through the Red Sea while the enemies who tried to follow them drowned in the Red Sea. Sing your unique song to God!

© By Dr. Sheila Hayford

November 26
Happy Thanksgiving!

Psalm 92, verse 1:

It is a good thing to give thanks unto the Lord, and to sing praises unto thy name, O Most High:

Prayer: Dear God, we thank you for so great a salvation and for all you give to humanity through our Lord and Savior Jesus Christ. We thank you for your protection and provision and are eternally grateful to you. We ask for your blessings as we celebrate this day. In Jesus' Name, Amen.

It is Thanksgiving Day in the United States. With all the many blessings God has given us, including life, health, family and friends, acquaintances, food, shelter, provision and most of all, the gift of the Lord Jesus Christ to humanity, it is our rightful duty to give praise and to thank our God. God desires us to worship Him out of reverence and love for Him and his wonderful works. We were still in sin when God sent the Lord Jesus to rescue and redeem us from sin, satan and death. Now we have an eternal future with God. So, as we enjoy the turkey and all the trimmings with family and friends, let us make sure to first give thanks and praise to God. Hallelujah!

© By Dr. Sheila Hayford

November 27
The Power Of Focus

Proverbs Chapter 4, verse 25:
Let thine eyes look right on, and let thine eyelids look straight before thee.

Prayer: Dear Holy Spirit, help us to keep our focus and not be distracted as we work on our assigned tasks. In Jesus' Name, Amen.

Focus is very powerful. A focused person does not allow distractions to interfere with their course of action and is more likely to complete the task at hand. A distracted person is drawn into just about anything and might not ever complete their assigned task. This verse encourages to look straight ahead at the goal in front of us and not allow ourselves to be distracted. God's work in us and through us is too important to be left unfinished; we will complete our work, In Jesus' Name.

© By Dr. Sheila Hayford

November 28
Do Not Slumber

Proverbs Chapter 6, verse 4:
Give not sleep to thine eyes, nor slumber to thine eyelids.
Prayer: Dear God; now is not the time to slumber so help us finish this year well. In Jesus' Name, Amen.

Do not slumber! We are about to enter the last month of the year and there might be the tendency to think that what has not gotten done for the year up to this time will not get done. It does not have to be so! The Lord Jesus spent thirty-three years on this earth but took only three days to die and rise again. Our God of acceleration knows how to accelerate what needs to be done. So take inventory of what you need to be done this year and re-evaluate your plans. With God on our side, it can be done!

© By Dr. Sheila Hayford

November 29
Precious!

Proverbs Chapter 17, verse 8:
A gift is as a precious stone in the eyes of him that hath it: whithersoever it turneth, it prospereth.
Prayer: Dear Heavenly Father; you are more precious to us than words could describe. We thank you for the gift of the Lord Jesus Christ and the gift of God the Holy Spirit. Thank you for your ever abiding presence in us. In Jesus' Name, Amen.

What do you value? We know there are some gifts that are very precious to us; what some call of sentimental value. They are not necessarily expensive, but we value the person who gave it, their thoughtfulness, the memories associated with it and in our eyes, the gift is irreplaceable. That is so with the Word of God, God's written gift to humanity. It is God speaking to us, God teaching and instructing us, God warning us, God promising us, God prophesying to us and much more. Moreover, the Lord Jesus Christ, who is the living Word of God, is our Lord and Savior and He reigns forever. The Holy Spirit, the Lord Jesus' gift to us, indwells us. How blest we are! Hallelujah!

© By Dr. Sheila Hayford

November 30
What Do You See?

Matthew Chapter 6, verse 22:
The eye is the lamp of the body. If your eyes are healthy, your whole body will be full of light. (NIV)

Prayer: Dear God; thank you for the gift of vision. Help us take responsibility for what we allow our eyes to observe. In Jesus' Name, Amen.

What do you see? Great question! In fact, the better question would be, "What do you choose to see?" This verse tells us that if what you choose to see is healthy or wholesome, your body will be full of light and you will walk in purity. If a person feeds their eyes with filth, their mind will be polluted or defiled and their body will respond likewise. As believers of our Lord Jesus Christ, we must take heed what we choose to see because that is a free-will choice. Choose wisely!

© By Dr. Sheila Hayford

December 1
A Child Is Born

Isaiah Chapter 9, verse 6:

For unto us a child is born, unto us a son is given: and the government shall be upon his shoulder: and his name shall be called Wonderful, Counsellor, The mighty God, The everlasting Father, The Prince of Peace.

Prayer: Dear Lord Jesus; we rejoice and are exceedingly glad for you have come, you are risen and you will come again. Hallelujah! Amen.

What a wonderful month of celebration; celebrating the birth of our Lord and Savior, Jesus Christ! Yes, the Lord Jesus was born to save mankind from sin and the punishment of sin when he died on the cross for us, but he had to first come to earth in the flesh and live a sinless life among us in order for that to happen. Yes, we share gifts with others; family, friends and strangers as a show of our appreciation for what God has done for us. However, we should never forget whose birthday we are celebrating for without the Lord Jesus Christ's birth on earth, there would be no Christmas. Unto us, a child is born! Celebrate Jesus, the Christ!

© By Dr. Sheila Hayford.

December 2
Prophecy Fulfilled

Isaiah Chapter 7, verse 14:

Therefore the Lord himself shall give you a sign; Behold, a virgin shall conceive, and bear a son, and shall call his name Immanuel.

Prayer: Dear All-knowing God; your words are so reliable! Thank you that we can depend entirely on what you say for you will never fail. In Jesus' Name, Amen.

It is astounding how accurate the prophecies of God are; to the smaller than minutest details. God prophesied through the prophet Isaiah that the Lord Jesus would be born of a virgin who would give birth to a son whose name means God with us. And that is exactly how it happened. Some wonder if the Holy Bible is relevant in the affairs of men today. The answer is: Yes, it is even more relevant. As we read the Bible, we read of several prophecies given with regards to humankind and this earth we now inhabit that have not yet been fulfilled. Each of these prophesies will have significant consequences depending on what you do with your life while you are on this earth. The Second Coming of the Lord Jesus will take place soon and this earth as we know it will be no more, two very important issues. Take time in personal Bible study to study some of the prophecies of God that are yet to be fulfilled with regards to humanity. What personal prophecies from God are you waiting for? Some promises and prophesies from God are conditional so find out God's terms and conditions. Then govern yourself accordingly. God's desire is to fulfil His good and great promises in and to us.

© By Dr. Sheila Hayford.

December 3
Godly Lineage

Matthew Chapter 1, verse 17:
So all the generations from Abraham to David are fourteen generations; and from David until the carrying away into Babylon are fourteen generations; and from the carrying away into Babylon unto Christ are fourteen generations.

Prayer: Dear God, thank you for the gift of godly families. May the "G.P.T." grow in families here on earth as your kingdom moves forward in the earth. In Jesus' Name, Amen.

Next to one's personal salvation and relationship with God the Father, God the Son and God the Holy Spirit, a godly family and a godly lineage is a blessing that goes beyond temporal benefits. Moreover, your godly family and heritage matter a lot to God. From Abraham, described in the Bible as a friend of God and Father of faith because he believed

God, to King David who was dearly beloved of God are fourteen generations. From King David's lineage, the Lord Jesus Christ was born. Are you the first in your family to receive the Lord Jesus Christ as your Lord and Savior and become a born again Christian? Then start what I call in Morning Glory - 365 Devotionals like no other! the "G.P.T."; my abbreviation for the Godly Parent Tradition. If you are part of a godly family heritage, respect and value your heritage and do not take your faith in Christ for granted. Determine by God's grace to teach and impart the knowledge of God and faith in God to young and upcoming generations as well as to your peers. Help others start their 'G.P.T. also. Many yet unborn are depending on you. Indeed, God's kingdom has been waiting for you.

© By Dr. Sheila Hayford.

December 4
The Promise Fulfilled

Luke Chapter 2, verses 25-32:

Now there was a man in Jerusalem called Simeon, who was righteous and devout. He was waiting for the consolation of Israel, and the Holy Spirit was on him. It had been revealed to him by the Holy Spirit that he would not die before he had seen the Lord's Messiah. Moved by the Spirit, he went into the temple courts. When the parents brought in the child Jesus to do for him what the custom of the Law required, Simeon took him in his arms and praised God, saying: "Sovereign Lord, as you have promised, you may now dismiss your servant in peace. For my eyes have seen your salvation, which you have prepared in the sight of all nations: a light for revelation to the Gentiles, and the glory of your people Israel." (NIV)

Prayer: Dear God; thank you for being the Ultimate Promise Keeper. We honor you and do not take your blessings lightly. In Jesus' Name, Amen.

Simeon was a devout man, who had been promised by God that he would live to see the Lord Jesus Christ on this earth. It may have been a long time before he saw the fulfilment of that promise and it might have seemed at times that it might not happen. Maybe Simeon felt unwell at times, but knew he could not die before God's promise came to pass and so Simeon held on to God's promise. Then one day, the Holy Spirit led Simeon into the temple courts and in the course of doing what was customarily being done according to their Law, God's promise to Simeon was fulfilled. Just like that, without any advance fanfare! Wow! With much gratitude, thankfulness and appreciation, Simeon gave God glory in public for the fulfillment of God's promises and was ready to leave this earth. Did God grant him more days on this earth? Probably! What is important for us is that God kept God's words to Simeon and God will keep God's words to us. And when God keeps His good promises to us, let us show God gratitude, appreciation and thankfulness both in private and in public.

God's promises are sure worth waiting on God for!

© By Dr. Sheila Hayford.

December 5
Widowed and Satisfied

Luke Chapter 2, verses 36-38:

And there was one Anna, a prophetess, the daughter of Phanuel, of the tribe of Aser; she was of a great age and had lived with her husband seven years from her virginity, and she was a widow eighty-four years, who departed not from the temple, serving night and day with fastings and prayers. And she coming in that instant gave thanks likewise unto the Lord and spoke of him to all those that looked for redemption in Jerusalem.

1 Corinthians Chapter 7, verses 8, 9:

Now to the unmarried and the widows I say: It is good for them to stay unmarried, as I do. But if they cannot control themselves, they should marry, for it is better to marry than to burn with passion. (NIV)

Prayer: Dear God, thank you for inspiring and challenging us with the testimony of Anna. To you is all the glory! In Jesus' Name, Amen.

What an amazing woman Anna is! Anna was married for only seven years and was living as a widow for eighty-four years. What makes Anna's life so remarkable is that she spent her eighty-seven years as a widow in the temple of God praying with fastings. Amazing! There is certainly a lot Anna could say to younger and older women alike. Anna was not interested in being the center of attention. She was content and satisfied serving God in God's temple and no doubt God shared some amazing insights with Anna that not everyone was privy to experience. The Holy Spirit led Anna to come in at the very time the Lord Jesus was in the temple. She immediately recognized the Lord Jesus Christ, gave thanks to God and preached salvation through the Lord Jesus for those who were anticipating redemption in Jerusalem. Is Anna's lifestyle for everybody? It depends on the person. The Apostle Paul was single and satisfied but recognized that it was better for single individuals and widows to get married than to engage in sinful acts. Be the authentic you and allow God to use you in the "spiritually authentic you" capacity.

© By Dr. Sheila Hayford.

December 6
Joseph – Entrusted With The Son Of God

Matthew Chapter 1, verses 18-21, 24-25:
This is how the birth of Jesus the Messiah came about: His mother Mary was pledged to be married to Joseph, but before they came together, she was found to be pregnant through the Holy Spirit. Because Joseph her husband was faithful to the law, and yet did not want to expose her to public disgrace, he had in mind to divorce her quietly. But after he had considered this, an angel of the Lord appeared to him in a dream and said, "Joseph son of David, do not be afraid to take Mary home as your wife, because what is conceived in her is from the Holy

Spirit. She will give birth to a son, and you are to give him the name Jesus, because he will save his people from their sins." When Joseph woke up, he did what the angel of the Lord had commanded him and took Mary home as his wife. But he did not consummate their marriage until she gave birth to a son. And he gave him the name Jesus. (NIV)

Prayer: Dear God: Thank you for Joseph; chosen, faithful and highly favored. Thank you for your keeping grace and empowerment and that Joseph did not let you down. May we individually be found faithful to you and in your service. In Jesus' Name, Amen.

Joseph is one amazing gentleman! Wow! Entrusted by God the Almighty to be the earthly father of our Lord and Savior, Jesus Christ, Joseph is a highly favored man of God. Some people have the personality that does a lot of talking, others have the gift of being very sociable. Joseph was a quiet person. When he found out that the woman he was engaged to be married to was pregnant with child, he was quiet about it. Joseph did not make a public spectacle of Mary, nor ask that Mary be stoned which was the practice at that time if she was pregnant by another man out of wedlock. Joseph's plan was to quietly let Mary go. However, Joseph had already gotten God's attention and so God sent his angel to reveal to Joseph in a dream the miraculous virgin birth that would take place and asked that Joseph should take Mary home as his wife. Joseph obeyed God, took Mary home as his wife and abstained from any sexual relations with her until after Mary gave birth to the Lord Jesus. How many men would the Lord God trust to do that? If a person is not faithful in the way they behave to the one they are engaged to marry, can God trust them to be faithful to each other after they are married? Joseph certainly got God's attention and he received a favor no other earthly father has received. As I read what God shares in the Holy Bible of Joseph, Joseph most certainly has gotten my attention. Do we have God's attention? And if we do, what is God saying to us and about us? That is something to meditate on.

© By Dr. Sheila Hayford.

December 7
Can God Use A Census?

Luke Chapter 2, verses 1-5:

And it came to pass in those days, that there went out a decree from Caesar Augustus that all the world should be taxed. (And this taxing was first made when Cyrenius was governor of Syria.) And all went to be taxed, every one into his own city. And Joseph also went up from Galilee, out of the city of Nazareth, into Judaea, unto the city of David, which is called Bethlehem; (because he was of the house and lineage of David:) To be taxed with Mary his espoused wife, being great with child.

Micah Chapter 5, verse 2:

But thou, Bethlehem Ephratah, though thou be little among the thousands of Judah, yet out of thee shall he come forth unto me that is to be ruler in Israel; whose goings forth have been from of old, from everlasting.

Prayer: Dear God; the hearts of Kings and Queens are in your hand and your purpose and plans will be established as you influence the affairs of man. May our lives be in full accord with your Words. In Jesus' Name, Amen.

Can God use a census? The short answer is: Yes! The Lord God had prophesied that the Lord Jesus would be born in Bethlehem so somehow Joseph and Mary had to be in Bethlehem when Mary was ready to give birth to the Lord Jesus. And so when the time came that Mary was about due, God had Caesar Augustus issues a decree that everyone should go their own city to be taxed and there in Bethlehem, the Lord Jesus was born. Yes, God can use anybody, Christian or not, to achieve God's purpose and to bring about the fulfilment of what God has declared. So do not place a limit on God as to how you want God to fulfil his Words or His promises. If you do, you might miss God. Let us allow God to prove himself and His words to be true in the way God chooses!

© By Dr. Sheila Hayford.

December 8
Herod: Insecurity Personified

Matthew Chapter 2, verse 16:

Then Herod, when he saw that he was mocked of the wise men, was exceeding wroth, and sent forth, and slew all the children that were in Bethlehem, and in all the coasts thereof, from two years old and under, according to the time which he had diligently inquired of the wise men.

Prayer: Dear God: Our security and our worth come from our relationship with your Son, our Lord and Savior, Jesus Christ, and for that we are thankful. Lead and direct us in all things and help us make wise decisions as to we choose whose authority we will submit to. Help us as we make the wise decision to submit to you first and foremost. In Jesus' Name, Amen.

How can a sitting King be so insecure about a baby who has just been born even if the baby is born to be king? At first, when Herod inquired of the wise men about the birth of Jesus, he pretended he wanted to go and worship the baby Jesus. However, God warned the wise men not to return to Herod. After two years when Herod realized the wise men would not get back to him, he had ALL the children two years of age and under who were in Bethlehem killed, in an attempt to kill the Lord Jesus Christ. So what happened? God had already told Joseph to get his family out of Bethlehem by that time so Joseph, Mary and the Lord Jesus were safe. King Herod died, the Lord Jesus still lives and King Herod will ultimately have to answer to the Lord Jesus, the one he tried to kill, when he is judged by the Lord Jesus on that Judgment Day. Sober thoughts! The lesson here is that insecurity in a person can have disastrous results; not just for them but for those under their authority. So be careful under whose authority you choose to submit. A person who is insecure might abuse or hurt his or her spouse or those close to them if they perceive a real or imagined threat to their person or their authority.

God wants you to know who you are in Christ in God and refuse to let satan or others make you feel less than you are.

© By Dr. Sheila Hayford.

December 9
The Shepherds

Luke Chapter 2, verses 8-11:
And there were in the same country shepherds abiding in the field, keeping watch over their flock by night. And, lo, the angel of the Lord came upon them, and the glory of the Lord shone round about them: and they were sore afraid. And the angel said unto them, Fear not: for, behold, I bring you good tidings of great joy, which shall be to all people. For unto you is born this day in the city of David a Saviour, which is Christ the Lord.

John Chapter 10, verse 11:
I am the good shepherd: the good shepherd giveth his life for the sheep.

Prayer: Dear Lord Jesus, we are so blessed to have you as our Good Shepherd. Thank you for dying on the cross for my sins and rising again with great authority and power. I confess my sins to you and ask you to cleanse me from all sin. I invite you to come into my heart as my Lord and Savior and know you will take utmost care of me. Thank you for the gift of the Holy Spirit to help me live for you and the free gift of eternal life to spend eternity with you. I bless you and I honor you, Amen.

Isn't it interesting that the Lord Jesus, the Good Shepherd, would be introduced to the shepherds by the angel of the Lord? There was something about the profession of the shepherds that was very appealing to the Lord Jesus. While some may have viewed the shepherd's jobs as mundane, the Lord Jesus saw a people concerned about the welfare of the flock under their care who would feed and protect their flock, even at great personal risk. And so, the Lord Jesus used the shepherds as a very fitting example when the Lord Jesus described himself as the Good Shepherd who gave his life for us. You see, the Lord Jesus saw humanity, left to the devouring ways of satan and condemned to hell as a result of the sins of Adam and Eve, but did not leave humanity in that condition. The Lord Jesus came to earth to live and sacrifice his life to pay the price for the sins of all humanity. However, the Lord Jesus Christ rose again and is seated at the right hand of God, our heavenly Father. Do you know the Lord Jesus Christ as your Good Shepherd?

© By Dr. Sheila Hayford.

December 10
The Wise Men

Matthew Chapter 2, verses 1-2:

Now when Jesus was born in Bethlehem of Judaea in the days of Herod the king, behold, there came wise men from the east to Jerusalem, Saying, Where is he that is born King of the Jews? for we have seen his star in the east, and are come to worship him.

Prayer: Dear God; help us to be wise and to seek you in sincerity and in truth. In Jesus' Name, Amen.

I love how accessible God is to all who are sincerely seeking God. The shepherds were out in the fields taking care of their sheep when the angel announced the birth of the Lord Jesus to them. In the case of the wise men, it was the wise men who came looking for God. In their desire to find the king of the Jews who had been prophesied about in the Old Testament, God led them by a star. Today, we do not have to go far to find God. We have the Holy Bible which not only reveals God our heavenly Father, the Lord Jesus Christ and the Holy Spirit, but also how we can invite and receive the Lord Jesus Christ as Lord and Savior in our individual hearts and become a part of God's family. How wonderful is that! The first priority of the wise men in their quest for the Lord Jesus shows why they were wise; their first priority was to worship God. They were not coming to God to find out how many blessings they could receive from God, even though we receive multitudes of blessing from God. They were coming to God because God is worthy of all praise. God is God and worthy of our praise, our adoration, our service and our worship. Are you seeking God sincerely? Are you, like the wise men seeking God to first and foremost worship and serve God? If yes, you will find God because God is longing to reveal himself to you.

© By Dr. Sheila Hayford.

December 11
From The East And From The West

Exodus Chapter 10, verses 1, 19:

And Moses stretched forth his rod over the land of Egypt, and the Lord brought an east wind upon the land all that day, and all that night; and when it was morning, the east wind brought the locusts.

And the Lord turned a mighty strong west wind, which took away the locusts, and cast them into the Red sea; there remained not one locust in all the coasts of Egypt.

Prayer: Dear God; we choose your blessing. Help us to serve you faithfully. In Jesus' Name, Amen.

Cursing or Blessing? We get to choose! God gave specific instructions to King Pharaoh through the prophet Moses. When King Pharaoh disobeyed God, King Pharaoh put himself under the curse of God and God sent an east wind that covered the land with locusts. When Pharaoh professed to be repentant and asked the prophet Moses to entreat God on behalf of King Pharaoh's professed repentance, God heard his prophet Moses and sent a strong west wind that took the locusts away. However, God knew King Pharaoh's heart and King Pharaoh continually made professions of repentance he never did follow through on until King Pharaoh was finally destroyed by God. So for those who want

God's blessings the choice is clear. Reverence, honor and serve God in obedience. Yes, God is our heavenly Father but he is our God first. So what if a person has disobeyed God and is under a curse? Can the curse be reversed? Yes, God will send His mighty strong wind; the wind of the Holy Spirit, the power of God and the blood of the Lord Jesus will reverse the curse if a person sincerely repents of sin, asks God for forgiveness and invites the Lord Jesus into their heart and life and Lord and Savior. Choose God's blessing!

© By Dr. Sheila Hayford.

December 12
Arise and Shine

Isaiah Chapter 60, verse 1, 3:
Arise, shine; for thy light is come, and the glory of the Lord is risen upon thee. And the Gentiles shall come to thy light, and kings to the brightness of thy rising.

Prayer: Dear God; it is our time to stand up and speak up for you and to show your light and your power at work in us. So help us, in the power of the Holy Spirit. In Jesus' Name, Amen.

Sometimes Christians can be too reserved. There are many people hurting, there are problems that require solutions for which they may have the answer but they just keep quiet and say nothing. That is selfish! God wants us to rise up for our Lord Jesus Christ, to share God's good plan for the salvation of humanity and to show the power of God at work in our lives. Why? It is because God's kingdom is not primarily about us, it is primarily about God. God has specific others waiting to hear you bring God's message. So stand up, speak up; it is your time to arise and shine. God's kingdom is moving forward; so do not stay behind!

© By Dr. Sheila Hayford.

December 13
Room At The Inn

Romans Chapter 12, verse 13:

Share with the Lord's people who are in need. Practice hospitality. (NIV)

Prayer: Dear God, it is such a joy to experience your custom tailored miracles. You provided a place for Mary, Joseph and the Lord Jesus and you continue to provide for us today. Help us to make room in our Inn to be a blessing to others. In Jesus' Name, Amen.

I was attending a Christian conference in a major city so I figured it would be easy finding a hotel room. I browsed online, called the hotels, looked in person and did all I knew to do. However, all the hotels were filled. Finally, the Holy Spirit gave me the idea to call the local Bed and Breakfast Inns in the area. It worked. I was able to book a place and I stayed in a gorgeous Bed and Breakfast Inn. Not only were they very hospitable, they prepared a hearty breakfast to start the day. However, what I really loved was how God custom tailored the experience for me. God knows I love history and there was some history there associated with the famous George Washington with some memorabilia. I was overjoyed! While the hotels were all booked, there was plenty of room at the Bed and Breakfast Inn. When Mary and Joseph were looking for a place for Mary to give birth to our Lord Jesus Christ, many turned them away. However, God had a place prepared for them and there in a lowly manger, our Lord and Savior, Jesus Christ was born. The Apostle Paul encourages us to practice hospitality and to share with Christians who are in need. Other places may be filled up and unavailable to them. God is asking each of us, "Is there room at your Inn?"

© By Dr. Sheila Hayford.

December 14
God Has Sent The Remedy

2 Chronicles Chapter 36, verses 15-17:

The Lord, the God of their ancestors, sent word to them through his messengers again and again, because he had pity on his people and on his dwelling place. But they mocked God's messengers, despised his words and scoffed at his prophets until the wrath of the Lord was aroused against his people and there was no remedy. He brought up against them the king of the Babylonians, who killed their young men with the sword in the sanctuary, and did not spare young men or young women, the elderly or the infirm. God gave them all into the hands of Nebuchadnezzar.

Prayer: Dear God; through your Son, our Lord and Savior, Jesus Christ you have provided humanity with everything we need for salvation from sin and the consequences and punishment of sin, from satan and from hell. Help us to accept and receive your remedy. In Jesus' Name with much thanksgiving, Amen.

As we celebrate the birth of the Lord Jesus Christ, let us remember that God sent humanity his Son, the Lord Jesus Christ as the remedy for sin and the consequences and curses of sin. As we read in the Scriptures above, God sent many people to warn humanity to repent and turn away from sin. Some heeded God's warning and those who rejected God's warning faced disastrous consequences. The choice to obey or reject God's Son, the Lord Jesus Christ, now rests with each individual. God has provided humanity with the remedy; no one can blame God for their personal decisions. Accept God's remedy and live!

© By Dr. Sheila Hayford.

December 15
Faith In Action

Mark Chapter 11, verses 22-23:

And Jesus answering saith unto them, Have faith in God. For verily I say unto you, That whosoever shall say unto this mountain, Be thou removed, and be thou cast into the sea; and shall not doubt in his heart, but shall believe that those things which he saith shall come to pass; he shall have whatsoever he saith.

Prayer: Dear God; you always outdo what we thought possible **for with God, all things are possible.** Help us to apply corresponding actions to our faith and see your mighty hand working custom tailored miracles on our behalf. In Jesus' Name, Amen.

A friend was believing God for a new home. She prayed, discussed it with God and needed the funds in order for her to be able to purchase a new home. She believed it was in God's will for her and she had faith to trust God to bring that to pass. So she began to apply corresponding actions to her faith. She packed her things and moved them into storage, ready to be moved to her new home. When she was asked where her new home would be, she said she did not know. When she was asked, what date she would move into her new home, she said she would let God take care of that. Then she went to see a Realtor. Unexpectedly, my friend received a fairly large amount of money. So she went with the Realtor looking at homes that would fit her budget. They found one but it needed fixing! She was elated. The miracles were continuing! They spoke with the seller and the seller agreed to fix the house. Then God allowed the seller to have my friend stay in the home free of charge before settlement until the needed repairs were done!! My friend said the Realtor said he had never seen anything like that in all his years working as a Realtor! The house was fixed, paid for in full at settlement and my friend still enjoys living in her home.

And yes, God is a God of overflow, and so after settlement, my friend still had funds left over! In keeping with God's will for us, what do we have faith in God for?

Let us apply corresponding actions to our faith and allow God to "show off" on our behalf.

© By Dr. Sheila Hayford.

December 16
***The Heart of an Overcomer:

John Chapter 16, verse 33:
In this world you will have trouble. But take heart! I have overcome the world.

Prayer: Dear Lord Jesus; how we love you! I am so grateful and thankful that you are our perfect example and that you would never ask us to do anything without giving us the power to do so. Enable us to look beyond any challenges to you. Let us trust Your Word and the Holy Spirit to transform our perspective, our situations and us. Enable us to live victoriously by giving us victory over sin, satan and all evil. May we renew our mind with and correctly apply your Holy Scriptures so that our lives will bring glory to our heavenly Father, God Almighty. Amen.

What is the Lord Jesus really saying to us? Is the life of a Christian always supposed to be full of trouble, or at the least, drama? Whenever I see the word 'trouble' I can usually replace it with the word 'challenge' or 'challenges'. So the text would be understood as: In this world you will have challenges. But take heart! I have overcome the world. Now I can relax! It means WHATEVER situation or challenge I am facing I can <u>always</u> have the victory. So how does victory in our challenges look like? It is victory God's way, in God's timing, and of God's choosing. When Joseph was going through all the earlier challenges that we read about in the Book of Genesis, it did not look anything like victory because in the eyes of men it seemed evil had gained the upper hand. But in God's eyes, every time Joseph refused to yield to sin, Joseph was victorious. Every time Joseph refused to give in to bitterness and unforgiveness, Joseph was victorious. And when Joseph was promoted to second in command to King Pharaoh, Joseph's overcoming victories were manifest to all. And who got all the glory? God. For ultimately, that is what our lives are all about; living lives that are glorifying to God.

© By Dr. Sheila Hayford.

*** Excerpt from 2017 Edition of Morning Glory -365 Devotionals like no other! By Dr. Sheila Hayford. Used with permission.

December 17
What Are You Praying About?

Exodus Chapter 14, verses 15-16:
And the Lord said unto Moses, Wherefore criest thou unto me? speak unto the children of Israel, that they go forward: But lift thou up thy rod, and stretch out thine hand over the sea, and divide it: and the children of Israel shall go on dry ground through the midst of the sea.

Prayer: Dear God; help us to move in sync with you, in the power of the Holy Spirit. In Jesus' Name, Amen.

We all know the importance of prayer. We know you cannot be in a relationshipship with God without prayer. And we are encouraged in the Bible to pray without ceasing. So why did God ask the prophet Moses why he was crying to God? It is because sometimes people are fearful and use prayer as an excuse for their inaction. They know what they should do but say, "I will pray about it." After they say that, that conversation ends because most people will not ask them not to pray to God since it might look like they do not want the person to pray. However, since God speaks in prayer, it is always better to pray than not to pray. In the end, when all is said and done, we must ultimately answer to God who sees all, knows our hearts, our thoughts, our intents and our actions. When we are determined to move forward with God, God will instruct us on what we should do, just as God gave the prohet Moses instructions on what to do. Of course we should pray. And when it is time for action, Act!

© By Dr. Sheila Hayford.

December 18
Kept by God's Power

Jude Chapter 1, verses 24-25:

To him who is able to keep you from stumbling and to present you before his glorious presence without fault and with great joy - to the only God our Savior be glory, majesty, power and authority, through Jesus Christ our Lord, before all ages, now and forevermore! Amen.

Prayer: Dear God; thank you for keeping me in faith all these years and continuing in the years to come. I appreciate your patience and long-suffering with me and the way you allow me to grow in my relationship with you; through our Lord Jesus Christ and in the power of the Holy Spirit. In Jesus' Name, Amen.

What assuring verses! I received the Lord Jesus as my Lord and Savior in my teenage years and during those times it was important for me to have the confidence that God was able to keep me in faith and faithful to God in my Christian life. It is the same today for our youth and for all who begin their Christian journey when they invite the Lord Jesus into their heart and life as Savior and Lord. Yes, we must desire to please God. Yes, as Christian disciples, we must pray and exercise the Christian disciplines of faith in Christ Jesus. However, ultimately, it is God who is keeping us for we could not live for God in our own strength. So whatever the challenge, trust God and trust God's keeping power.

© By Dr. Sheila Hayford.

December 19
Soul Prosperity

3 John Chapter 1, verse 2:

Beloved, I wish above all things that thou mayest prosper and be in health, even as thy soul prospereth.

Prayer: Dear God, we submit our body, our soul and our mind to your authority, through our Lord and savior Jesus Christ. May we wlak in wholeness in every area. In Jesus' Name, Amen.

God is saying to us in these verses that our physical health is tied to our soul prosperity. That does make sense. If a person is happy and grateful, they enjoy their relationships more and their general countenance is relaxed. If a person is bitter and ungrateful, it shows in the way they speak, their relationships are strained and scientists show their health may be affected by what is going on in their mind, their emotions and their will. The Lord Jesus came to earth and was born to make humanity whole again, whole in body, soul and spirit. Let us believe and trust God, accept the Lord Jesus into our heart as Lord and Savior and allow God to fulfill God's mission to make us whole in body, soul and spirit through His Son, the Lord Jesus Christ.

© By Dr. Sheila Hayford.

December 20
What You Say Matters

1 Peter Chapter 2, verses 1, 3:

Wherefore laying aside all malice, and all guile, and hypocrisies, and envies, and all evil speakings, If so be ye have tasted that the Lord is gracious.

Prayer: Dear God; thank you be being so gracious to us. Help us to extend your grace to others. In Jesus' Name, Amen.

The month of December is a season of goodwill. We are celebrating the Lord Jesus' birth on earth and there are many celebrations; family reunions, office parties, church events and the giving and receiving of gifts. It is therefore important, especially at this time, to remember that what we say matters. How many relationships have been ruined because of what was inappropriately or incorrectly said about them? Have many people have lost their jobs because of what they inappropriately said at the office Christmas party? Remember, once you say it, you cannot take it back. You may clarify what you said and you may correct what you said or you can be careful about what you say in the first place. God has been extremely gracious to us this year. Let us extend God's good grace to us in our speech and in our relationships with our fellow humanity; men, women, youth as well as children. What you say matters!

© By Dr. Sheila Hayford.

December 21
Are You Ready?

Matthew Chapter 5, verse 24:

Leave there thy gift before the altar, and go thy way; first be reconciled to thy brother, and then come and offer thy gift.

Prayer: Dear Lord Jesus; we celebrate you! As we celebrate your birth this month, help us to be mindful to spend personal time with you and to obey you in all things. Thank you for the gift of salvation and the gift of eternal life. Hallelujah! Amen.

It will be Christmas Day in a few days, the day when we celebrate the birth of our Lord and Savior, Jesus Christ, on earth. There is so much busyness going on; the hustle and bustle of shoppers, events and parties, plays and theatrical performances, church events, the list goes on. In the midst of this, God is asking us, "Are you ready?" Not ready as in; Do you have enough gifts to give to others? Should we invite more people to the celebrations? Are your home decorations all done? No! Ready as in, "Have you set aside personal time for you to celebrate the Lord Jesus, the one whose birthday we are celebrating in the first place? Have you set aside time to thank God for his gift to humanity? Have you taken the time to lay your gifts at God's altar and first go and seek forgiveness from those who you have offended and to make things right, where possible, with those who have offended you? Yes, we love our Lord Jesus and he tells us that if we love him, we will keep his commands. Are we ready to celebrate Jesus?

© By Dr. Sheila Hayford.

December 22
Seated At God's Right Hand

But from now on, the Son of Man will be seated at the right hand of the mighty God." (NIV)

Prayer: Dear Lord Jesus; thank you for coming to earth to save us. May we remember that you are now seated at God's right hand in power and with authority. May we willingly submit to your authority. Amen.

With His victory over sin, satan and death, the Lord Jesus is now seated at the right hand of God the Father and has been given all authority. Every knee will bow before Him, on this earth or at the Judgment. Yes, God the Son, the Lord Jesus came to earth as a baby but now lives and reigns on high. Hallelujah! Receive Him as Lord and Savior today!

© By Dr. Sheila Hayford.

December 23
What Are Your Expectations?

Psalm 33, verse 20:

We wait in hope for the Lord; he is our help and our shield. (NIV)

Prayer: Daer Lord Jesus; we are looking forward to your Second coming with joy. Help us to be ready and to be found faithful. Amen.

Our hope is in the Lord Jesus Christ and we are expecting His Second Coming. The Lord Jesus came to earth as a baby, fulfilled his mission on this earth and promised to come again to receive all those who have received him as Lord and Savior. At that time, he will take us to be with him **forever**. That is huge! So our hope and expectation is in our Risen Lord and King, Jesus the Christ. What are your expectations?

© By Dr. Sheila Hayford.

December 24
Anticipation Runs High!

Luke Chapter 1, verse 31:
You will conceive and give birth to a son, and you are to call him Jesus. (NIV)

Prayer: Dear God; we are extremely grateful for the gift of the Lord Jesus Christ to humanity. We know the Lord Jesus is coming again and we are eagerly anticipating a wonderful reunion; saints of yesterday, today and tomorrow rejoicing at the Second Coming of the Lord Jesus. Our anticipation runs high! Help us to live ready. In Jesus' Name. Amen.

Imagine how Mary and Joseph must have felt when the Lord Jesus was about to be born. He was the miracle child they were to name Jesus, because he would save humanity from their sins. Could they have imagined all the joys and the suffering they would experience as the Lord Jesus fulfilled his mission here on earth? Probably not, but they would consider nothing to be too much to do for God considering all God has done, continues to do and will do for humanity. And so, as we celebrate Jesus' birth, we are blessed to welcome the Lord Jesus into our hearts and our lives. The Lord Jesus died for our sins, rose from the dead and is preparing a place for born again children of God in glory. Yes, Jesus Christ is coming back again! The prophets anticipated Christ's birth and we are anticipating Christ's Second Coming: Anticipation runs high!

© By Dr. Sheila Hayford.

December 25
The Perfect Gift

Luke Chapter 2, verse 11:

For unto you is born this day in the city of David a Saviour, which is Christ the Lord.

Prayer: Dear God, thank you for sending humanity the perfect gift of our Lord Jesus Christ while we were yet sinners. We value and respect your gift and receive the Lord Jesus into our heart and our life with joy. Thank you that we are now born again and eternally a part of your family. In Jesus' Name, Amen.

I love giving gifts. I try to find a gift that will be valuable to the person and that I would enjoy if I received as a gift. I just so enjoying the experience of giving! Well, God has a gift for humanity. In fact, all over the world, today we are celebrating God's gift of the Lord Jesus Christ to humanity. God enjoys giving gifts and he made sure this gift would be the most valuable gift humankind would receive. Our earthly gifts may be temporal. However, God knew that humankind had an eternal problem that needed an eternal solution. For when Adam and Eve sinned, all humanity fell and were condemned to a forever burning hell. So, God sent us the perfect gift of the Lord Jesus Christ. The Lord Jesus saves all who freely receive the Lord Jesus from hell and gives them the gift of salvation, the gift of the Holy Spirit and the gift of eternal life with God; all wrapped in one package, our Lord and Savior Jesus the Christ. And so make sure to thank God for his perfect gift to you and unwrap God's gift first. Then enjoy your giving and receiving of gifts as we commemorate God's gift to us.

© By Dr. Sheila Hayford.

December 26
Boxing Day

Colossians Chapter 2, verses 14-15:

Blotting out the handwriting of ordinances that was against us, which was contrary to us, and took it out of the way, nailing it to his cross; And having spoiled principalities and powers, he made a shew of them openly, triumphing over them in it.

Prayer: Dear Lord Jesus; we rejoice as we celebrate your victory over sin, satan and death. You have won the victory on our behalf and on this Boxing Day, we declare, "Jesus Christ has triumphed over satan and over all evil principalities and powers; therefore, we live victoriously in the power of the Holy Spirit who is gifted to us by our Lord and Savior, Jesus Christ." Thank you. You are blessed forever! Amen.

Today is celebrated in some parts of the world as Boxing Day. So to boxing fans and as well as those who do not like the sport of boxing, all Christians should be celebrating the Lord Jesus' triumph over satan, sin, evil principalities, evil powers and over death itself. For you see, the Lord Jesus died on the cross for the sins of humanity and rose from the dead victorious. Yes, we are celebrating the birth of the Lord Jesus this month. However, we must remember that the Lord Jesus came to earth with a mission. The punishment for the sins of Adam and Eve in disobedience to God had been pronounced against humanity and the evil principalities and powers were having a field day until the Lord Jesus showed up on earth and put a stop to their party. Through our Lord Jesus Christ our sins are forgiven, our slate is wiped clean by God and we are welcomed into God's family. So it is time for our celebration and our celebration continues all through eternity. Our celebration won't stop!

© By Dr. Sheila Hayford.

December 27
Be Born Again

John Chapter 3, verses 5-7:

Jesus answered, Verily, verily, I say unto thee, Except a man be born of water and of the Spirit, he cannot enter into the kingdom of God. That which is born of the flesh is flesh; and that which is born of the Spirit is spirit. Marvel not that I said unto thee, Ye must be born again.

Ezekiel Chapter 36, verse 26:

I will give you a new heart and put a new spirit in you; I will remove from you your heart of stone and give you a heart of flesh. (NIV)

Prayer: Dear God, I know that my decision to receive the Lord Jesus as my Lord and Savior is the best decision I ever made. It is so for me and so for many others. Help me to share this great news so many more will have this testimony. In Jesus' Name, Amen.

When Nicodemus asked the Lord Jesus if he must enter his mother's womb a second time to be born again, the Lord Jesus gave the explanation we read of here. When we are born the first time, we are born naturally in the flesh. When a person is born again, they are born supernaturally or spiritually into the family of God. God takes away their heart that is spiritually hardened by sin and gives the person a regenerated spirit that is tender towards God and the things that pertain to God. Thus, we ought not to be surprised when the Lord Jesus says we must be born again in order to enter God's kingdom. Be Born Again! And if you are already born again, share this salutation with someone who might not be: Be Born Again!

© By Dr. Sheila Hayford.

December 28
Move On!

Matthew Chapter 13, verse 53:

When Jesus had finished these parables, he moved on from there. (NIV)

Prayer: Dear God; help us to obey your instructions promptly. In Jesus Name, Amen.

Has God ever asked you to do something and you procrastinated? I had been asked my God to do a Project and God gave me enough time to do it, and then extended the time. When I had not completed it within that time period, I knew it was entirely my fault. I could not blame God. I was still going to finish it, but I could not get past the fact that I had not finished it on time. It was becoming a "weight" that was hindering my progress. So, one day when I had rehearsed my delay one more time, God said to me in conversation, "Move On!" And then, God spoke very kind and gentle words to me and gave me the opportunity to do the project and incorporate it in a different way. This Year is almost over and a New Year is at hand. What are you going to take with you into the New Year? What are you going to leave behind? God wants you to "Move On With God!"

© By Dr. Sheila Hayford.

December 29
No Returns Here!

Luke Chapter 16, verse 26:

And beside all this, between us and you there is a great gulf fixed: so that they which would pass from hence to you cannot; neither can they pass to us, that would come from thence.

Prayer: Dear God; help us to love others enough to introduce them to our Lord and Savior Jesus Christ. In Jesus' Name, Amen.

This time of the year, many stores experience high rates of return. Some may have received clothes with the wrong dress size that they want to exchange or return, others are dissatisfied with their gift for whatever reason and just want to return it. The stores are accommodating during this time, they may have more store clerks to take care of the large crowds and those returning items wait patiently in line for their turn. The verse today is very sobering. The rich man had many opportunities to live for God but he did not and after he died, he went to hell. God did not condemn him to hell because of his riches but because of his rejection of God. The poor man was so poor that he would beg for food and the dogs licked his sores while many did nothing to help him. However, the poor man trusted God and when he departed this earth he was with God. Note what happened next. In hell, the rich man wanted Father Abraham to send the poor man, now on the other side of this earth, to go and warn his five brothers about hell and to ask the poor man to send a few drops of water to him to cool his lips. That is very, very sad. That is when Father Abraham explained and essentially said, "No returns here!" Once a person departs this earth, their eternal destiny is sealed. The opportunity to accept or reject the Lord Jesus Christ as Savior and Lord takes place as long as a person is alive on this earth. God is warning humankind not to take chances when it comes to our eternal destiny. We must decide where we want to spend eternity and then take the necessary steps. I encourage you to choose to spend your eternity with God.

© By Dr. Sheila Hayford.

December 30
We Are Grateful, Lord!

Isaiah Chapter 12, verse3:
With joy you will draw water from the wells of salvation. (NIV)

Prayer: Dear God; we are so thankful for your provision, your protection, your healing and most of all, for the gift of our Lord and savior Jesus Christ. We are looking forward to the coming year with joy. In Jesus' Name, Amen

As we approach the end of this year, our hearts are filled with gratitude to God; for saving us, for protecting us, for providing for us, for healing us and for securing for us an eternal future with Him, through our Lord and Savior Jesus Christ. God has this promise for us as we enter the coming New Year. With joy we will continue to draw water from the wells of salvation, for God the Holy Spirit dwells in us. Hallelujah!

© By Dr. Sheila Hayford.

December 31
The Dawn Of A New Year

Leviticus Chapter 26, verse 9:
I will look on you with favor and make you fruitful and increase your numbers, and I will keep my covenant with you.

Prayer: Dear God; what an extraordinary year it has been! You have come through for us in ways we had not imagined and provided for us beyond our expectations. We are blessed to know you through our Lord and Savior Jesus Christ and to experience your favor. Empower us, by the Holy Spirit, as we enter into the New Year for our hope and our joy is in you. We honor you, we reverence you and we bless you. Thank you! In Jesus' Name, Amen.

As we enter a New Year, it is reassuring that we are entering with God's favor. God will continue to favor us and keep His covenant with us, through our Lord Jesus Christ. We will be fruitful, we will experience God's abundance and we will bring God joy; in the power of God the Holy Spirit, Amen. Happy New Year!

© By Dr. Sheila Hayford.

Directory of Featured Business Resources

1. Barksdale & Affiliates Realty ....page 50
Telephone: 302-533-8606
Home Buying and Selling, Free Home Market Analysis

2. Wealth Wisdom Group ....page 51
Telephone: 302-651-9191
Tax and Income Planning

3. Dance Delaware Studios ....page 62
Telephone: 302-9981222
Dance. Tap. Ballet. Jazz. Hip-Hop. Acrobatics.

4. U. S. Tax Pros ....page 66
Telephone: 484-821-7904.
Tax, Accounting and Business Support

5. Laurece West ....page 80
Telephone: 919-383-4876
Voice Coach. Singer. Speaker

6. Mr. Income Tax ....page 86
Telephone: 919-526-4829
Personal and Business Taxes, Small Business Accounting

7. Simpsons Hobbies and Gifts ....page 188
Telephone: 302-654-5022
Toys. Collectibles. Antiques. Gifts. Repairs.

8. Tina's Timeless Threads ....page 221
Telephone: 302-399-3224
Clothing. Accessories and Novelty Gifts.

9. Power Up 4 Success ....page 269
Telephone: 302-898-4013
Monthly Training Meetings.

A Celebration of Book Writing

What A Word Publishing and Media Group is on a mission to promote Book Reading, Writing and Publishing nationally and globally.

Services for Authors, Businesses and Companies include:

- Customized Book Coaching Services
- Editing and Proof Reading
- "Book from Scratch" Services
- Printing and Publishing Services
- "Featured Business" showcase Specials
- Publicity and Marketing Services
- Book Launch Events
- Seminars, Workshops "ON LOCATION, OURS OR YOURS!"
- Promotional items to promote your publication and your organization such as customized business cards, mugs, pens, tee shirts, tote bags, magnets.
- Press Releases. Advertising Services. Logos
- Screen play writing
- Documentary screen play writing –customized
- Enrollment in services, conferences and seminars Custom Tailored to your needs.

For information or to set up a Seminar, Workshop or Book Consult Appointment, please email: info@whatawordpublishing.com

What A Word Publishing & Media Group:
Published Book Titles include:

- ❖ Morning Glory - 365 Devotionals like no other!

- ❖ Sailing Into Destiny - The Providential Way and Sharing

- ❖ Snatched From The Fire - One Man's Compelling Story

- ❖ God's Sound Bites

- ❖ SUPER - A Life of Challenges and Changes to a Life of Accomplishments

- ❖ I Love My Family - Liberian Literacy Series

- ❖ Zack Exact – The Case of The Missing Trophy

Isn't it time **you** published your book?
Let's talk!
Email: info@whatawordpublishing.com
Visit www.whatawordpublishing.com/contact us

Thank You!

Month of January Notes:

Month of February Notes:

Month of March Notes:

Month of April Notes:

Month of May Notes:

Month of June Notes:

Month of July Notes:

Month of August Notes:

Month of September Notes:

Month of October Notes:

Month of November Notes:

Month of December Notes: